oops

Also by Martin J. Smith
and Patrick J. Kiger

Poplorica

oops

20 Life Lessons from the Fiascoes That Shaped America

MARTIN J. SMITH and PATRICK J. KIGER

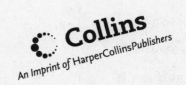

Collins

An Imprint of HarperCollinsPublishers

The authors are grateful to Gray & Company of Cleveland, Ohio, for its permission to use the transcript of the Ten-Cent Beer Night broadcast from Bob Dyer's *Cleveland Sports Legends: The 20 Most Glorious & Gut-Wrenching Moments of All-Time.*

HarperCollins books may be purchased for educational, business, or sales promotional use. For information, please write: Special Markets Department, HarperCollins Publishers, 10 East 53rd Street, New York, NY 10022.

FIRST COLLINS PAPERBACK EDITION PUBLISHED 2007

Designed by Mary Austin Speaker

Printed on acid-free paper

The Library of Congress has Catalogued the hardcover edition as follows:

Smith, Martin J., 1956–
    Oops : 20 life lessons from the fiascoes that shaped America : with handy recipes for disaster / Martin J. Smith and Patrick J. Kiger.—1st ed.
        p. cm.
    Includes bibliographical references and index.
    ISBN-10: 0-06-078083-5
    ISBN-13: 978-0-06-078083-8
        1. United States—History—Anecdotes.   2. United States—Civilization—Anecdotes.   3. Popular culture—United States—History—Anecdotes.
        4. Errors—Anecdotes.   5. Fads—United States—Anecdotes.
        6. Disasters—United States—Anecdotes.   7. Conduct of life—Miscellanea.   I. Kiger, Patrick J. II. Title

E179.S653 2006
973—dc22   2005051199
978-0-06-078084-5 (pbk.)

ISBN-10: 0-06-078084-3 (pbk.)

07 08 09 10 /RRD 10 9 8 7 6 5 4 3 2 1

M.J.S.

To William Leford Smith, whose dimming eyes
still see the humor in almost everything

P.J.K.

To Beastboy and his momster

**Good judgment is usually the result of experience.
And experience is frequently the result of bad judgment.**

*—An attorney in a lawsuit involving Boston's John Hancock
Tower, after the skyscraper's windows fell out*

**Some said I couldn't sing, but no one
could say I *didn't* sing.**

*—Florence Foster Jenkins, widely recognized
as the worst opera diva ever*

contents

Lesson #1 READ THE FINE PRINT
The Eroto-Utopians of Upstate New York

John Humphrey Noyes's sexually adventurous Perfectionist commune was one of the most successful utopian religious groups in 19th-century America. Alas, the devil was in the details.

Lesson #2 ACCENTUATE THE POSITIVE
How Thomas Edison Invented Trash Talk

Why would one of America's iconic inventors publicly electrocute a full-grown carnival elephant? The answer reveals a little-known story of ego, failure, and the moment when America began "going negative."

Lesson #3 BEWARE SOLUTIONS THAT CREATE NEW PROBLEMS
The Global Underarm Deodorant Disaster

Thomas Midgley Jr. was among America's greatest problem solvers. Unfortunately, his landmark "Eureka!" moments had an echo that sounded a lot like "Oops!"

Lesson #9 BEWARE OF UNPROVEN TECHNOLOGIES
The Lingering Reek of "Smell-O-Vision"

Sound revolutionized motion pictures, but the tortured effort to bring smell to the silver screen proved that some things are best left to the imagination.

{ 94 }

Lesson #10 CONVENIENCE ISN'T ALWAYS ENOUGH
The Paper Dress

In the mid-1960s, ordinary housewives and the fashion elite thrilled to the notion of cheap, disposable garments. The fad lasted about as long as the clothes themselves.

{ 106 }

Lesson #11 DUBIOUS NOTIONS SEDUCE EVEN THE BRIGHTEST MINDS
The U.S. Psychic Friends Program

The federal government dabbled in paranormal espionage for decades, using clairvoyants for everything from spotting enemy subs to "reading" documents on Nikita Khrushchev's desk. And for fun, they bent spoons.

{ 115 }

Lesson #12 UNDERSTAND THE MARKET
The 1967 Jimi Hendrix–Monkees Concert Tour

Perhaps the greatest rock guitarist ever, Jimi Hendrix's flamboyant fusion of blues, psychedelia, and sex changed popular music. But to the prepubescent fans of a fictional TV pop group, he was boh-ring!

{ 126 }

Lesson #13 DESPERATION IS THE CRADLE OF BAD IDEAS
The Cleveland Indians' Ten-Cent Beer Night

Lagging attendance. Latent hostility. Limitless lager. Add them up, and you get the most ill-conceived sports promotion in American history—and a pivot point in the new temperance movement.

{ 139 }

Lesson #14 SWEAT THE DETAILS
The Sixty-Story John Hancock Guillotine

If you're going to build a masterpiece of modern high-rise architecture, make sure the five-hundred-pound windows don't fall out during windstorms.

{ 151 }

Lesson #15 CULTURAL NORMS RESIST RADICAL CHANGE
Male Fashion's Fabulous Faux Pas

The leisure suit is reviled as the ultimate icon of 1970s-era bad taste. But what was hyped as a harbinger of a male fashion revolution actually turned out to be just that, in a flammable, double-knit way.

{ 161 }

Lesson #16 THINK LONG TERM
The Abbreviated Reign of "Neon" Leon Spinks

The tragicomic heavyweight boxing champ was neither the first nor the last American sports hero to badly mismanage fame and fortune. But by rising higher and falling faster than most, he brought schadenfreude to the masses.

{ 173 }

Lesson #17 KNOW "HELPFUL" FROM "ANNOYING"
Clippy—Microsoft's Relentless Software Irritant

The bizarre, bug-eyed anthropomorphic paper clip was supposed to make Microsoft software easier to use. Instead, Clippy became such an unpopular pest that even its creator ended up mocking it.

{ 184 }

Lesson #18 BEWARE THE PROFITING PROPHET
The Y2K Scare

To nervous Americans on the eve of the 21st century, a couple of missing digits in a computer program foretold a looming techno-apocalypse. So a few entrepreneurs did what they do best: turned fear into cash.

{ 195 }

Lesson #19 DON'T MESS WITH SUCCESS
The XFL's Quick Takedown

In a single season of televised T&A, backstage buffoonery, and second-rate football, the league launched by wrestling impresario Vince McMahon and NBC recorded the lowest prime-time ratings in network history.

{ 206 }

Lesson #20 OCCASIONALLY LOOK UP FROM YOUR WORKBENCH
The Quixotic Quest for the Flying Car

As they have for generations, aviation wonks and *Popular Mechanics* subscribers continue working toward the Holy Grail of private transportation: the flying car. Never mind that nobody needs one anymore.

{ 219 }

acknowledgments

WE SEE OURSELVES as miners as well as writers. The stories in *Oops* were buried in the nation's great repositories of information—public libraries, universities, corporate histories, print and broadcast archives, Web sites—and our job was simply to identify the most promising claims, dig out the sparkly stuff, and arrange it on the page. We were preceded in that task by many prospectors, and we owe those journalists, historians, humorists, and researchers a great debt. We hope they'll accept our gratitude and this book as our way of honoring their contributions, because frankly, no further payment will be forthcoming.

The most productive mines, in our case, were the Carnegie Library in Pittsburgh; the University of Maryland's Theodore R. McKeldin Library; the Montgomery County, Maryland, Public Libraries; the Library of Congress; and the Los Angeles Public Library system, in particular the Richard J. Riordan Central Library. We'd also like to express our appreciation to the growing number of Web-based sources of information that we've used extensively in our work. They include Nexis-Lexis, Thomson Gale's InfoTrac OneFile, NewspaperArchive.com, which is making tens of millions of newspaper pages dating back to the 18th century available online, and Questia.com, which offers a vast library of digital books and magazine articles.

In addition to our impossibly tolerant wives, Judy Smith and

Martha Kiger, two other dynamic women have been partners in this project from the beginning. Toni Sciarra, our editor at HarperCollins, shares our twisted senses of humor and history. We thank her for her advocacy and editorial advice, which greatly improved this book and its predecessor, *Poplorica*. And Susan Ginsburg, our agent at Writers House, remains a cherished friend and champion. She's one of the good ones.

introduction
THE JOY OF OOPS

WHETHER WE'RE SHOCKED by a "wardrobe malfunction" or hooting as a reality-show contestant is humiliated on national television, Americans are none-too-secretly fascinated with failure—and with good reason. From embarrassing fashion faux pas to architectural disasters, recent history is filled with flops that not only were bizarrely spectacular, but have had lasting cultural impact.

Now, finally, here's a book that not only celebrates some of the most significant flops, goofs, misjudgments, and fiascoes of the past century and a half, but also extracts a meaningful lesson from each.

Oops: Twenty Life Lessons from the Fiascoes That Shaped America examines in excruciating detail twenty strange and amusing stories, from the ill-fated 1967 Monkees–Jimi Hendrix concert tour to the preposterous collapse of the Tacoma Narrows Bridge. It's peopled with eccentric visionaries, misguided geniuses, and well-intentioned incompetents, ranging from the Reverend John Humphrey Noyes, the 19th-century minister who created a libidinous utopia in upstate New York, to Dr. Hans Laube, inventor of that dubious cinematic advance known as "Smell-O-Vision." We've carefully weighed the topics and personalities to create a book that will, like its predecessor, *Poplorica: A Popular History of the Fads, Mavericks, Inventions, and Lore That Shaped Modern America*, offer an entertaining, informative, and eclectic mix of topics, but with a crystal clear organizing principle.

Ultimately, the book offers twenty complementary lessons about the general conduct of life—lessons that can be used for everything from a personal mantra to a philosophy of business. Each story serves as a vivid example of the stated lesson, and each lesson is accompanied by a handy clip-'n'-save "Recipe for Disaster" that details the essential "ingredients" of each grand failure.

At the same time, we've retained the qualities that readers liked so much about *Poplorica*. Each of these twenty miscues in some way helped spawn a trend, phenomenon, or motif whose influence is still felt in contemporary culture. We trace the sometimes obscure and often amusing connections between the forgotten failures of the past and the world in which we now live.

—*Martin J. Smith and Patrick J. Kiger*

the eroto-utopians of upstate new york

John Humphrey Noyes's sexually adventurous Perfectionist commune was one of the most successful utopian religious groups in 19th-century America. Alas, the devil was in the details.

IF YOU FOUND yourself living near Putney, Vermont, in 1847, it would have been hard to ignore the gossip that was rampant in local sewing circles, and harder still to resist the temptation to ask a few curious questions. For the past six years, John Humphrey Noyes, a local boy and renegade former licensee of the Yale Theological School, had been leading a rather unorthodox Christian community in that orthodox New England town. Utopian experiments weren't unusual during that period; similar groups such as the Shakers and the Mormons were just getting started as well. But Noyes's "Perfectionist" gospel had a particularly interesting twist—its enthusiastic embrace of sex as a means of spiritual enlightenment.

In marketing terms, this is what later became known as a unique selling proposition. The Shakers had one, too, but they were pushing celibacy, a tough sell even in Victorian America, and certainly a deterrent to recruiting and a hindrance to long-range viability. The Mormons allowed men to take more than one wife, but not everyone saw that as a win-win. Noyes and the Perfectionists, on the other hand, were suggesting that the way to godliness was by doing the nasty—early, often, and with a smorgasbord of willing and like-minded partners. Their approach to spirituality was built around a marginal theological concept that, in more ways than one, promised heaven on earth. By the end of 1846 at least four couples among Noyes's approximately forty followers were actually practicing the "complex marriage" system that they preached (including Noyes, his wife, two of his sisters, and their husbands), and in doing so they embarked on one of the most remarkable—and controversial—social experiments in American history.

But to the pious citizens of Putney in those fledgling days of Noyes's grand plan, the defrocked preacher appeared to be hosting a kinky Victorian-era swingers' club under the convenient guise of religion. Even today, a skeptic might draw the same conclusion, especially after a recent revelation that Noyes once suggested that the Perfectionists could "conquer shame" by having sex onstage in front of an audience. The scandalous tales of spouse swapping and Noyes's unapologetic defense of complex marriage were enough to work the locals into a lather, and on October 25, 1847, a county court in Putney issued a writ for Noyes's arrest on two counts of adultery and "adulterous fornication." His arrest was preceded by dark threats and loose talk about lynch mobs in this life and eternal damnation in the next, and the controversy eventually prompted Noyes and his followers to flee Vermont for New York State, where they joined with another group of Perfectionists on land along Oneida Creek in Madison County to build what outsiders imagined was a 19th-century version of Plato's Retreat.

In fact, what came to be known as the Oneida Community was a much more complicated endeavor—one that lasted for a remarkable thirty-two years but which ultimately proved unsustainable. That's not to say it was a complete failure; in fact, Noyes's experiment succeeded on many levels. The group gradually built a magnificent mansion complex in which to house a population that at one point swelled to more than 250 people. The members fused into a community in the purest sense of the word, with an admirable and lively spirituality at its center. Smoking, drinking alcohol, and the consumption of coffee and tea were discouraged long before the health risks were known. The businesses the Perfectionists created to support themselves were quite successful, and often were run using the kind of enlightened labor practices—safe working conditions, free transportation, generous wages—that later became hallmarks of the nation's most dynamic 20th-century employers. The corporate manifestation of the original community, Oneida Ltd., remains one of the world's largest manufacturers of stainless steel and silver-plated flatware. Even critics at the time conceded that the Perfectionists seemed well-adjusted and upstanding, striving constantly for both self-improvement and selflessness.

But anyone tempted by craven lust to pursue Noyes's Perfectionist ideals was in for a rude surprise. Noyes and his free-loving followers didn't just approach the practice of sex with sacramental zeal; they applied such a dizzying array of arcane rules to its practice that it's not hard to imagine bewildered new recruits to Perfectionism as first-time car buyers, dazzled by a shiny new toy on the showroom floor, but suddenly sobered by their loan documents and wondering, "Just what have I gotten myself into here?"

What from the outside may have seemed like a nonstop orgy was, in fact, something quite different. Membership in Noyes's group involved one of the most mind-boggling social contracts ever imagined, and potential "joiners" lured by leering fantasies of a varied and unlimited sex life at Oneida were well-advised to read its fine print. The devil, it turns out, was in the details.

In the Beginning . . .

The spiritual seeking that took place in pre–Civil War America was a lot like the New Age movement of the 1980s, minus the crystals and sensory-deprivation tanks. Noyes and his Perfectionists were an extreme expression of the great American idea of the 1840s that New Worlders could transcend the ancestral European model, devise their own indigenous philosophy, and create their own perfect society—if they could just come up with the right rules and stick to them. The idea still flourishes in American culture, as demonstrated by any Anthony Robbins infomercial or Dr. Phil television special.

But the movements that flourished during the 1830s and 1840s were efforts to create something new from the nation's religious and social diversity, and New York State became the same kind of magnet for utopian kookiness and alternative lifestyles that California did a century later.

Noyes, a smart and precocious mama's boy, was one of the more audacious of those spiritual seekers. For years he had been convinced that there were no absolute standards of morality. After completing his studies at Dartmouth with high honors in 1830, he studied one year at the conservative Andover Theological Seminary. In the fall of 1832 he transferred to the more liberal divinity school at Yale, where a year later he was granted a license to preach even though some of his classmates and teachers considered him—let's not mince words here—a complete wack-job. Noyes had become a zealous preacher of an ascendant theology: Perfectionism.

What attracted Noyes to that particular branch of the Christian tree was the uplifting notion that people are more than just sin-blackened scum wads stuck to the bottom of God's sacred sandals. Perfectionists believe that people are actually holy, and can attain a state of perfect love between themselves and God. As a newly licensed preacher, the young Noyes felt qualified to take that concept even further. His reading of the Old and New Testaments led him to believe that the Second Coming to which Christians were so looking forward actually had already happened, pretty much unnoticed, with the destruction of Jerusalem in AD 70, and that since then it had been possible for man to achieve perfection in this life instead of waiting for the afterlife. Not only that, but Noyes declared publicly on February 20, 1834, that he already *was* perfect and incapable of committing sin, which led eventually to a decision by the appalled Yale faculty to ask Noyes to return his preaching license.

That setback was minor compared to the one Noyes received soon thereafter when, in June 1834, he traveled from New Haven, Connecticut, to New York City to attend a prestigious annual meeting of ministers and theologians. At twenty-three, he was convinced that, given the chance, he could engage some of the country's greatest theological minds in fervent discussion about his Perfectionist philosophy, and perhaps even convince them of the rightness of his cause. The trip was a low point for Noyes, as the gathered men of God basically treated him like a punk. Virtually ignored, the tormented Noyes went on a three-week bender, wandering the city's streets, drinking, tempting himself by forgoing food and sleep as he blathered on about Perfectionism to New York's bums and prostitutes.

During his time in New Haven, Noyes's first successful conversion to Perfectionism was a woman eight years his senior named Abigail Merwin, upon whom he apparently developed a serious crush. Her feelings about Noyes were less intense, but she cared enough about him to arrange his rescue from the streets of New York and return him to the Perfectionist church he had established in Connecticut.

"The incident caused a certain coolness among some of the New Haven Perfectionists," wrote Oneida biographer Maren Lockwood Carden in her 1969 book *Oneida: Utopian Community to Modern Corporation,* but Noyes again was undaunted. He spent the next two years preaching his peculiar gospel in New York State and throughout New England. In 1836, after little success, he returned home to Putney, Vermont, and a family that, according to Carden, "wondered if he was deranged."

Merwin's marriage to another man the following year nudged Noyes close to the edge of reason. The same month she wed, Noyes wrote a letter to a follower in which he first sketched out his groundbreaking theory of complex marriage. Convinced that Merwin was the wife that God intended for him, he wrote that "my claim on her cuts directly across the marriage covenant of the world." He went on: "When the will of God is done on earth as it is in heaven there will be no marriage. Exclusiveness, jealousy, quarreling have no place at the marriage supper of the Lamb."

Noyes had given his follower permission to publish the letter, and its subsequent appearance in a Perfectionist publication set Noyes on an irreversible course. Having publicly declared his belief in the free exchange of marriage partners, he became openly dedicated to the proposition. While that made it tough for his less radical disciples to publicly support him, a different kind of flock began to gather, including a reasonably wealthy and generous woman named Harriet A. Holton who credited a previous Noyes article with saving her from sin. She began sending money to support his ministry, and in 1838, Noyes proposed marriage in a letter that read like a tomcat's prenup. It emphasized, in no uncertain terms, the sexually open nature of the relationship he envisioned.

Holton accepted, and for nearly a decade she and Noyes worked together to build a following among the native Vermonters. Things went pretty well until 1846—the year after they moved Noyes's ideas about "complex marriage" from theory to practice.

Heaven on Earth, but with a Catch

Call him what you will, but John Humphrey Noyes was without question a great communicator. After he and his followers were run out of Vermont and relocated to Oneida, he continued to articulate his Perfectionist principles and share his ideas in nightly "home talks" and in published newsletters and theological tracts.

And while the brand of Perfectionism he preached offered a broad and holistic approach to living, emphasizing both the pursuit of individual perfection and communal good, even a casual reading of Noyes's public writings and comments suggests that he spent a *lot* of time thinking about sex, often with the same obsessive focus on precious bodily fluids that the fictional General Jack D. Ripper displayed in the film *Dr. Strangelove* more than a century later.

According to Louis J. Kern, author of the book *An Ordered Love: Sex Roles and Sexuality in Victorian Utopias—the Shakers, the Mormons, and the Oneida Community,* Noyes considered the term "spirit" analogous to "semen," and considered the sexual fluids of both men and women to be "the vital element, the power of life." He even had a theory about the creation of the first mortal soul resulting from God's "vital fluid" entering Adam's body. Kern wrote that, to Noyes, "the sexual act had all the significance of a sacrament." He opined often about the tendency of men to waste their precious "seed" during recreational sex. (You'll be forgiven here if the "every sperm is sacred" chorus to the parody song from Monty Python's 1983 film *The Meaning of Life* is running through your head.)

As Noyes and his followers began to fully practice their unorthodox social and sexual community, Noyes found it necessary to set down a few ground rules—a lot of them, actually, covering everything from the protocol males were supposed to follow in requesting an "interview" with a woman in the community, to the time of day and place that the liaison was supposed to take place, to how long that session was supposed to last, to the preferred position in which the interview should be conducted. He forbade exclusive romantic relationships, and couples who fell in love were separated, often by sending one partner to another of the several Perfectionist communes that Noyes later established. The community kept detailed records of who was interviewing whom and how things went during the encounter, mostly to make sure no one grew too attached to another individual.

Noyes also developed a system known as "ascending fellowship," which was based on the premise that sexual partnerships should be arranged according to spiritual need rather than physical compatibility—a spiritual mentoring program, of sorts. In practice, that meant that older, experienced, and presumably more spiritually perfect men in the community—in particular, Noyes and his increasingly wizened inner circle—were almost always paired with the most nubile and less experienced (and therefore spiritually unsophisticated) females. The converse, of course, meant that the studliest young Perfectionists were usually paired with the community's postmenopausal women, the trade-off being that, since those women were least likely to get pregnant, the young men were allowed to finish what they started. (You'll understand the significance of this shortly.) Draw your own conclusions about Noyes's real motive here. The system did keep unwanted pregnancies to a minimum, and ensured that lines didn't form for access to the most attractive members of the community. But suffice it to say that the ascending-fellowship system led to a lot of grumbling among the community's younger men and women and ultimately hastened the demise of the Oneida Community.

But the rule that best qualifies as the Perfectionist catch-22 was Noyes's rule about "male continence." Because his own wife had known the tragedy of four stillbirths during her five difficult pregnancies, Noyes decided that reliable birth control was of primary importance in a community that drew a distinct line between the ideas of sex for pleasure and sex for procreation. (Why, he wrote, should men "sow seed habitually where they do not *wish* it to grow?") In his relations with the fertile but delicate Harriet, he had avoided unwanted pregnancy for two years by employing the challenging practice of *coitus reservatus,* or simply refusing to ejaculate during or after sex. The metaphor Noyes used to explain the technique to his followers was that of a boatman on a river near a waterfall. Basically, he said, the closer you row your boat to the falls, the harder it becomes to turn back. Therefore, he advised, paddle only in the calm waters far upstream. Noyes claimed the practice was satisfying for both himself and his partner, and in fact Oneida may have been the only place in Victorian America where the female orgasm was the primary goal of sex. Perhaps the most telling evidence of Noyes's charismatic leadership is that the community's men agreed to practice *coitus reservatus* as well.

Of course, rules mean nothing unless there's a way to enforce them. To help keep the community's men from straying from the righteous path, Noyes created a process called "mutual criticism." According to author Kern, it was "a kind of proto-encounter-group therapy, in which an individual was publicly judged by his peers and frankly told of his faults, annoying habits, idiosyncrasies, and virtues." A man who displayed what the community derided as a "rooster spirit" in his pursuit of sexual partners, or who was branded a "leaker" for going over the falls, might be placed in the same sexual purgatory as the community's young boys, with sexual access restricted only to the community's older women, or denied altogether. If you wanted to play at Oneida, you played by Noyes's rules.

"Love at Oneida was not 'free,' " wrote Kern, "and those who confused complex marriage with free love erred gravely in their conception."

As a result, the Oneida Community was a roiling stew of weirdness. Noyes and his followers willfully violated every conceivable sexual taboo, from the routine deflowering of preteen girls by the community's older men, to institutionalized incest, to eugenics. To manage so complicated a social structure, the Oneida Community had a rule book that, were it not evolving constantly in Noyes's head, might have been as dense as the modern U.S. tax code, and just as bizarre. And in Noyes, the Perfectionists had an autocratic leader who oversaw the most intimate details of his followers' lives with the same attention to detail that Hugh Hefner once brought to Playmate photo shoots.

"This was rational sex, one might say, with a vengeance," wrote editor Kaz Dziamka in the journal *American Rationalist*. "No other utopian experiment before or since has so drastically overhauled the existing system of sexual, moral and social conventions. . . . One would expect that the system would never work, that human nature being what it is, no sensible woman or man would ever be glad to share sexually his lover [and that] any utopia based on Male Continence, Complex Marriage and Christian Perfectionism would be doomed to fail from the start. But the rather uncomfortable fact is that the Oneida Community did succeed."

For a while.

As with any organization built around a charismatic leader, the Oneida Community began to unravel during the 1860s as Noyes's powers began to fade. He stayed at Oneida less and less, and started delegating responsibilities to others in his inner circle, including the initiation of the community's virgins. (For much of his life at Oneida, Noyes had reserved the job of "first husband" mostly for himself, and by various followers' accounts, he was quite gentlemanly about what to less sympathetic ears might sound like a regular regimen of statutory rape.) He lost much of his hearing, making it difficult for him to participate in conversations, and his once-fierce emphasis on religious study, discussion, and contemplation evolved into an overarching interest in science. By the late 1860s, Noyes had read Charles Darwin's *Origin of Species* and began a selective breeding program among community members that he called "stirpiculture."

Although couples sometimes applied together to the breeding program, the stirpiculture committee at Oneida, guided by Noyes, had the final say on which pairings were allowed to propagate. Between 1869 and 1879 the community intentionally produced forty-five live children under that program—nine of them sired by Noyes himself, and three others fathered by Noyes's son Theodore. Wrote Carden in her 1969 account of the community's history: "Noyes believed sincerely in the superiority of his family line."

In the end, that was a big part of the problem. Oneida's younger generation became part of the community by accident of birth rather than by choice, and they didn't necessarily buy what Noyes was selling. The leader they knew was not the dynamic religious firebrand that the elders chose to follow, but a deaf old man who seemed to have engineered an elaborate utopian social system that in matters of the flesh benefited him more than most. "Dissent focused on Noyes and on the subject of virginity, but it really extended to the whole manner in which the Community was governed," Carden wrote.

The complex marriage system was abandoned in August 1879; monogamy and celibacy became the recommended alternatives. A year later, the community agreed to divide and reorganize, and on January 1, 1881, the Oneida Community members voted to transform the group's businesses into a joint-stock company, which would be owned and operated by former members of the society. "The Community was valued at $600,000 and stocks were distributed according to each member's original contribution and length of service," according to the Oneida corporate Web site. "The stock was divided among 226 men, women, and children, the majority of whom received between $2,000 and $4,999 in shares."

In the end John Humphrey Noyes's grand social experiment came down to numbers, and it would be hard to imagine a more sexless ending.

A METAPHOR RUN AMOK

The end of John Humphrey Noyes's public life turned out to be as unusual and controversial as its beginning.

According to Robert S. Fogerty, who in 2000 published an intimate and revealing seventy-page memoir written by Noyes's niece, Tirzah Miller, Noyes decided to flee the Oneida Community because, once again, he feared prosecution by local authorities—possibly for statutory rape for his role as "first husband" to many of the community's adolescent girls.

Leaving behind a community that was irreparably divided by philosophical disputes and unfocused leadership, Noyes and a colleague left Oneida for the last time after midnight on June 23, 1879, and drove thirty miles to Holland Patent, New York. From there, they boarded a train and later crossed into Canada by ferry. Nearly two hundred miles from the utopian community he founded, Noyes lived in a stone cottage overlooking Niagara Falls until his death in 1886, supported by a group of loyal friends and family. It was a smaller group than Noyes had hoped. "At the time of the [Oneida] breakup 112 members signed a document agreeing to go to Canada to form an alternative community," Fogarty wrote. "But in the end only about 15 stalwarts made the journey."

Wrote Oneida historian Louis J. Kern: "It was one of those little ironies of history that found John H. Noyes, who had metaphorically warned men against venturing in the sexual act too near the 'verge of the fall where he has no control over his course,' in the twilight of his career living in exile within sight of Niagara Falls, the most powerful rushing waters in America. . . . The cultural and biological forces of sexuality he had tried to dam up in the toils of his sexual system had in the end burst their bonds and broken the man who would have mastered them."

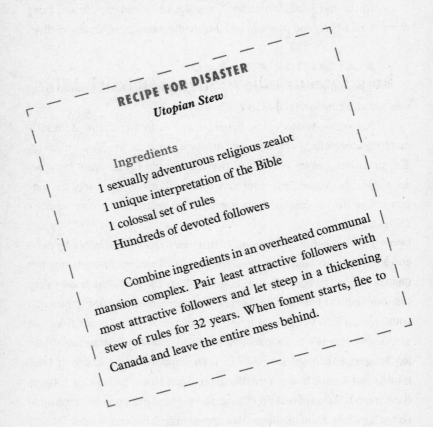

RECIPE FOR DISASTER
Utopian Stew

Ingredients
1 sexually adventurous religious zealot
1 unique interpretation of the Bible
1 colossal set of rules
Hundreds of devoted followers

Combine ingredients in an overheated communal mansion complex. Pair least attractive followers with most attractive followers and let steep in a thickening stew of rules for 32 years. When foment starts, flee to Canada and leave the entire mess behind.

how thomas edison invented trash talk

Why would one of America's iconic inventors publicly electrocute a full-grown carnival elephant? The answer reveals a little-known story of ego, failure, and the moment when America began "going negative."

LONG BEFORE THE provocative multimedia weenie-wagging between marketplace rivals Coke and Pepsi, Burger King and McDonald's, and Visa and American Express, inventor Thomas Alva Edison was pioneering the loathsome and now common art known as "going negative"— the use of modern media and trash-talking surrogates to smear your chief competitor.

But the story of Edison's extended public-relations campaign against his rivals to electrify the world is so bizarre, so spectacularly misguided, that the failure of Edison's effort is underscored every time an American homeowner today flips a light switch or plugs in a vacuum cleaner. Worse, Edison managed to preserve forever the saddest chapter of the whole sorry episode—the one a biographer dubbed "America's longest and most splenetic howl of corporate outrage"—in a one-minute motion picture whose title perfectly echoes the unsubtle way in which Edison conducted the campaign. The enduring 1903 snuff film *Electrocuting an Elephant* offers proof that, in matters of judgment, the great man really wasn't all that smart.

To appreciate the full glory of Edison's goof, it helps to understand the times and the extraordinary stakes for which the nation's most prolific inventor was gambling. In the late 1880s, the world was at a crossroads. Electricity had been discovered and harnessed, and clearly had the potential to change the world, but the era's leading technologists hadn't yet figured out the best way to generate and distribute it on a large scale.

It also helps to understand the two different types of electricity. Any electrical device requires the movement—a "current"—of electrons for power. At the time Edison created the first commercially practical incandescent lightbulb in 1879, all of the electricity used in the United States was direct current, or DC. With direct current, electrons flow constantly along a wire like water through a hose, with users siphoning off power along the way. That type of low-voltage electricity is reliable and safe, but not very efficient because it requires a generating station every half mile or so to refill the "hose." Edison, holder of a record 1,093 U.S. patents, was a DC man because he had invested heavily to develop systems and equipment that relied on direct current, and he intended to make a lot of money electrifying the world with his DC-powered inventions.

There was just one problem: Edison was wrong. An eccentric Eastern European immigrant named Nikola Tesla, along with visionary Pittsburgh industrialist George Westinghouse and others, was pursuing a different course, developing motors and related systems that ran on alternating current. AC electricity keeps electrons moving (and producing power) by quickly cycling them back and forth along a wire between positive and negative charges. It can be distributed at much higher voltages, making it more powerful and efficient than direct current, and it's far easier to deliver across large geographic areas. Also, if properly handled, AC electricity is perfectly safe. Although the Edison Electric Light Company's 1887 annual report dismissed rival AC as "having no merit [and] notoriously destructive of life and property," it didn't take long for most reasonable people, including some of Edison's own engineers, to realize that the future belonged to AC.

Edison's choice at that point was to (a) take the high road and convince the world that his DC electricity was better than their AC electricity, or (b) take the low road by trashing the other guys and everything they stood for. He chose b, focusing on the one aspect of alternating current that he knew might give the public and politicians pause: high-voltage meant potential danger. All Edison needed, he figured, was to link AC electricity with death in the public mind, and to do it in some ghastly and unforgettable ways.

The Hot Dog–Roast Beef Strategy

Thus began what today is known as the "War of the Currents," a pitched battle for the hearts and minds of America's early electricity consumers. How appalling were Edison's tactics in that fight? Imagine, for example, if Apple Computer cofounder Steve Jobs, sensing the growing demand for rival IBM-based personal computers in the early 1980s, had begun a fact-free advertising and public-relations campaign linking PCs to, say, colorectal cancer. Or if the makers of Tylenol launched a national ad campaign suggesting that those who prefer rival Advil are more likely to be hacked to death by men with machetes.

Yes, it was that bad, but Edison knew from past experience that fear could work wonders. When he was trying to convert residential consumers from gas to his newfangled electricity, for example, he'd played smartly on common fears about gas leaks and fires. His first Grinchy impulse to demonize alternating current apparently came in late 1887, when one member of the three-member New York State Death Commission wrote a letter asking him if electrocution might be a more civilized alternative to hanging, the state's standard method of dispatching condemned criminals. There had been a spate of botched hangings, each covered in splendid detail by the newspapers, each involving either an agonizingly slow strangulation (knot too loose) or decapitation (knot too tight). Neither scenario played well with the assembled witnesses, and the sitting governor was looking for something a bit "less barbarous."

Edison at first refused to get involved, citing his moral opposition to capital punishment. Then, within a month, he had second thoughts and wrote back to the commission member with a radically different opinion. Electricity would be an excellent way to execute a human being, Edison had decided. He noted, too, that "the most suitable apparatus" for killing people was a generator that produced—you guessed it—alternating-current electricity. And, ever helpful, Edison offered that "the most effective of those are . . . manufactured principally in this country by Geo. Westinghouse."

With that self-serving recommendation, Edison deftly linked his chief rival's primary product with death. But he was just getting started.

By happy coincidence for Edison, during the spring of 1888, New Yorkers were treated to some vivid demonstrations of electricity's fatal power. A snarl of overhead electrical wires had been blooming for years on poles along New York streets, but most people considered them an eyesore rather than a danger. That began to change in mid-April that year. The phrase "death by wire" entered the lexicon after an exuberant young man fried to death after picking up a downed power line. Less than a month later, an electric company lineman inadvertently cut the wrong wire while doing repairs on a second-story Broadway cornice. That death, in particular, became macabre street theater as the lineman's body roasted on the cornice for an excruciatingly long time before onlookers were able to pry his charred and smoking remains from the current's grasp.

By then, the Edison Electric Light Company had already launched a frontal assault on the AC forces. It had issued a helpful eighty-four-page booklet that focused on the technical and moral failings of Westinghouse and other competitors, and also chronicled in glittering detail the gruesome deaths of various people felled by AC electricity. With its bright red cover and fire-alarm title ("WARNING!"), Edison's first public rant had all the subtlety of a trench coat flasher. According to author Jill Jonnes in 2003's *Empires of Light: Edison, Tesla, Westinghouse, and the Race to Electrify the World*, the booklet reduced the whole debate to a simple matter of good versus evil. "DC was a gentle, friendly current," she wrote of the booklet. "AC was a stone killer. Edison suggested the AC people were criminally indifferent to safety just to save a buck and get ahead."

When Tesla and Westinghouse joined forces in June 1888, Edison should have known he was in trouble. The primary advantage of DC electricity to that point was that all electric motors ran on DC current, and electric motors were what made electricity useful on an industrial scale rather than just for residential lighting. But Tesla had created an effective AC motor that was far more efficient and effective than Edison's offerings, and it was exactly what Westinghouse needed to fulfill the promise of the alternating-current power systems he had been building.

Edison could have recognized that reality and adapted his company to better compete. Instead, he embarked on the next phase of the low-road campaign that ultimately led him to his fateful rendezvous with Topsy the elephant. His avatar in that phase of the battle was an aspiring self-taught electrical engineer named Harold P. Brown. The same month that Tesla joined Westinghouse, Brown wrote a letter to the editor of the *New York Evening Post* lamenting the springtime deaths of the boy and the electrical worker. He presented himself to the public as a concerned citizen who simply wanted to ensure public safety, but his frothy denunciation of "damnable" AC electricity echoed the arguments Edison had been making since the release of his "WARNING!" booklet. It was later revealed that Brown was on Edison's payroll, though precisely when Brown became Edison's surrogate slanderer isn't clear.

Beyond dispute, however, is that Edison quickly opened the doors of his brand new West Orange, New Jersey, laboratory to Brown to begin a series of "experiments" designed not only to discredit AC electricity, but to build a case that its use should be severely restricted, or possibly even outlawed. How? Let's just say the summer of 1888 was a bad one for the stray dogs of West Orange, for which Brown was paying a 25¢-per-head bounty to unwitting local children.

On July 30 that year, Brown unveiled his long-term strategy for demonizing AC at a festive little gathering for seventy-five invited guests. They met in a private lab at the Columbia College School of Mines in Manhattan, and Brown, without forewarning the audience of electricity experts and others, dragged a seventy-six-pound, part Newfoundland dog onto the stage, muzzled and tied the creature, and placed it in a wooden cage with heavy copper wire woven through the bars. "Sensing their discomfort, Brown assured the audience that although the dog appeared friendly, he was actually a 'desperate cur' who had already bitten two people," wrote author Richard Moran in *Executioner's Current: Thomas Edison, George Westinghouse, and the Invention of the Electric Chair.*

The crowd wasn't much comforted as Brown administered an increasingly powerful series of direct-current shocks to the frantic dog, which at one point tore off his muzzle and nearly escaped from the cage. Brown's point was that while the DC shocks had hurt the dog, they hadn't killed him. One witness reported that "many spectators left the room, unable to endure the revolting exhibition." An animal lover in the audience suggested that the dog immediately be put out of its misery, and that was all the invitation Brown needed. He tied the dog down again, switched to alternating current, and, after assuring the group that the dog would experience far less pain with AC, promptly zapped it to death. The demonstration horrified the gathered crowd, with a newspaper reporter asking Brown to stop the "inhuman performance," and a representative from the Society for the Prevention of Cruelty to Animals demanding that Brown use something other than animal torture to promote DC electricity over AC.

Brown, and presumably his patron, Thomas Edison, didn't take the hint. Four days later, Brown conducted a more elaborate demonstration for a crowd of about eight hundred people. This time he decided not to prolong the torture of the dogs. Using only AC electricity at what he felt were lethal voltages, he quickly dispatched two smallish dogs. But the third, a friendly Irish setter–Newfoundland mix, struggled for more than five minutes, during which time it was in obvious agony. The crowd recoiled at the scent of slow-roasted dog flesh, among other off-putting aromas. Brown quickly declared the whole thing a great success, and suggested with a straight face that the dog felt no pain whatsoever. Again to his surprise, Brown found himself playing to a hostile crowd.

Still, the DC forces didn't quite grasp that, as a persuasive technique, electrocuting furry animals in gaudy public demonstrations wasn't working as well as they might have hoped. By December 1888, Brown had decided to stage the most ambitious of his little set pieces for an invited audience of reporters and influential New Yorkers. This time it was held at Edison's West Orange lab, and Edison decided to witness the public demonstration himself—the first time the nation's preeminent electrician stepped into public view after so artlessly guiding the War of the Currents from behind the scenes. Stung by suggestions that dogs were more vulnerable to electrocution than larger human beings, Brown had lined up a veritable barnyard of new victims, including a doe-eyed 124-pound calf, a slightly larger 145-pound calf, and finally, to cap the event, a healthy 1,230-pound horse. By then, Brown had his act down pretty well, and the animals died without undue struggle. That, along with Edison's august presence, carried the day. The *New York Times* concluded in its report that AC electricity was "the most deadly force known to science" and predicted that AC would "undoubtedly drive the hangman out of business" in the state.

The following month, electrocution became the legally accepted method of execution in New York. More important, Harold Brown—not yet unmasked as an Edison toady—was hired in the spring of 1889 as the electrical expert for the state prison system. He was put in charge of designing the first electric chair, and eventually made sure that the very first electrocution in the United States was carried out using alternating current generated by Westinghouse equipment. (That 1890 electrocution of murderer William Kemmler was a botched and prolonged affair that recalled some of Brown's more gruesome animal demonstrations, and prompted Westinghouse to say "they could have done better with an axe.") But executives at Edison's company saw nothing but victory in that lethal climax to their years of effort. A giddy Edison lawyer at one point even suggested that the state of New York introduce the term "westing-housed" into the lexicon, as in "that criminal was westinghoused" in the "westinghouse," much like the French named the guillotine after the doctor who invented it. Doing so, the lawyer suggested, would "be a subtle compliment to the public services of this distinguished man."

Electrocuting the Elephant

Those were the best of times in Edison's DC camp, but the wider War of the Currents didn't exactly go their way. DC electricity was never able to overcome its inherent flaws—not to mention the miscalculated early snuff shows staged by the Edison forces—and public support for alternating current grew steadily stronger. By November 1889, the war was pretty much over. An investigation by the journal *Electrical Engineering* laid waste to claims advanced by Edison and Brown that Westinghouse AC systems had killed thirty people the previous year. In fact, according to the journal's investigation, only one or two of those thirty victims were killed by a Westinghouse system. Three years later, Edison's company was absorbed into an AC-oriented conglomerate called General Electric, marking what Edison biographer Mark Essig called "the Edison company's full surrender in the battle of the currents."

By 1897, Edison was focusing on new enterprises, including a system to separate and concentrate iron ore, improved versions of his original phonograph, and early motion pictures. Ironically, his motion picture business ultimately brought him out of retirement as the nation's preeminent trash-talking critter killer.

In 1903, the year before the Edison studio's film *The Great Train Robbery* transformed motion pictures from short novelties into vehicles for elaborate visual storytelling, Edison got word of a dilemma facing the operators of Coney Island. Topsy, a ten-foot-high, twenty-foot-long female Indian elephant, was going to be euthanized because she had killed one of her handlers. (This was not Topsy's first homicide, though from all accounts it may have been her most justifiable. She attacked the handler, according to many reports, after he fed her a burning cigarette.) Special scaffolding had already been built to hang the pachyderm, but animal-rights advocates stepped in to prevent that spectacle.

Edison's reasons are far from clear, but the inventor decided to offer his services as both executioner and documentarian. Edison, never a slouch at publicizing himself and his inventions, may have been trying to promote electrocution nationwide as a means of execution, or perhaps he was simply hoping to use the public fascinations with electricity, elephants, and death to introduce the public to his latest creation—the motion picture. Whatever his reasons, Edison knew from experience that a certain type of spectacle would guarantee public attention.

And so, on a gray January morning, Edison set up his crude movie camera in the then-unfinished Luna Park section of Coney Island, right in front of the gallows. Word spread and a crowd began to gather, eventually swelling to about 1,500 people. Around 1:30 p.m., park employees led the six-ton Topsy, wearing copper-lined sandals, onto the platform. An Edison company employee attached electrodes, and final adjustments were made. Around 2:45, Edison started his camera and somebody threw the switch. Six thousand volts of alternating current shot through the elephant. Smoke wafted from where the electrodes met her leathery skin, and her knees buckled. Within ten seconds, Topsy was history. "The big beast died without a trumpet or a groan," reported one newspaper, the *Commercial Advertiser*. The *New York Times* later called the event "a rather inglorious affair." Looking back in a 2003 newspaper article, Dick Zigun, the proprietor of the Coney Island Museum, described Topsy's death as "a seminal moment" for electricity, film, and public entertainment that kept Coney Island "at the forefront of popular culture at the turn of the century."

Edison is said to have taken his film on the road as part of his continuing campaign to discredit AC electricity, but if that's true it was no less misguided than the event itself. By then the AC forces clearly had the upper hand. More likely, Edison may have been using *Electrocuting an Elephant* as a macabre advance trailer for the new medium of film.

Topsy, for her part, remains an iconic figure in American popular culture. Film director Errol Morris used the footage of her electrocution in his 2000 documentary about a Holocaust revisionist called *Mr. Death: The Rise and Fall of Fred A. Leuchter Jr.*, and writer John Haskell's critically lauded 2003 debut short-story collection included an extended piece called "Elephant Feelings" in which Haskell imagined the sad inner life of Topsy as she was led to her death. To mark the centennial of Topsy's death in 2003, the Coney Island Museum and various Topsy supporters unveiled a memorial sculpture which the *New York Times* described as "rife with symbolism and larger suggestions about the relationship between humans and animals." The memorial involves a coin-operated, hand-crank Mutoscope through which to watch the execution film, as well as chains and cables which suggest confinement. Viewers stand, as Topsy did, on copper plates.

The legacy of Edison and the Topsy debacle extends far beyond the actual event, of course. America still runs on AC electricity, as it pretty much has for the past century. Edison's endorsement of electrocution as a humane way to execute condemned criminals led to more than 4,300 legal executions by electricity in the U.S. during the 20th century. And the kind of disinformation Edison spewed during the War of the Currents—a long and often successful tradition in American politics—has become a Darwinian fact of life in American commerce. Pepsi challenges Coke in blind taste tests, then airs the results in national ads. Anheuser-Busch once launched a radio campaign revealing that rival Coors Brewing ("A Taste of the Rockies") actually makes its beer with non–Rocky Mountain water. Burger King has mocked rivals that fry rather than flame-broil. Visa touts all the places that don't take American Express. Worse are the whisper campaigns, below-the-radar assaults, and arm's-length slanders designed to discredit competitors, such as the persistent and pernicious rumors about certain movie stars at Oscar time, or that urine is among the ingredients in a particular brand of imported beer. That's all happened despite credible studies that suggest "going negative" may work in politics, but it's risky at best when used as a strategy against a marketplace competitor, and often can backfire. The negative approach "is akin to taking drugs," wrote business professor Philip Patton in an essay urging those in the marketing industry to avoid the tactic, which was published in the June 1990 issue of *Marketing & Media Decisions*. "In the short run we may feel good, but in the long run we will be worse than when we started. If we stop now, we may not have the problems of the

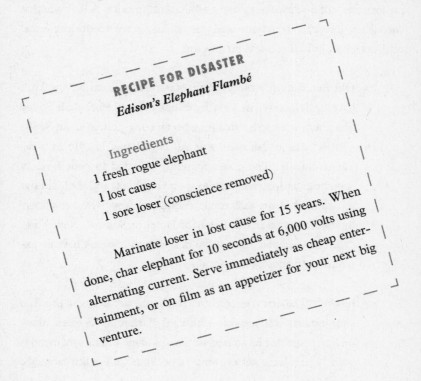

RECIPE FOR DISASTER
Edison's Elephant Flambé

Ingredients
1 fresh rogue elephant
1 lost cause
1 sore loser (conscience removed)

Marinate loser in lost cause for 15 years. When done, char elephant for 10 seconds at 6,000 volts using alternating current. Serve immediately as cheap entertainment, or on film as an appetizer for your next big venture.

addict and will heal rather quickly. If we continue, we will have very painful problems to overcome."

Despite those cautionary words more than a decade ago, consumers today are being manipulated by a virulent new strain of trash talkers who employ ever more sophisticated techniques and media such as television, talk radio, and the Internet. But, the truth be told, they're all just following the lead of the American icon who made "negative" so much more than an electrical term.

AN ELEPHANT GRAVEYARD

Topsy's inglorious 1903 electrocution was not the first or last major fiasco involving a celebrity elephant, but her death is emblematic of the misfortunes suffered by many other elephants in America. A Web site that chronicles unusual attractions and memorials, www.roadsideamerica. com/pet/eleph.html, includes epitaphs for:

- **Old Bet.** The African elephant was rescued from a New York City cattle market in 1804 by circus pioneer Hachaliah Bailey and put to work in his fledgling performing-animal show. Sadly, Old Bet was assassinated near Alfred, Maine, in 1816 by a religious fanatic. The man apparently objected to poor farmers spending hard-earned cash to see an elephant, and shot Old Bet to death. Perhaps that tragic ending explains why her cheesy monument outside the Elephant Hotel in Somers, New York, "the oldest elephant memorial in America," doesn't have an explanatory plaque or inscription.

- **Jumbo.** "The first true celebrity elephant," according to the Web site, Jumbo's starring role with P. T. Barnum's "Greatest Show on Earth" made him so famous that his name is now synonymous with "a very large person, animal, or thing" in English-language dictionaries. Jumbo, unfortunately, was struck and killed by a speeding freight train in St. Thomas, Ontario, Canada, on September 15, 1885. For a while, local hucksters charged gawkers a small fee to see the famous carcass as it lay on a trackside embankment. Barnum later sent taxidermists to reclaim Jumbo's skin and skeleton, which later were displayed at Tufts University in Medford, Massachusetts. Recalled writer Peter Unwin in a 2003 article in *Canadian Business and Current Affairs:* "All that remained was a flood of elephant grease, bottled and sold as a curative ointment for aches and pains." A hundred years later, the St. Thomas town council commissioned a concrete elephant sculpture so large that its legs had to be removed so it could pass beneath bridges along the Trans-Canada Highway while being trucked to St. Thomas.

- **Big Mary, aka Murderous Mary.** After the circus elephant stomped a malicious trainer to death in Kingsport, Tennessee, in 1916, the town fathers decided that Mary had to go. Unable to find a gun large enough to do the job, they approached the neighboring town of Erwin, which had a railroad crane hefty enough for a hanging. A crowd estimated at five thousand watched the hoist chain break during the first attempt, sending the elephant to the concrete and knocking her unconscious. Justice was done on the second attempt. No memorial exists ("The town is not real proud of it," explained the local museum curator), but the episode is chronicled in a 1992 book by Charles Edwin Price, *The Day They Hung the Elephant.*

- **Norma Jean.** The 6,500-pound star of the Clark and Walters circus was struck by summer lightning on July 17, 1972, while chained to a tree in the town square of Oquawka, Illinois.

Elephants, by tradition and common sense, are supposed to be buried where they fall. Norma Jean was, and the circus went out of business a year later. One of the town's main attractions today is a twelve-foot tombstone topped by a concrete elephant, to which tourists are directed by signs reading: "Elephant killed by lightning."

BEWARE SOLUTIONS THAT CREATE NEW PROBLEMS

the global underarm deodorant disaster

Thomas Midgley Jr. was among America's greatest problem solvers. Unfortunately, his landmark "Eureka!" moments had an echo that sounded a lot like "Oops!"

IF YOU TRAVELED back in time to the flashpoint of the 20th century's two most significant environmental fiascoes—the addition of toxic lead to gasoline, and the invention of ozone-eating chlorofluorocarbons—you might be surprised to find the same brilliant and well-intentioned scientist standing at ground zero of both, grinning with pride but nonetheless holding a lighted match. His name was Thomas Midgley Jr., and when in 2000 historian J. R. McNeill wrote that Midgley "had more impact on the atmosphere than any other single organism in earth history," it wasn't necessarily a compliment.

But let's first give credit for all of the good things Midgley did throughout his illustrious career. Midgley, who died in 1944, was the human incarnation of the slogan "Better things for better living . . . through chemistry." His work solved problems as diverse as engine knock, rampant food poisoning, and noxious, exploding refrigerators. His achievements in chemistry included breakthroughs that not only overcame confounding scientific problems, but also led to other innovations and inventions that immeasurably changed life in America, including guided missiles, more powerful engines for cars, home refrigeration, and air-conditioning. In 1952, *Popular Mechanics* magazine celebrated its fifty-year anniversary by honoring fifty Americans for their "contributions to the welfare of mankind during the past half-century," and Midgley was listed among luminaries such as Orville and Wilbur Wright, Charles Lindbergh, and Albert Einstein. He also was inducted into the National Inventors Hall of Fame in 2003, where he rightfully took his place in the pantheon of architects of modern American living alongside Alexander Graham Bell, Thomas Edison, and Henry Ford.

At the same time, though, Midgley's two landmark inventions were, by century's end, linked to untold deaths, widespread disease, and a potentially cataclysmic change in the very atmosphere of the planet. As epic goofs go, leaded gas and chlorofluorocarbons together had the same destructive potential as global nuclear holocaust. We are assured that, were he alive today, the ever-creative Midgley would be leading the effort to solve the problems he inadvertently created. Given his track record, though, maybe it's best that he *isn't* trying to help.

"Midgley was an engineer by training," wrote author Bill Bryson in his 2003 bestseller *A Short History of Nearly Everything*, "and the world would no doubt have been a safer place if he had stayed so."

Midgley's transformation from mechanical engineer to renowned chemist began in 1916 while he was working for the fabled Charles Kettering at Dayton Research Laboratories (which later became the General Motors Research Division) in Dayton, Ohio. In the fall of that year, Kettering asked Midgley to figure out why internal-combustion engines had an annoying knock which seemed to rob them of power. Midgley's work on the problem was delayed by the start of World War I. But by 1921 he'd not only identified the source of the knock but figured out a way to stop it by adding a measure of tetraethyl lead—a long-known neurotoxin—to gasoline. By 1922, according to several accounts, Midgley's experimentation with leaded gasoline was taking a toll on his own health. He was suffering from lead-poisoning symptoms, which he described in a letter as "almost identical to the . . . second stage of tuberculosis," and had to take six weeks off work. Still, he claimed tetraethyl lead was safe in the diluted form sold to the public, and defended that unverified theory when the U.S. Public Health Service started asking questions about the health risks. In a letter to a professional acquaintance concerned about the potential damage leaded gasoline might cause, Midgley wrote: "The exhaust does not contain enough lead to worry about, but no one knows what legislation might come into existence fostered by competition and fanatical health cranks."

Midgley and his employers clearly ignored safer alternatives for decades while marketing leaded "ethyl" gasoline to an enthusiastic driving public, according to "The Secret History of Lead," a damning twenty-one-thousand-word article by Jamie Lincoln Kitman in the March 20, 2000, issue of the *Nation*. Unfortunately, car engines make terrific aerosolizers, and thus began decades of unnecessarily toxic spew from car exhaust pipes that left an estimated 7 million tons of lead in soil, air, and water, not to mention in the flesh and blood of every organism exposed to it. According to U.S. government statistics, by the mid-1980s, an estimated five thousand Americans were dying each year from lead-related heart disease, and 68 million young children were exposed to lead between 1927 and 1987. It took more than sixty years before the federal government had the gumption to stand against General Motors, Du Pont, and Standard Oil of New Jersey (now known as Exxon) to outlaw lead in gasoline in favor of less toxic additives.

Despite the scope of that disaster, Midgley's discovery of leaded gasoline pales when compared to the potential ecological devastation of chlorofluorocarbons, or CFCs, which he discovered in 1928. General Motors had bought a small Detroit refrigeration business and renamed it Frigidaire. Although the company was able to improve the performance, design, and manufacturing of its home refrigerators through the 1920s, Kettering, by then the company's head, suspected that America was ready to embrace home refrigeration in a big way—provided his company could address the unsettling tendency of those early refrigerators to kill their owners.

While the early appliances were more effective and less messy than old-fashioned iceboxes, the chemicals that pulsed through their cooling coils were noxious and nasty, including ammonia, methyl chloride, and sulfur dioxide. Those chemicals were explosive, and even a small leak could spoil all of the food inside the refrigerator. Large leaks were more dangerous. According to Seth Cagin and Philip Dray, authors of the 1993 book *Between Earth and Sky: How CFCs Changed Our World and Endangered the Ozone Layer,* twenty-nine people died of refrigerator-related methyl chloride poisoning between August 1928 and July 1929—and that was just in Cook County, Illinois. Then, on May 15, 1929, an explosion at a Cleveland hospital sent methyl chloride fumes through the building, killing 125 patients and employees.

Just a few months before that disaster, in the fall of 1928, Kettering had challenged Midgley to find a safer chemical refrigerant. Within days, Midgley and his research team had hit upon the idea of using a chemical compound called chlorofluorocarbons, which later became commonly known as Freon after chemical giant Du Pont trademarked the name. Chlorofluorocarbons showed great promise. They were nontoxic, inflammable, and inert, meaning that they stubbornly refused to mix or react with anything—the molecular equivalent of wallflowers. Frigidaire patented the formula for chlorofluorocarbons on December 31, 1928, and secretly set to work developing ways to make the compound cheaply and easily in industrial quantities. By April of 1930, Midgley was ready to unleash his chemical breakthrough on the world.

He did so at a gathering of the American Chemical Society in Atlanta by conducting a dramatic experiment. Ever the showman, Midgley lit a candle, inhaled two lungs full of CFCs, and calmly blew the candle out. Had he tried the same experiment with the common refrigerant chemicals of the day, the inhaled fumes would have seared Midgley's lungs and left him on stage choking and gasping, and his exhaled breath would have exploded upon contact with the flame. Word about Midgley's demonstration—and the potential of CFCs—spread quickly. By 1931, according to Cagin and Dray, Frigidaire had launched a $7 million ad campaign for home refrigerators focusing not only on the safety of CFC coolant, but on the appliances' more obvious innovations, including a special "hydrator" drawer for storing vegetables and the hand-crank ice-cube tray that promised to "End Cube Struggle!"

Soon CFCs were the preferred coolant in refrigerators, freezers, and air conditioners for both cars and buildings. New uses were discovered. Their insulating value makes them good for insulating foam. Eventually, CFCs turned up in various types of foam, including the kind of rigid foam in cheapo ice chests and fast-food containers, as well as flexible foam, such as that used in furniture cushions, car upholstery, and foam pillows. CFCs also power fire extinguishers and provide the cushion in urethane shoe soles. Low surface tension and low viscosity make CFCs good cleaning agents because they can wet even tiny spaces easily. (Water, by contrast, cannot get into small spaces.) As cleaning agents, CFCs eventually would be used to wash hundreds of products, from computer chips to artificial hip joints.

But the chemical compound's most notable use was as a propellant. With the invention of the spray-can top after World War II—with its simple plastic valve that releases or restrains a pressurized aerosol—the world's cars, homes, garages, kitchen cupboards, and medicine cabinets began to fill with hundreds of everyday products loaded with CFCs. Each can was a miniature version of those aerosolizing car engines. Those products made possible a comfortable, convenient, portable way of life that many people began to regard as a birthright. All over America and in other developed parts of the world, each day began with a collective and satisfying spritz of underarm deodorant or hairspray, or a billowing blast of shaving cream. Spray deodorant became a potent cultural metaphor for our cultural obsession with leading convenient, pleasantly sanitized lives.

By the early 1970s, the manufacture of CFCs had become an $8-billion-a-year industry. An estimated two hundred thousand jobs depended upon their manufacture, sale, and distribution. Entire regional economies were built around them. According to Sharon L. Roan, author of *Ozone Crisis: The 15-Year Evolution of a Sudden Global Emergency,* "By 1973, more than 2 billion aerosol cans rolled off production lines, which meant the average American purchased about 14 aerosol cans a year."

The Sunscreen Generation

Every party has a pooper, but in this case the party pooper may have saved the world. His name was F. Sherwood Rowland, and in 1972 the avuncular chemist began to question the seemingly unshakable belief that lighter-than-air CFCs were harmless. That year he met a British scientist who had documented an odd phenomenon: the amount of CFCs drifting slowly up into Earth's stratosphere—good old nontoxic, nonflammable, inert CFCs—was approximately equal to the amount of CFCs produced to that point by the chemical industry. This wasn't surprising, since, once released, the chemical compound basically hung around doing nothing. That inert quality had been Midgley's main selling point in 1930, and ever since had been considered the primary advantage of CFCs.

But Rowland wondered what might happen when that massive, rising cloud of CFCs reached the stratosphere, between twenty and thirty miles above the planet. Up there, environmental conditions are quite different than on Earth's surface. Would the CFCs still be inert? In June 1973, Rowland, a professor of chemistry at the University of California, Irvine, recruited a postdoctoral student name Mario Molina to help him investigate what might happen when the CFCs reached the upper atmosphere.

As it turns out, CFCs do react with something: intense sunlight. That's not a problem on the ground, because the atmosphere filters the sunlight to a point where it has no effect on a CFC molecule. But when a CFC molecule finally reaches the outer limit of the stratosphere, the sunlight there splinters it and frees a chlorine atom into the fragile bubble of ozone that surrounds the planet.

Let's take a breath here because, let's face it, chemistry can be boring as hell. But there is something vital you should know about that layer of ozone above us. That ozone filters out the sun's dangerous radioactivity and makes Earth habitable. Without it, a lot of unpleasant things would happen. The sea's plankton would die, a consequence that would echo all the way up the food chain. Skin cancer rates would soar. Worst-case scenario, humans would begin to die off either from the effects of the unfiltered rays or from the snowballing damage to the ecosystem. Without the ozone layer, this planet would be toast.

In science, questions don't always lead to "Eureka!" answers. Sometimes they lead to more questions, and that was the situation Rowland and Molina faced once they had documented the behavior of CFCs in the upper atmosphere. So they began to wonder: What happens to all that chlorine once it's released up there in our delicate, life-preserving ozone layer? The scientists began to calculate based on what they already knew about chlorine and ozone. And as they calculated, they began to get very, very nervous. Chlorine and ozone are a bad combination. Each freed chlorine atom theoretically would set up a chain reaction that could destroy as many as one hundred thousand molecules of ozone, a horrific multiplying effect. CFCs "weren't just bullets cutting holes in the ozone," wrote Pulitzer Prize–winning journalist Edward Humes. "They were shrapnel from a chemical grenade, shredding whole swaths of the vital layer high above us."

As the two scientists checked and rechecked their calculations and tested their theory for loopholes, the magnitude of their discovery began to sink in. They already knew that four decades' worth of CFCs from all that Right Guard and Aquanet was drifting slowly upward. If they were correct, CFCs released during World War II were just arriving to do their dirty work. The world was only just beginning to see the results of the folly that Midgley had unwittingly unleashed that day in 1930, and it would only get worse. Rowland often tells the story of the day he first recognized the danger. He arrived home dejected, and his wife, Joan, asked him how work was going. "Very, very well," he conceded. "But it looks like the end of the world."

Rowland began urging a total ban on CFC production and sharing his sky-is-falling theory with other scientists, as well as industry and government officials. Because a scientist's credibility is based on objectivity, Rowland paid a heavy price for that advocacy. The main CFC manufacturers were Dow and Du Pont, huge corporations loaded with money and bristling with PR people and scientists. Industry reactions were predictable and straightforward: Rowland was a nut, a scientific charlatan, an environmental extremist.

Academic scientists weren't much kinder. They considered it wrong for a professor to mix it up with industry and politicians. Federal officials eventually piled on. They stopped inviting Rowland to participate in scientific conventions and panels during the four years after the ozone discovery—even as he was gathering prestigious awards from his peers. When Rowland spoke at colleges and press conferences, CFC industry officials sometimes watched from a distance or peppered him with hostile questions. Sometimes he was invited to speak on CFCs at professional meetings, then found the invitation quietly withdrawn. Anne Burford, President Ronald Reagan's first chief of the Environmental Protection Agency, scornfully dismissed Rowland's claims as the scare tactic of a man with an anti-industry agenda.

Fixing a Hole

The debate turned a corner in 1985, when a team of British scientists released the results of independent research that confirmed the existence of a never-before-documented hole in Earth's ozone layer high above Antarctica. Some accounts claim the drop in ozone levels in the stratosphere was so dramatic that, after taking their first measurements, the scientists thought their instruments were faulty. Replacements were built and flown to the test site several months later, but those, too, showed an alarming drop in ozone levels. Other research soon confirmed a link between the disappearing ozone and the CFCs that were still being dumped into the air.

In March 1987, a report by the National Aeronautics and Space Administration showed that CFCs were destroying ozone far more rapidly than previously believed. The new measurements showed that from 1969 to 1987, ozone levels above the United States fell 2.3 percent, with losses of up to 6.2 percent in the winter. That smoking-gun study vindicated the two California scientists, who eventually would share the 1995 Nobel Prize for Chemistry with Dutch chemist Paul Crutzen. Du Pont, the world's largest CFC manufacturer, reacted to the 1987 NASA study by promising for the first time to phase out production of the compounds. Three weeks later, fifteen manufacturers of foam food containers pledged to convert from CFCs to safer compounds by the end of the year.

That same year, at a United Nations–sanctioned meeting in Montreal, scientists and officials from dozens of nations, including the United States, forged an unprecedented agreement to phase out CFC propellants and refrigerants. The so-called Montreal Protocol was the beginning of the end of worldwide CFC production and use.

About sixty years passed between Midgley's initial discovery and that global ban—about the same time lapse that followed Midgley's leaded-gas discovery and its ban. During those sixty years, Rowland estimates, the unrestrained use of CFCs depleted the ozone layer by 10 percent worldwide. Another 5 percent loss is likely, he says, as the remaining CFCs reach the upper atmosphere. Eventually, if the world stops sending those molecular grenades aloft, the holes in the ozone layer may begin to close.

A recent study by New Zealand researchers found that the ozone hole over Antarctica shrank 20 percent between 2003 and 2004, from 11 million to 9 million square miles. While encouraging, the researchers also warned not to read too much into the fluctuation, which could have been caused by natural climate variations. With luck and continued vigilance, the planet's self-inflicted wound may be healed a century from now. But things may get worse before they get better.

"In the first 25 years of the ultraviolet century [1970–2070], perhaps 1 to 2 million excess cases of skin cancer derived from stratospheric ozone loss," wrote McNeill in *Something New Under the Sun: An Environmental History of the 20th Century*. "That translated into about 10,000 to 20,000 early deaths, mainly among fair-skinned people in sunny lands such as Australia. . . . No one knows the full effect of excess UV radiation on immune response, so the real impacts of CFCs' erosion of the ozone layer on human health (let alone the rest of the biosphere) remain entirely unclear. But stratospheric ozone depletion—another combination of bad luck and Midgley's ingenuity—will surely kill many thousands more before the close of the ultraviolet century."

Midgley's own death came at age fifty-five, after a long, difficult struggle with polio. His inventiveness was apparent even during that ordeal when he devised a complex pulley-and-harness lifting mechanism to help himself get into and out of bed without assistance. Sadly, Midgley's wife found her husband's lifeless body tangled in that device on November 2, 1944. "The newspapers reported Midgley's demise as a freakish accident, but the friends and family who had witnessed his recent suffering knew better," wrote Cagin and Dray in *Between Earth and Sky*. "Columbus cemetery records list 'Suicide by strangulation' as the official cause of death."

At Midgley's funeral service, the minister noted that we all enter and leave this world with nothing. Kettering later told a colleague that he'd wanted to interrupt the minister to say, "In Midge's case, it would have been so appropriate to have added, 'But we can leave a lot behind for the good of the world.' " Indeed, the Detroit section of the American Chemical Society has, since 1965, bestowed the Thomas Midgley Award to honor "outstanding research contributions in the field of chemistry related to the automotive industry." But Midgley's most enduring legacy may be a better understanding that the planet's ecosystem is far more fragile than we ever imagined, and an acute awareness that solving today's problems can sometimes have unintended, and profound, consequences for tomorrow.

TOM MIDGLEY'S OTHER LANDMARK INVENTION

Without Thomas Midgley, one could argue, global environmental awareness might not exist.

By creating toxic leaded gasoline and ozone-eating chlorofluorocarbons in the 1920s—man-made substances that threatened the existence of every living creature on Earth—Midgley inadvertently created public-health crises so formidable that people began to understand just how drastically human behavior can affect what once seemed like a limitless ecosystem.

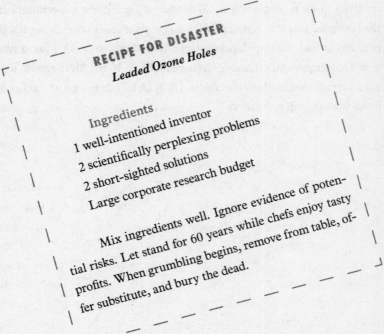

RECIPE FOR DISASTER

Leaded Ozone Holes

Ingredients

1 well-intentioned inventor
2 scientifically perplexing problems
2 short-sighted solutions
Large corporate research budget

Mix ingredients well. Ignore evidence of potential risks. Let stand for 60 years while chefs enjoy tasty profits. When grumbling begins, remove from table, offer substitute, and bury the dead.

When the widespread damage done by Midgley's chlorofluorocarbons became undeniable in the 1970s, thanks to the work of University of California, Irvine, chemist F. Sherwood Rowland and others, "the idea that a little hair spray and a little deodorant in the morning could affect our children's children changed everything," said Don Blake, a Rowland research partner at UCI. "When it comes to the atmosphere, there are no longer any [geographical] or political boundaries." The university's chancellor, Ralph Cicerone, agreed, telling *OC Metro* magazine in May 2000 that the idea that "people with little spray cans could affect the global environment seemed preposterous to almost everyone" before atmospheric ozone depletion was discovered.

Realizing that little things could do big damage changed the way many scientists looked at the world. And their work took on added urgency when they realized that the environmental problems they were studying knew no boundaries. "Whenever we are doing experiments in the lab or field we are thinking of the larger picture, of how the results fit into and impact the interdependent global environment," UCI earth system sciences professor Susan Trumbore told *OC Metro*. "It is easy to forget how new that kind of thinking is. [But] globalism is a natural concept to scientists of my generation."

kudzu: a most tangled tale

What began as a well-intentioned effort to stop soil erosion in the American South became a dramatic example of what can happen when you mess with Mother Nature.

A BRONZE HISTORICAL marker along Highway 90 on the outskirts of Chipley, Florida, commemorates a commercial nursery that once operated in that small town. The nursery was established in the early 1900s by Quaker conservationists Charles and Lillie Pleas, a couple who, were they alive today, might not recognize the transformed landscape of the American South for which they were partly, and inadvertently, responsible. In just a few short words, the marker tells a tale of good intentions gone horribly wrong; of inflamed passions and misguided love; of unstoppable ecological menace and strange, gothic beauty. It reads in part: "Kudzu developed here."

But to credit, or blame, the couple with developing what's now known as "the vine that ate the South" is a vast oversimplification. The Pleases were early boosters of kudzu (pronounced *kud*-zoo), a Japanese import that grows with the approximate speed and intensity of a tsunami, but they eventually were joined in their crusade to promote the vine by, among others, an outspoken Atlanta newspaper columnist and, eventually, the New Deal Democratic government of Franklin Delano Roosevelt. Each saw in kudzu a logical solution to critical erosion and agricultural problems that were plaguing the South in the early part of the 20th century, and, in fact, kudzu was as effective as promised in that regard.

But none of those well-intentioned cheerleaders foresaw the unintended consequences of their enthusiasm.

Despite emerging evidence that kudzu is useful in everything from cooking to basket weaving to curing alcoholism, the creeping vine these days is generally considered what *Deliverance* author James Dickey described as "a vegetable form of cancer." It's pernicious, destructive, and pretty much unstoppable in the warm-weather states. Barely a century after its introduction in the United States, kudzu now covers more than 7 million acres, or an area roughly the size of Massachusetts. According to one recent report, the vine has established itself in at least twenty-eight of the fifty states and beyond, with each new colony greeted with alarm in locales from Peoria, Illinois, to Long Island to the island of Bermuda.

"Throughout the South," wrote Janet Lembke, author of the 1999 book *Despicable Species: On Cowbirds, Kudzu, Hornworms, and Other Scourges,* "kudzu creeps with stealthy swiftness over brushpiles and fences. It climbs trees and telephone poles and casts its soft but heavy net over thickets and hedgerows. It enshrouds abandoned houses, tumbledown tobacco barns, rusted appliances, and junked cars. It sneaks into gardens and plowed fields. Displacing innocent native vegetation, it twines, curls, shoots upward and outward with relentless green insistence."

Power companies spend millions each year to keep kudzu from disrupting power lines, and great snarls of the plant are said to have derailed trains. Employing everything from angora goats to powerful herbicides, those trying to stop kudzu's advance report few long-term successes. They might as well swat an attacking swarm of bees one bee at a time.

There were plenty of warnings. Long before the modern environmental movement schooled even average Americans about the dangers of introducing nonnative species into a new ecosystem, those who understood kudzu's dangerous potential, including many farmers, were advising against it. The public debate was passionate; the red flags were waved, the doomsayers given their chance to object. But, of course, we decided to plant it anyway.

How Kudzu Came to Visit

Kudzu arrived in North America as a Trojan horse. The vine, a member of the pea family, had an ancient history in the Far East, dating at least to 2699 BC, when the Chinese emperor Chon-nong included kudzu in a catalog of herbs. By 200 BC, the Chinese were using its mighty taproots (which in a mature vine can have the girth of a dinner plate and weigh hundreds of pounds) as an herbal medicine. By the 18th century kudzu had been imported into Japan, and from there, in 1876, it migrated to the United States when it was featured as a fast-growing agricultural novelty at the Japanese Pavilion at the United States Centennial Exposition in Philadelphia. Seven years later, the Japanese featured it again at an exposition in New Orleans, where the plant found the sunny, warm, humid southern climate particularly to its liking.

By 1900, kudzu was the preferred "porch vine" in the South because its flowers were pretty and exuded the alluring scent of grapes; its mitten-shaped leaves provided ample shade, and during the warmest months of the year it reaches its top-speed growth of a foot a day—so fast some people joke that the best way to plant kudzu is to drop the seeds and run like hell. As the new growth races along, the plant divides at nodes spaced about a foot apart along the stem, and each node that touches soil sets down new roots, eventually forming a sprawling web between two and eight feet thick. Once it begins to climb, things get particularly dramatic. Telephone poles, trees, and entire buildings disappear beneath a curtain of green. Scientists estimate that a single acre of kudzu will expand to 5,250 acres if allowed to grow unchecked for a hundred years—a reality Dickey had in mind in describing the vines as "green, mindless, unkillable ghosts."

In the early 1900s, though, a botanist named David Fairchild began to worry. He was chief of the U.S. Department of Agriculture and had served for a time in Japan, where he came to believe in nutrient-rich kudzu's potential as a forage crop for grazing animals. He brought samples of it home to Washington, D.C., and planted the seedlings in his yard. As chronicled in his autobiography *The World Was My Garden: Travels of a Plant Explorer,* things got quickly out of control. The kudzu became "an awful, tangled nuisance" by quickly covering everything in his yard that didn't move. Writing in 1902, he cautioned strongly against use of the plant which had so enchanted him. Unfortunately, that warning wasn't published until 1938.

By then, Charles and Lillie Pleas had been feeding kudzu to their livestock for decades. It was as rich as alfalfa in protein and starch and far better suited to the South's climate. They touted the stuff through the 1940s "with the intensity and fervor of true believers," according to author Lembke, and eventually began their Florida nursery to develop the vine from seeds, cuttings, and root crowns. Their kudzu mail-order business was boffo, and they converted their share of doubters. Researcher Kurt E. Kinbacher, writing in the spring 2000 issue of the *Vulcan Historical Review,* notes that agricultural experts at the Alabama Polytechnic Institute (later renamed Auburn University) were by 1917 exploring the feasibility of planting kudzu as a cash crop.

The vine also began to generate support from unlikely quarters, including a central Georgia railroad whose executives imagined great profits in shipping bales of kudzu hay to market—overlooking that kudzu is notoriously hard to harvest, bale, and cure—and began providing free seedlings to farmers as a promotional gimmick. In 1927, an Atlanta newspaper columnist named Channing Cope picked up the chant, proclaiming: "Cotton isn't king here anymore. Kudzu is king."

The underlying reason for their enthusiasm was the dire condition of southern soil. During the boom years of the early 1900s, southern farmers had been working hard to supply the growing nation with cotton, corn, and other crops. But their traditional—some say reckless—method of planting the same crops year after year had depleted the region's soil of vital nutrients, and eventually the land became less productive. Fallow land is susceptible to erosion (the same problems that led to wind erosion in dust-bowl states such as Oklahoma), and over time parts of the American South became a moonscape of jagged gullies. A 1936 government survey of nearly 2 billion acres found that 700 million of them were severely eroded, with much of the topsoil in the South scoured to the infertile subsoil.

With its ability to stop soil erosion *and* feed livestock, kudzu promised salvation. Franklin Roosevelt had made soil conservation a centerpiece of his administration, establishing the Soil Erosion Service in 1933 as a division of the Department of the Interior. The agency dedicated itself to using "every feasible method to prevent soil erosion." Between 1933 and 1935, Hugh Hammond Bennett, the department's head, traveled nationwide preaching the gospel of soil conservation, urging farmers to plant soil-conserving crops, including kudzu.

Between 1935 and 1942, kudzu actually *was* king. The federal government was paying farmers between $6 and $8 an acre to plant it, and that was a pretty good deal in those lean times, especially for a crop that pretty much raised itself. The renamed Soil Conservation Service shipped an estimated 100 million plants from nurseries in Georgia and Alabama. A half million acres of kudzu took root in the South as a result, and in 1944 *Business Week* magazine touted the government's wonder crop as "cash on the vine."

By the late 1940s, though, the same farmers who'd heeded the government's call were complaining that the recommended cure-all was behaving like the cannibalistic plant Audrey in *Little Shop of Horrors*. It was overrunning their outbuildings and parked farm equipment. There was talk that cows that stood too long in one place were at risk of being swallowed by fast-growing tendrils, and motorists were jokingly advised to keep their windows rolled up when driving past kudzu colonies, just in case.

Indiana gardener Diana Craft's story is not uncommon. She recalled to researchers Derek and Donna Alderman an incident that happened during the two decades that she lived in Florida. She had collected a bag of kudzu roots in a brown paper grocery bag and put them on a low shelf in a closet, intending to plant them a few months later. When she opened the closet the following spring, she "noticed a white rope that I didn't remember having. I started pulling the rope, and pulling the rope, and pulling the rope, until finally I realized it was not a rope at all. The kudzu root had grown to about fifty feet over the winter, in a bag and in the dark."

Ranchers also reported that kudzu, a member of the bean family, had a rather unfortunate side effect for those who used it as forage food for their livestock: methane. Ed Bostick, a biology professor at Kennesaw State College in Georgia, told the *Atlanta Journal-Constitution* in 1993 that cows that graze on kudzu are excessively flatulent—which contributes to global warming—and that "they actually came up with a lance to stab cow bellies and let out the gases. I have this image of cattle shooting through the sky like balloons."

The environmental havoc was undeniable, and overwhelming. One kudzu booster, quoted years later by writers for *Mother Earth News*, said: "It was like discovering Old Blue was a chicken killer."

By 1953, with foresters and transportation engineers reporting similar concerns about runaway growth, the federal government stopped recommending kudzu for any purpose; farmers were demanding compensation for land and income lost to kudzu. The Kudzu Club of America, which in 1943 boasted a membership of twenty thousand, was quietly disbanded. Studies on how to best eliminate the vine began in 1956, at least one of them at the university now known as Auburn, which had led the way in promoting the plant. The feds officially labeled kudzu a common weed in 1970, but the policy shift had the approximate impact of epithets shouted at a charging rhino.

The balance of nature in the South was wobbling noticeably. As kudzu's own nitrogen-fixing qualities improved the region's depleted soils, the vine itself began to grow like a postapocalyptic Godzilla feeding off of ambient radiation. The monster was moving fast, and today kudzu claims at least 120,000 additional acres each year. In 1993, the same federal government that once so boldly touted kudzu cultivation as a great idea estimated that the vine was costing Americans about $50 million a year.

That's not to say kudzu is invincible. Certain fungi common to beans can retard its growth, and animals as diverse as deer, goats, rabbits, slugs, moth larvae, and some Japanese beetles find it delectable. Overgrazing by ruminants can eliminate a stand of kudzu within two years, even if it creates a methane problem in the process. Some herbicides are effective, but that sort of human intervention requires both vigilance and persistence, with treatment seldom effective unless it's carried out consistently every year for a decade. John Byrd, a professor of weed science at Mississippi State University who tested various chemicals to control the vine, suggested in a 2000 issue of *Smithsonian* magazine that the surest way to control a patch of kudzu is to build a Wal-Mart on top of it.

Some have simply tried to make the best of the situation by finding new and imaginative uses for kudzu, from baskets woven from the vines to skin lotions to deep-fried kudzu leaves, but there's an unmistakable whiff of surrender to it all. The most intriguing possibility is modern medical research that confirms the ancient Eastern practice of using kudzu root to treat alcoholism, though to this point it has proven effective only on a certain breed of hard-drinking hamster.

Touting the upside of kudzu, though, is a zero-sum game. Kudzu additives and products would need to become as ubiquitous as sugar in this culture to make a significant dent in this country's approximately eleven thousand square miles of the stuff. The editors at *Time* magazine understood this when, in a special end-of-the-millennium issue, they listed the introduction of kudzu to the United States among the "100 worst ideas of the century." The list also included asbestos, DDT, driftnet fishing, Barney, spray-on hair, *Jerry Springer,* and thong underwear for men.

Where Kudzu Has Crept

Kudzu's impact on American culture, particularly in the South, is as hard to ignore as the vine itself. Worldwide, the word is now used as a synonym for unchecked and obnoxious growth, with everything from e-mail spam to suburban housing to the World Wide Web said to be growing like, well, you know.

In terms of culture, pick a topic. Music? You have your choice, from rock (the cover image of R.E.M.'s 1983 *Murmur* album showed kudzu covering a railroad right-of-way), to punk (who remembers the now-defunct band Kudzu Ganja?), to alternative country (Kudzu Kings), to bluegrass (the Kudzu Quartet), to barbershop (the Kudzu Krooners used the motto "We grow on ya"). Film? A sixteen-minute documentary called *Kudzu* was an Academy Award nominee (best live-action short) in 1976. Literature? Kudzu turns up as both the central metaphor and in the title of novelist William Doxey's 1985 *Cousins to the Kudzu* and Hal Crowther's 2000 essay collection *Cathedrals of Kudzu,* both published by Louisiana State University Press. Mass media? Doug Marlette's *Kudzu* comic strip, begun in 1981, won the Pulitzer Prize in 1988. Management expert Stephen M. Gower uses kudzu as the organizing image of *The Art of Killing Kudzu: Management by Encouragement,* his 1991 book about eliminating negative attitudes in the workplace.

Individuals and communities throughout the South have embraced kudzu in their own unique ways, with kudzu festivals and even local sports events such as the Birmingham (Alabama) Track Club's annual 5K Kudzu Run and the Kudzu Classic youth soccer tournament in Clinton, Mississippi. A recent survey by an Atlanta public-relations firm, Kudzu Communications, revealed that the word "kudzu" turns up in at least thirty-six business and street names in the states of Georgia, Alabama, and North Carolina.

Kudzu's darker side surfaced in the early 1980s, when Atlanta actually declared out-of-control kudzu a misdemeanor. The overgrowth, which offers shelter and privacy to many of the city's homeless, also had made it distressingly easy for the city's notorious child killer to hide victims' bodies. And at the turn of the 21st century, there was a creeping political irony to it all: The states that now form the core of conservative Republican power in America are slowly being strangled by one of the few thriving parts of Franklin Roosevelt's legacy.

"Good, bad, or indifferent: no matter how we see it, kudzu has settled in and won't be budged," wrote Lembke in *Despicable Species*. "Roots in the earth, leaves to the sun, it will persist until the last trump. I've thought of comparing it to phenomena I find obnoxious, like the wild proliferation of pounding boom boxes or the unchecked spread of concrete lawn geese and decorative nylon banners, but no, there's nothing faddish about the plant. It's a force of nature, more on the order of azaleas and tobacco, country music, coon hunts, NASCAR races, and good old boys. It just plain *is*. Certainly, nothing obliges us to like it, but because we must live with it, the least painful way to come to terms with the doggone stuff may indeed be to see it as a heritage."

If you listen closely to Lembke's words, though, you can hear the unambiguous snap of a briskly waving white flag.

DID KUDZU KILL THE KUDZU KING?

Channing Cope, an agricultural columnist for the *Atlanta Constitution* in the late 1930s and early 1940s, did everything he could to promote kudzu as a wondrous plant capable of solving any number of the problems that plagued the American South during that period. Part evangelist, part huckster, Cope labeled himself the "Kudzu King" and hailed the plant in print and on radio. He also established the Kudzu Club of America in the early 1940s, and its stated goal was to plant a million acres of kudzu in Georgia and 8 million acres of it across the South.

What few people know, however, is that kudzu played out in Cope's life like the demon in a novel by Stephen King, who has, in fact, used kudzu colonies in his fiction as the dark realm of monsters.

At the height of his fame, Cope delivered a daily radio broadcast extolling the vine from the front porch of his house at Yellow River Plantation, near Atlanta. At the time he bought the farm, it "consisted of seven hundred eroded, unproductive acres," according to author Janet Lembke. "But kudzu, which he set in to improve the soil and serve as pasturage for cattle, worked its thickety green magic almost overnight."

Cope refused to let county workers cut back the large kudzu patches on his property even after the U.S. government labeled the vine an ecological threat. In time, the vine overtook many of the farm's trees and enclosed the road leading to the farmhouse, giving local teenagers private

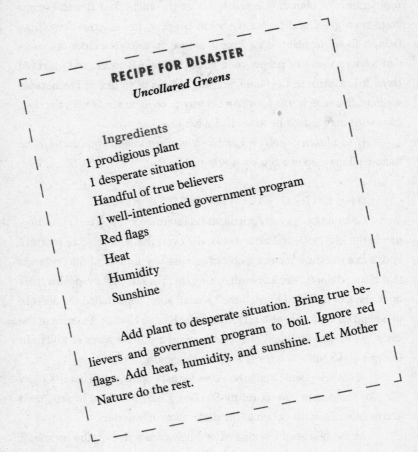

RECIPE FOR DISASTER
Uncollared Greens

Ingredients

1 prodigious plant
1 desperate situation
Handful of true believers
1 well-intentioned government program
Red flags
Heat
Humidity
Sunshine

Add plant to desperate situation. Bring true believers and government program to boil. Ignore red flags. Add heat, humidity, and sunshine. Let Mother Nature do the rest.

places to park and party. Philip S. Cohen, a Cope friend, told researchers Derek and Donna Alderman in 2001 that when the Kudzu King "came off his porch one evening to run off these trespassers, he walked only three feet before dying of a massive heart attack."

That was in 1961. Many years later, a reporter for Cope's old newspaper visited the farm and spoke to its new owner. According to a 1993 *Journal-Constitution* story, "when [the new owner] bought the place, he had found the strangest thing. The farmhouse—it was covered in kudzu."

the preposterous collapse of
"galloping gertie"

The completed Tacoma Narrows Bridge stood for four months in 1940 as a landmark of machine age design and aesthetics—qualities that are less apparent now that it's at the bottom of Puget Sound.

SUCCESS CAN BE the harshest prelude to failure, because the fall of the high and mighty seldom ends well. And it's safe to say that Leon Moisseiff, who helped engineer New York's George Washington Bridge and San Francisco's Golden Gate Bridge during the late 1920s and 1930s, was at the top of his game in 1938 when the Washington State Toll Bridge Authority hired the New Yorker as a consultant and principal engineer for its most ambitious bridge project ever—a suspension bridge across the Tacoma Narrows, a half-mile gap between Washington State's mainland and the Olympic Peninsula.

But on November 7, 1940, a little more than four months after the Tacoma Narrows Bridge opened as one of the sleekest, lightest, and most beautiful suspension bridges ever built, Moisseiff's reputation lay in a twisted heap, much like the bridge itself. What his employers had wanted in those money-strapped, post-Depression years was a serviceable bridge to link the rural Olympic Peninsula to commercial and military centers near Tacoma and Seattle. What they got was a beautiful bridge equipped by Moisseiff with a fatal engineering flaw—a flaw its Latvian-born, Columbia-educated engineer-designer should have foreseen based on numerous suspension-bridge failures of the past. But thanks to the triumph of beauty over brains, as well as the amplifying effect of having amateur filmmakers and a newspaper photographer capture for posterity the absurd final moments of the Tacoma Narrows Bridge, Moisseiff went from being one of America's best-known bridge designers and theorists one day to the butt of endless jokes the next.

Only a few today remember his name, and the panel that investigated the bridge collapse eventually decided to blame the entire engineering profession rather than Moisseiff in particular. But an official history of the incident complied by Richard Hobbs for the Washington State Department of Transportation notes with some understatement: "After November 7, 1940, [Moisseiff's] services were not in high demand." Moisseiff died three years later, before the film footage and photos of his big goof became an enduring pop-culture metaphor for hubris, careless planning, and aesthetic folly, and before the study of his judgment errors became part of the core curriculum in engineering schools around the world. But from the moment the Tacoma Narrows Bridge went down, the pieces of the fallen structure became what surely is every bridge builder's worst nightmare, and what it remains today: a magnificent underwater reef.

The "Search for the Graceful and Elegant"

Proposals to bridge the Tacoma Narrows had been circulating since 1889, when the Northern Pacific Railroad first studied the possibility of building a functional train trestle across that part of Puget Sound. Momentum grew, and between 1928 and 1938 no fewer than seven different bridge plans were developed and discussed. So how could a group of intelligent and well-meaning civil engineers spend four decades coming up with a bridge that eventually crumbled into infamy after just four months of use?

The answer involves the quest for aesthetic elegance that was so much a part of design and architecture in machine age America of the 1920s and 1930s. In that new era of streamlined airplanes, cars, and mass-produced everything, the nation dreamed of greatness and wanted its structures to reflect that vision. "Even after the stock market crash of 1929 and the hard times of the Great Depression that followed, the dream of greatness persisted," wrote Hobbs in his comprehensive narrative of the Tacoma Narrows Bridge on a Washington State Department of Transportation Web site. "Skyscrapers came to symbolize the strengths of American civilization. The soaring towers represented America's vision of greatness, efficiency, elegance, power, courage, and even rebirth." The phrase "frozen fountain" was bestowed upon those high-rising structures that celebrated what architect Louis H. Sullivan in 1896 had described as "the force and power of altitude."

In that era, building a utilitarian train trestle or a merely functional passenger-car bridge across a spot as magnificent as the Tacoma Narrows would have seemed like putting yard gnomes on the White House lawn. The site—a divide that featured picturesque bluffs topped by tall evergreens—was a blank canvas in need of an artist.

As luck had it, Moisseiff's design aesthetic meshed perfectly with the times for several reasons. Bridges, he believed, needed to be "safe, convenient, economical in cost and maintenance, and at the same time satisfy the sense of beauty of the average man of our time." Engineers should strive for "the pleasure of good form," and continuously "search for the graceful and elegant." As luck also had it, "graceful and elegant" usually meant thinner and lighter, which also meant cheaper—an appealing notion to taxpayers and government accountants during the scarce-money years after the 1929 crash.

When the state of Washington applied to the federal Public Works Administration for money to build the Tacoma Narrows Bridge, the feds decided that the safe and practical preliminary design by state bridge engineer Clark Eldridge was, at $11 million, too expensive. The precise reasons why the federal officials balked aren't clear, but dark rumors have swirled for decades. Suspecting the fix was in, Eldridge later suggested in his unpublished autobiography that Moisseiff had met with PWA officials before their decision and convinced them that he could design a bridge that could be built for far less money than Eldridge's design. That suggestion seems plausible because the PWA's decision to fund the project came with two telling caveats. It required the state to hire outside design consultants, and it offered only $6.4 million to get it built—the same amount Eldridge claims Moisseiff estimated *his* bridge design would cost. Federal officials later denied trying to steer the job into the hands of any particular designer, but Moisseiff eventually got the gig as design consultant for the superstructure, and the New York firm of Moran & Proctor was hired to design the substructure. And Eldridge, who'd spent years on his own design and scavenging money for what he considered his pet project, was eventually put in charge of building Moisseiff's design.

That design was so stunning that Moisseiff, boldly overcoming humility, described the completed Tacoma Narrows Bridge as "the most beautiful in the world." It was a classic modernist span with streamlined features, a showpiece of period design. He'd given it two soaring 425-foot towers and accentuated their height by incorporating supporting cables and other vertical lines that swept the eye skyward. The roadway that stretched across the mile-plus length of the bridge was a slender two-lane ribbon of asphalt only 39 feet wide. The whole thing was secured at both ends by massive art deco anchorages of concrete and steel. "It was not merely a road for cars and trucks," Hobbs wrote, "but an artistic and engineering statement. It was the culmination of [Moisseiff's] outstanding career."

Had Moisseiff paid a bit more attention to the history of suspension bridges, though, he would have realized that he'd overlooked something rather critical. Bridge builders of the 19th century had followed the same path as Moisseiff, striving to build suspension bridges that were longer, lighter, and more flexible. But they had also cataloged a persistent problem with such designs: the lighter and more flexible the bridge, the more it tended to move in the wind.

Engineers then didn't fully understand the destructive potential of "lift"—the physical force capable of raising a heavy airplane into the air—but they realized that something was clearly wrong with those delicate bridges, and not just because travelers often reported getting seasick while crossing them. The first recorded wind-buffeted collapse of a suspension bridge was in 1817, when a 260-foot footbridge across Scotland's river Tweed went down just six months after it was finished. The Menai Straits suspension bridge in Wales, which opened in 1826, was badly damaged and nearly fell during an 1839 gale.

In 1854, in Wheeling, West Virginia, wind wasted a 1,010-foot span across the Ohio River that had been the world's longest suspension bridge when it was completed five years earlier. According to Henry Petroski, author of the 1985 book *To Engineer Is Human: The Role of Failure in Successful Design*, the West Virginia bridge's final moments were chronicled by a reporter for the *Wheeling Intelligencer* in language that could have been used to describe the final moments of the Tacoma Narrows Bridge nearly a century later. The bridge was "lunging like a ship in a storm" as it "twisted and writhed" and fell "with an appalling crash and roar." Wrote Petroski: "If the designers of the Tacoma Narrows had known the story of the Wheeling suspension bridge . . . they would have had no excuse for overlooking wind as a possible cause of failure to be anticipated during design, not a problem to be dealt with after construction."

The last major suspension bridge failure before Tacoma Narrows was in 1889, with the wind-whipped collapse of the Niagara-Clifton Bridge between Niagara Falls, New York, and Clifton, Ontario, Canada. Other lightweight suspension bridges had survived, but most had had to be retrofitted with stiffening trusses. In all, Petroski wrote in 1994's *Design Paradigms: Case Histories of Error and Judgment in Engineering*, ten suspension bridges were severely damaged or destroyed by the wind between 1818 and 1889.

By the late 19th century, bridge engineers were building less flexible and heavier bridges to avoid problems with wind. John Roebling, for example, had incorporated the lessons of the past into his landmark 1883 Brooklyn Bridge, which he consciously designed to handle strong wind. But by the early 20th century, those earlier lessons were fading. Princeton civil engineering professor David P. Billington wrote that Roebling's "historical perspective seemed to have been replaced by a visual preference unrelated to structural engineering." A major suspension bridge hadn't failed since 1889, but as Petroski points out, "the absence of failure does not prove that a design is flawless. . . . it appears to be a trait of human nature to take repeated success as confirmation that everything is being done correctly."

It wasn't. By the 1930s, even the massive Golden Gate Bridge, for which Moisseiff had been a consulting engineer, was behaving badly on windy days. Its chief engineer reported a 1938 incident in which a cluster of ripples traveled along the bridge's roadway like an incoming set of surfable waves. That landmark bridge eventually was retrofitted to make it more stable.

Moisseiff was aware that wind posed a problem, but according to Hobbs he believed, like most other engineers at the time, that wind was far less a factor in stressing a bridge than heavy traffic and poor workmanship. He'd even tempted fate by designing the Tacoma Narrows Bridge with an impermeable, eight-foot-high side panel running along the outside of the roadway that acted like a sail, maximizing the wind's impact. Bridge designers knew that wind occasionally moved bridges from side to side, and they usually adjusted their designs for that lateral movement, or deflection—a theory credited mostly to Moisseiff, who claimed his Tacoma Narrows design would withstand a broadside wind of 120 miles per hour, and could deflect twenty feet.

But up and down? And twisting like an angry serpent? That wasn't part of anybody's plan.

The "Pearl Harbor of Engineering"

An estimated seven thousand people attended the official opening of the Tacoma Narrows Bridge on July 1, 1940, and a parade of two thousand cars trekked from one side to the other that first day. The lead car carried the state's governor, who proudly paid the toll (75¢ each direction) as photographers snapped away. But by then, the bridge already had a reputation among workers and others who knew it well as something of a thrill ride. Even a wind of less than 5 miles per hour sometimes rippled the road structure, and those ripples sometimes reached five feet high and left the road surface undulating for hours. Motorists reported that driving across was like bobbing among ocean waves, with cars ahead and behind rising to peaks and disappearing into troughs. Within a couple of months of its opening, the bridge bore the jovial nickname "Galloping Gertie"— a nickname Hobbs notes was first assigned to the doomed bridge in Wheeling.

"Suspension bridges are supposed to move," he wrote, "but this was different."

Transportation officials were publicly delighted that traffic across the bridge during its first months was much heavier than expected—more than triple their projected figures—and it appeared the financial gamble of building the bridge had paid off. They also dismissed the bridge's bouncing as normal conduct for a new suspension bridge.

Privately, though, they were worried. They had already contacted Moisseiff with their concerns, and he acknowledged that two other recently opened suspension bridges, the Deer Isle Bridge in Maine and the Bronx-Whitestone Bridge across the East River in New York (for which he had been a consulting engineer), had similar problems. The state also had contacted an engineering professor at the University of Washington, F. Bert Farquharson, to begin scale-model wind testing to find a solution to the problem. As a stopgap measure, they installed shock-absorbing jacks at the towers and tie-down cables on the sides. Those measures helped a little in controlling the movement, but not enough.

Ominous warnings began to accumulate. About a week before the collapse, one of the tie-down cables snapped, requiring repairs. And in his lab, Farquharson sometimes noticed an unexpected "twisting motion" when wind passed through his scale model of the Tacoma Narrows Bridge. According to Hobbs, the engineer predicted "if that sort of motion ever occurred on the real bridge, it would be the end of the bridge."

Farquharson finished his study of the bridge on November 2. Along with Eldridge and others, the engineers immediately began developing specific plans and shopping for wind deflectors and other materials they needed to streamline the structure. But the improvements were expected to take about forty-five days, and early on the morning of November 7, the winds from the southwest began to pick up.

It was hardly a hurricane-force assault, with measurements topping out at around 42 miles per hour. According to Hobbs, Eldridge stopped by about 8:30 a.m., but saw no reason to be any more concerned than usual. A thrill-seeking local college student paid the 10¢ pedestrian fee just so he could walk across the undulating bridge for kicks. Not long after Eldridge left, though, the toll collector on the bridge's west side was concerned enough that he was reluctant to let Leonard Coatsworth, a copy editor for the *News Tribune* in Tacoma, drive across the bridge. He told Coatsworth that he'd be one of the last motorists allowed to pass until things settled down.

They didn't.

"Just as I drove past the towers, the bridge began to sway violently from side to side," Coatsworth recalled. "Before I realized it, the tilt became so violent that I lost control of the car." He stepped out and was thrown to the concrete, which he could hear cracking all around him. When he tried to coax his daughter's black cocker spaniel, Tubby, from the car, the panicked dog bit his hand. It was all he could do to crawl off the bridge to save himself. He called the newspaper office to say he was coming in to write about the experience, and urged the city desk send a reporter and photographer to the scene.

Reporter Howard Clifford grabbed his camera, and he and fellow reporter Bert Brintnall drove to the bridge to look for a story, ultimately deciding that, if nothing else, they could rescue Tubby from Coatsworth's abandoned car and write about that. They arrived about the same time as Farquharson, who had driven an hour from Seattle to take film and photos of the bridge's behavior in the wind. Barney Elliott and Harbine Monroe, co-owners of the Camera Shop in Tacoma, had grabbed their Bell & Howell 16mm camera with the same idea in mind.

A few minutes after 10 a.m., reporters Clifford and Brintnall started walking out to Coatsworth's car. They didn't get far, maybe twenty yards, when the bridge's swaying motion first mutated into the violent twist that Farquharson had observed during his wind-tunnel tests. By 10:07, the roadway was tilting up to a 45-degree angle, with one side twenty-eight feet above the other. The question of why that twisting began under those conditions has been the subject of intense aerodynamic study in the decades since, but as Farquharson had predicted, it was the moment when the bridge was clearly doomed.

"I'd gone just a short distance when I heard a popping sound, like rifle fire," Clifford recalled to the *Seattle Times* in 1990. "It was the cables that supported the bridge deck. They were breaking and flying around in the air."

The next forty-five minutes were painfully well chronicled. The wind ebbed and flowed, but around 10:30 a large chunk of the center span broke loose and dropped 195 feet into the water below. Thirty minutes later, the twisting motion resumed, and the end began. "Massive steel girders twisted like rubber," Hobbs wrote. "Bolts sheered and flew into the wind. Six light poles on the east end broke off like matchsticks. Steel suspender cables snapped, flying into the air 'like fishing lines,' as Farquharson said." (Accounts differ, but Hobbs concludes that the engineering professor probably was the last person off the collapsing bridge.) At 11:02, a six-hundred-foot-long section of the center-span roadway broke free, flipped over, and fell, taking Coatsworth's car and Tubby, the day's only casualty, down with it. The splash reached one hundred feet high. By 11:10, Puget Sound had a new thirty-fathom-deep reef that eventually proved so suitable for underwater life that, even after extensive salvage operations, it was named in 1992 to the National Register of Historic Places.

An after-the-fact reference to the 1940 Tacoma Narrows Bridge collapse in the collection of the University of Washington Libraries refers to the event as "the Pearl Harbor of engineering," and in some ways it was. But in other ways, the catastrophe may have been one of the most constructive events in modern engineering. Petroski, a Duke University civil engineering professor, wrote in 2001 that "unfortunately, it often takes a catastrophic failure to provide clear and unambiguous evidence that the design assumptions were faulty. It provided the counterexample to the implicit engineering hypothesis under which all such bridges were designed, namely, that wind did not produce aerodynamic effects in heavy bridge decks sufficient to bring them down. Thus, the failure of the Tacoma Narrows Bridge proved more instructive than the success of all the bridges that had performed satisfactorily—or nearly so—over the preceding decades."

Even now, the far sturdier and more conventional $14 million replacement bridge that began carrying traffic across the Tacoma Narrows in 1950 is "one of the most studied in the United States," engineering manager Joe Collins told the *News Tribune* in Tacoma in 2002. Its builder, Tacoma Narrows Constructors, began precautionary tests that year to make sure its five-year, $615 million plan to resurface the bridge roadway wouldn't end up changing the behavior of the bridge in the wind or under stress. "The world as a whole got much smarter about suspension bridges as a result of Galloping Gertie's failure," Collins said.

The Tacoma Narrows Bridge collapse is still mentioned alongside other spectacular and embarrassingly public engineering failures that were far more recent, including the 1979 sinking of the west half of Washington's $26.6 million Hood Canal Floating Bridge, and the tragic 1981 collapse of two suspended walkways at the Hyatt Regency Hotel in Kansas City. That may be because nothing compounds a failure or tragedy like the inconvenient presence of someone with a camera, and that aspect of the bridge failure pushed it into another realm entirely. As one of the earliest and most spectacular caught-on-tape American touchstones, its visceral impact is much the same as Abraham Zapruder's 1963 film of the assassination of President John F. Kennedy in Dallas, or the televised 1986 and 2003 explosions of the space shuttles *Challenger* and *Columbia*.

Fortunately, a cocker spaniel was the only casualty that day in 1940, but only if you don't count the careers and reputations that were ruined in the aftermath of the collapse. Moisseiff wasn't the only victim. Two days after the bridge went down, Eldridge publicly blamed the moneylenders who insisted on hiring "an eastern firm of engineers" for the project. By the following spring, he'd decided he needed a change of scenery. He took a job with the U.S. Navy and moved to Guam in the South Pacific.

On January 11, 1941, about two months after the collapse, the *Tacoma Times* broke the news that the federal Public Works Administration's own field engineer in Tacoma, David L. Glenn, had warned of faults with the bridge design and recommended that the agency refuse to accept the structure. The PWA ignored that recommendation, and fired Glenn two weeks after his dissent was made public.

The fallout included inquiry hearings, insurance scandals, and generalized acrimony that lasted the better part of a decade. The salvage operation was a disaster, too, with the Toll Bridge Authority paying nearly $650,000 to recover seven thousand tons of scrap steel that later was sold for less than $300,000. Another insult came many years later, when leading bridge engineers studied Eldridge's original design for the Tacoma Narrows Bridge and declared that, had it been built, it would "without a doubt" still be standing.

The final ironic twist was left to residents of the Olympic Peninsula. The peninsula had about four thousand residents when the replacement bridge opened in 1950, but the population ballooned in the decades that followed, especially after authorities stopped charging a toll to cross it in 1965. It wasn't long before locals were talking about blowing up the new Tacoma Narrows Bridge to stop the runaway population growth.

A TACOMA NARROWS SUCCESS STORY

Not everything about the 1940 collapse of the original Tacoma Narrows Bridge was a disaster.

Barney Elliott and Harbine Monroe, cofounders of the Camera

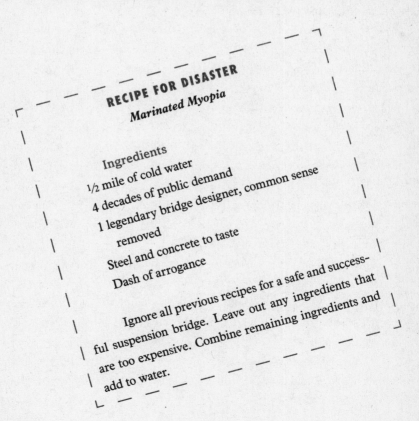

RECIPE FOR DISASTER
Marinated Myopia

Ingredients
½ mile of cold water
4 decades of public demand
1 legendary bridge designer, common sense removed
Steel and concrete to taste
Dash of arrogance

Ignore all previous recipes for a safe and successful suspension bridge. Leave out any ingredients that are too expensive. Combine remaining ingredients and add to water.

Shop in Tacoma, continued to sell their famous film of the bridge's flailing final moments to engineering colleges and for use in advertising campaigns. Their descendants continue to operate the original shop and a second store in Puyallup, Washington, and offer the footage via their Web site for $55 per copy, including ground shipping in the continental U.S.

In addition, the National Film Preservation Act requires that the Librarian of Congress, with advice from the National Film Preservation Board and suggestions from the public, identify twenty-five valuable films each year and ensure they are preserved for all time. In 1998, the film shot by Elliott and Monroe was added to the National Registry of Film, along with other classics such as 1925's *Phantom of the Opera*, 1935's *Bride of Frankenstein*, and 1982's *Tootsie*.

Lesson #6
PERSISTENCE CAN OUTWEIGH TALENT

the screeching diva

With a voice that one critic described as like that of a "maudlin cuckoo," Florence Foster Jenkins may have been the worst operatic singer of all time. But the do-it-yourself diva was able to charm audiences with unabashed, joyful ineptitude.

IN JANUARY 2004, a twenty-one-year-old engineering student named William Hung had the audacity to sing in the TV talent competition *American Idol* on a dare, even though he had no performing experience beyond singing karaoke, and no discernible talent. Hung's atrocious rendition of the Ricky Martin hit "She Bangs" was cut off in midsong by the judges, who were unable to restrain their laughter when the Hong Kong native earnestly explained, "You know, I have no professional training of singing." But when the guffaws subsided, Hung's irrepressibly cheerful incompetence provided him with an unlikely express lane to fame. As the *Los Angeles Times* subsequently reported, Hung's vocals, sampled and remixed with hip-hop and techno instrumentals, became a Top 10 hit on a Chicago radio station. Hung fans created several Web sites devoted to him, one of which had to be moved to a server with more capacity after it attracted 4 million visitors in four days. He quickly signed a $25,000 recording contract.

When Hung's CD of Elton John and R. Kelly covers came out a few months later, it was savaged by critics, including an *Entertainment Weekly* reviewer who called his singing "pathetic" and suggested that the record company was cruelly exploiting him. No matter. Hung's record went on to sell a respectable one hundred thousand copies, undoubtedly leaving many more musically adept would-be stars bitterly envious.

But Hung is merely the latest in a long line of performers who have developed enthusiastic followings despite their own painful lack of ability—whose work, to borrow a phrase from author Susan Sontag, is "good *because* it's awful." The genre of "outsider" or "incorrect" music, as aficionados call it, includes overreaching luminaries in other fields, such as TV actor turned lounge singer Telly Savalas and quarterback turned country crooner Terry Bradshaw, as well as show-business naifs such as the Shaggs, a trio of New Hampshire sisters whose discordant 1969 guitar-rock album, *Philosophy of the World,* became such a cult classic that the *New Yorker* profiled them thirty years later.

Alas, the perverse appeal of appallingly bad music has never been subjected to thorough scientific study, so it's impossible to say what aberrant neural pathways were stimulated by Elva Connes Miller, a muumuu-clad Kansas grandmother whose off-key covers of pop songs such as "These Boots Are Made for Walkin' " earned her a spot on Bob Hope's Vietnam tour, or by the frenetic, atonal rants of Chicagoan Wesley Willis, who reportedly kept in his apartment ten thousand CDs filled with compositions with titles such as "Vultures Ate My Dead Ass Up."

But it seems to take more than mere incompetence to capture an audience's heart. To become a cult favorite, a performer must be as unabashedly passionate as he or she is woefully untalented. Irwin Chusid, author of *Songs in the Key of Z: The Curious Universe of Outsider Music,* put it aptly in describing an inept country singer: "He's got an awful toupee. He can't sing worth a lick . . . the rhythm falters, he's constantly off key, his enunciation is terrible. . . . He's thoroughly inept, and yet his ineptitude is so sincere, the intent is so genuine."

But in the annals of musical awfulness, one nonvirtuoso rises above the others. During the course of a vocal career that stretched from 1912 to 1944, she earned an enduring spot in music history as perhaps the most breathtakingly awful singer ever to perform in front of a paying crowd. Her outlandish costumes, mock-profound stage presence, and penchant for doing violence to the works of Brahms, Mozart, and other great composers surely made her one of the most preposterous. A 1942 *Time* magazine reviewer noted that "she will intrepidly attack any aria, scale its altitudes in great swoops and hoots, and assay its descending trills with the vigor of a maudlin cuckoo." All the same, Florence Foster Jenkins still managed to win the affections of the most aesthetically exacting, hypercritical audience imaginable—the highbrow elite of the New York music world. And by proving it was possible to be both bad and beloved, the screeching diva who signed her publicity stills "Lady Florence" paved the way for countless William Hungs to come.

"The Bel Canto Banshee"

Just how bad a singer was Lady Florence? The verdict of contemporary critics is that she was very, very bad. British reviewer Marc Brindle, after listening to a recently rediscovered recording of Jenkins, notes that "where notes should be floated, they have a gale force choppiness" and that lines "crack as loudly as the splitting hull of the *Titanic*." Fergus Gwyneplaine MacIntyre, who wrote a retrospective for the *New York Daily News* in 2004, dubbed her "the Bel Canto banshee." *Opera News* writer Brooks Peters has compared her screechy voice to that of the fictional Susan Alexander, who was forced against her will to become a singer in the 1941 Orson Welles film *Citizen Kane*.

But part of Jenkins's charm was that nothing—not even a total lack of talent—was going to stop her from singing. Born in 1868, she was the only daughter of Wilkes-Barre, Pennsylvania, lawyer and banker Charles Dorrance Foster, who for a time served in the state legislature. Her mother, Mary J. Hoagland Foster, was a member of forty-two different society clubs and organizations. Florence started music lessons as a young child, and at age eight she gave her first piano recital. She loved to sing as well, and as she grew into a young woman, her head was filled with dreams of pursuing a musical career in Europe. Her father nixed that notion—by some accounts, because he thought a young woman's place was at home, though he may simply have been realistic about his daughter's musical talents. Not long afterward, Florence eloped to Philadelphia with a young doctor, Frank Jenkins. The marriage turned out to be an unhappy one, and the couple divorced in 1902. Jenkins spent seven years eking out a living as a music teacher.

Lady Florence might have ended up just another embittered matron contemplating her crushed ambitions, except that in 1909, her father died and, in addition to a piano, left her a quarterly stipend that made her independently wealthy. By then, she was in her early forties, too old to even dream of studying opera at the Paris Conservatoire. But Jenkins wasn't content to spend the rest of her life contemplating what outfit she should wear to the Long Branch horse show. Within her substantial body still beat the heart of an aesthete. She would find a way to become a singer after all.

There was one problem. Jenkins, simply put, could not sing. Her inability to discern pitch, some believe, nearly matched that of legendary tin ear Ulysses S. Grant (who once confessed that he knew only two tunes—"one is 'Yankee Doodle,' and the other isn't"). "Her voice was not even mediocre—it was preposterous," recalled Daniel Dixon, who profiled her in *Coronet* magazine in 1957. The wealthy widow was unable to carry a tune, or even keep to a rhythm. At times, she squawked like a barnyard fowl, or rumbled along in an atonal caterwaul. When she struggled to hit difficult notes, her vocal cords sometimes simply refused to cooperate, leaving an awkward silence in the piece. Jenkins worked to overcome her limitations, apparently to no avail. Actor St. Clair Bayfield, who was Jenkins's manager—and by his account, romantic companion— for more than three decades, told Dixon that the would-be diva took singing lessons from "a great opera star." Bayfield, however, declined to reveal the instructor's identity, apparently for fear of damaging the virtuoso's reputation. (Opera writer Brooks Peters has identified him as Carlo Edwards, a maestro at the Metropolitan Opera.)

For someone who was such a lover of music, Jenkins's vocal ineptitude was a cruel blow—or it would have been, had she accepted the reality that she was awful. Instead, Lady Florence blithely carried on as if she were a gifted coloratura, a singer capable of flowery trills and runs. In April 1912, while the headlines were still filled with news about the sinking of the *Titanic*, Jenkins began her singing career with a recital in New York. She made the rounds of society affairs in Newport and Saratoga, singing for small audiences of women in her blue blood club circuit, who were either too polite or too hearing-impaired to respond to her efforts with anything other than applause. In 1919, a newspaper clipping notes that she provided entertainment at a soiree put on in New York by the Little Mothers Aid Association, which benefited young girls from impoverished families.

Lady Florence's vocal cords may have been deficient, but she had other gifts that helped her performing career. An adept fund-raiser and organizer, she founded the Verdi Club, which aided the careers of American musicians, and became a familiar and well-liked member of New York society. Her numerous loyal friends included musical luminaries such as tenor Enrico Caruso and composer-songwriter Cole Porter (who seldom missed one of her performances, and even wrote a song for her).

In 1931, emboldened no doubt by her famous acquaintances' tolerance for her oddball obsession, Lady Florence gave the first of her annual concerts in the ballroom of the Ritz-Carlton Hotel. Admittance was by invitation only; anyone not part of her social and artistic circle could obtain a ticket only by showing up in advance at her apartment in the Hotel Seymour on West Forty-fifth Street, where Jenkins personally questioned such visitors to ascertain whether they were sufficiently sincere lovers of music. (They also were invited by the convivial diva to stay for a glass of sherry.)

Quite a few people went to the trouble to obtain tickets, because a Lady Florence concert was a spectacle not to be missed. The curtain rose on a stage piled high with flowers, whose fragrance, Jenkins believed, would enhance her voice. The diva herself was equally florid visually, clad in one of the numerous outlandish costumes she would don during the course of the show. (Her trademark accessory: a pair of golden wings and a tiara.) At her side was longtime accompanist Cosme McMoon. Lady Florence opened by shrieking through the "Queen of the Night" aria from Mozart's *The Magic Flute*. "In the back of the hall men and women in full evening dress made no attempt to control their laughter," a *Time* magazine critic wrote after attending her 1934 performance. "Dignified gentlemen sat with handkerchiefs stuffed in their mouths and tears of mirth streaming down their cheeks."

After her rendition of Brahms's song "The May Night," Jenkins would take a short intermission. Then she would return dressed in a lace shawl, carrying castanets and a wicker basket of rosebuds, and perform a screechy version of her favorite song, Spanish composer Joaquín "Quinito" Valverde's lively "Clavelitos." At the conclusion, she tossed handfuls of rosebuds into the crowd. On one occasion, she was so carried away with excitement that she tossed the basket as well, striking a man in the audience on the head. "When her delighted listeners roared for an encore, she had an assistant hurry out front and gather up the blossoms," Dixon recalled. "Then she repeated the whole routine."

After a second intermission, the elderly diva would return, dressed as the chambermaid Adele from Strauss's light opera *Die Fledermaus*, and sing "The Laughing Song" as her final number. The audience's uproarious applause, as critic MacIntyre has observed, was "possibly accompanied by the rattles of dead composers turning over in their graves."

Appalling at Carnegie Hall

One of the enduring mysteries of Jenkins's career is the otherwise dignified and seemingly sane society matron's motivation for putting on her bizarre performances. McMoon decided that she was tone-deaf, and genuinely believed that audiences adored her superlative voice. "The audience always tried not to hurt her feelings by outright laughing," McMoon recalled in a radio interview after her death. "So they developed a convention that whenever she came to a particularly excruciating discord or something like that, where they had to laugh, they burst into these salvos of applause and whistles, and the noise was so great that they could laugh at liberty."

After a 1943 taxicab accident, she claimed that she could reach a higher F than ever before, and sent the unfortunate driver a box of Havana cigars as a reward. (Jenkins tended to accentuate the positive—as writer Irving Johnson once put it, "a ripe tomato was an orchid and the faintest hiss a roar of applause.") Of course, it may also have been that she simply was unconcerned about her talent, or lack of it—and that to Jenkins, simply having the taste to sing Brahms and Mozart was the important thing. "It was a different era, when there was still a distinction drawn between high- and lowbrow art," playwright and opera historian Albert Innaurato explained to *Opera News* in 2001. "Florence represented the last gasp of that world."

In October 1944, Lady Florence staged her most ambitious performance ever—a concert at Carnegie Hall, which she rented for the occasion. After all two thousand seats were sold weeks in advance, tickets remained in such demand that scalpers reportedly were able to sell them for $20 apiece, a princely sum in 1944. On the evening of October 25, Jenkins took the stage, accompanied by McMoon, flutist Oesto De Sevo, and a string quartet. Her opening number was "Bell Song" from Delibes' opera *Lakmé,* delivered in her usual faltering form. The seventy-six-year-old Jenkins was a bit worse for wear, as were her costumes—at one point, one of her trademark wings collapsed, and she had to interrupt her performance until repairs were made. The bigger audience was a bit rowdier than her usual following. "Where stifled chuckles and occasional outbursts had once sufficed at the Ritz, unabashed roars were the order of the evening," a *Newsweek* critic noted.

But in the end, La Jenkins's irrepressible love of performing won them over. When she concluded with her flower-tossing rendition of "Clavelitos," the crowd gave her an ovation. Afterward, she presented McMoon with a gold medal, which columnist Mel Meimer would later joke was, "presumably, for valor."

Not long after the concert, the elderly diva suffered a heart attack, and a month later she died at her apartment in the Hotel Seymour. Her obituaries in the *New York Times* and the *Herald Tribune* respectfully downplayed her eccentricities, but in the decades that followed, Lady Florence evolved into a minor legend and lasting, albeit offbeat, part of

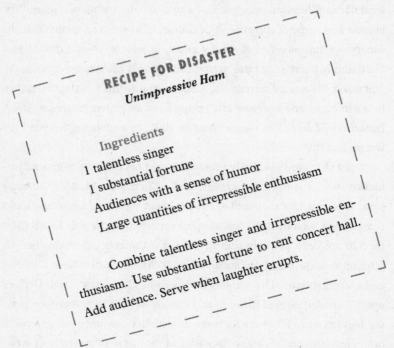

RECIPE FOR DISASTER

Unimpressive Ham

Ingredients

1 talentless singer
1 substantial fortune
Audiences with a sense of humor
Large quantities of irrepressible enthusiasm

Combine talentless singer and irrepressible enthusiasm. Use substantial fortune to rent concert hall. Add audience. Serve when laughter erupts.

operatic lore. Her 1941 studio recording—which consisted entirely of single takes, since Jenkins loathed tinkering with perfection—became a collector's item, and was reissued several decades later as a CD. In recent years, Jenkins's story has been retold a number of times on the stage, most recently in British playwright Stephen Temperley's *Souvenir,* with Broadway musical star Judy Kaye suppressing her vocal virtuosity to portray Jenkins.

But Jenkins's most enduring legacy is America's continuing fascination with would-be vocal virtuosos who are as unrelenting as they are untalented. As Jenkins herself supposedly once explained, "Some may say I couldn't sing, but no one can say I didn't sing."

THE ACCOMPLICE . . . ER, ACCOMPANIST

Over the years, Jenkins aficionados have speculated that the unusual name of her accompanist, Cosme McMoon, was a pseudonym employed by some professional musician to protect himself from embarrassment. However, Social Security Administration records indicate that Cosme McMoon was an actual person, who was born in Texas in 1901 and died in New York in 1980.

In 1936, the *New York Times* published a short review of a recital by McMoon, whom the paper described as a Texas-born composer and pianist. He reportedly got the job working for Jenkins after she fired her previous accompanist, Edwin McArthur, for laughing during one of her performances.

the kaiser-hughes flying boat

If you're crazy enough to take on an incredibly difficult project in an unrealistically short deadline, don't ask an even crazier person to help you get it done.

ON NOVEMBER 2, 1947, a pack of reporters and photographers crowded onto a motorboat in Long Beach, California, harbor with their host, Howard Hughes. They had come for a close-up look at what promised to be either the most outlandish, astonishing triumph in human flight since the Wright brothers, or else the most ill-conceived, embarrassingly costly aviation fiasco ever.

Since Hughes was involved, it was a safe bet that they would get one extreme or the other. To the tall, mustachioed forty-two-year-old multi-millionaire, a dandyish figure in his snap-brim fedora and gaudy two-tone sports jacket, prudence was a thoroughly alien concept. The scion of a Texas oil-well drill-bit fortune, he sank much of the vast wealth he inherited as a teenager into two of the riskiest ventures around—moviemaking and designing airplanes. He pursued both with a perfectionism that was extreme, perhaps even for a clinically obsessive-compulsive personality whose brain tissue had been battered like a piñata in a series of near-fatal car and plane crashes. As a Hollywood producer-director, he thought nothing of shooting as much as 166 feet of film for each foot that ended up in the finished product, and once invented a special cantilevered metal brassiere in an attempt to showcase his star's ample figure. As an aircraft builder, he pushed the envelope even more, lavishing his millions on radical, brilliantly innovative designs that turned out to be impractical.

On this particular chilly, windswept morning, Hughes had summoned the press to witness the unveiling of Hughes Aircraft Company's most controversial project, which now loomed before them in the water. Even among a bunch of jaded scribes who thought they'd seen it all already, jaws no doubt dropped at the sight of the Hughes H-4 Hercules seaplane. Tall as an eight-story building and with a wingspan longer than a football field, it was by far the most gigantic airplane ever built. Its eight engines had propellers seventeen feet in diameter. But size was just one of the aircraft's mind-boggling attributes. Due partly to wartime metal shortages and partly to Hughes's stubbornness, the two-hundred-ton craft was made of plywood instead of metal. It was held together not by nails, but by a special sort of glue—almost as if it were a twelve-year-old boy's hobby project instead of a military prototype in which the U.S. Treasury and Hughes had invested a sum equal to $225 million in today's dollars.

When defense officials commissioned the project in 1942, they envisioned a fleet of supertransports that would turn the tide of World War II by rushing an army of soldiers and tons of supplies across the Atlantic while soaring safely above the German U-boats that menaced the Allies' oceangoing ships. But the war ended with Hughes still laboring on the prototype, fixated inscrutably on details such as the perfect arrangement of instrument gauges in the cockpit. Hughes, who had once been honored with a ticker-tape parade in New York for his exploits as an aviator, had metamorphosed in the public eye from American hero to profligate pariah. Critics ridiculed the now unneeded H-4 as the "flying lumberyard" and the "Spruce Goose"—and questioned whether it could even fly at all. Worse, they insinuated that Hughes was a corrupt grafter, whose lavish lifestyle and succession of affairs with beautiful movie actresses was somehow subsidized by taxpayers.

In truth, the H-4's plywood hull and wings were mostly birch—

which was lighter and more durable than spruce—and Hughes lost millions of his own money on the project. But after staring down a hostile Senate inquiry in Washington, Hughes desperately needed some public-relations damage control. That was why he had invited reporters to come out and see the H-4—which he preferred to call "the flying boat"—and to ride along for some surface cruising tests. Little did they know that Hughes secretly intended to show them all. Even if the flying boat was a monumental flop, he was still going to prove that he could get the thing up in the air.

"And Besides, You're Crazy"

Today, the gargantuan flying boat is so closely identified with Hughes's distinctively over-the-top brand of craziness that Henry J. Kaiser's role in the debacle is seldom even mentioned—even though he was the one who dreamed up the idea.

Today Kaiser, a pioneer in providing medical coverage for workers, is probably best known for the health-care company that bears his name. But in his day, he was a steel, concrete, and construction mogul famed for accomplishing seemingly impossible feats. In the 1920s and 1930s, he laid down the roads that helped build the West, paving more miles in a week than his competitors could do in a month. To transport concrete to build California's Shasta Dam, he erected the world's longest conveyor belt, nearly ten miles from one end to the other. When World War II started and the United States desperately needed freighters to transport armaments and men overseas, Kaiser became a shipbuilder. By adapting automotive-style assembly lines to shipbuilding, he was able to finish ten-thousand-ton vessels that once took a year to build in just seven weeks. But he watched with dismay as German submarines sank his "Liberty Ships" faster than he could churn them out.

Kaiser soon came up with an audacious way to evade enemy torpedoes. At the July 1942 christening of a Liberty Ship in Portland, Oregon, Kaiser boldly proclaimed: "Our engineers have plans on the drafting boards for gigantic flying ships beyond anything Jules Verne could ever have imagined." There was one small problem. Kaiser knew nothing about building airplanes, and didn't have anyone in his employ that did. When he took his concept to the nation's major aircraft manufacturers, they quickly passed on it. With a booming demand for military airplanes, they didn't want to share engineering talent, which was in short supply, with a newcomer. The government's War Production Board tried to persuade Kaiser to give up on the flying boat. Its members believed that Kaiser's plan to develop a flying boat from design to prototype in ten months was ludicrous, and didn't want to waste resources on it. Just as Kaiser's brainchild seemed hopelessly stalled, he got a phone call from a Portland engineer. The man was a friend of a friend of Howard Hughes, and knew that Hughes Aircraft had about two hundred engineers who needed work. Initially, Kaiser had difficulty arranging a meeting, because Hughes's aides were oddly evasive about their boss's whereabouts. Finally, Kaiser learned that Hughes was staying in a hotel in San Francisco under an assumed name as he recuperated from what by some accounts was a severe case of pneumonia. Hughes had worn himself out with obsessive overwork on the final cut of *The Outlaw*, a tawdry western starring bosomy actress Jane Russell, for whom he had designed his famous high-tech bra. That glimpse of Hughes's weirdness should probably have tipped off Kaiser that working with him was a likely ticket to disaster. But the industrial mogul was an irrepressible optimist. As investigative journalists Donald L. Barlett and Charles B. Steele describe in their 1979 book, *Empire: The Life, Legend, and Madness of Howard Hughes*, Kaiser bustled into Hughes's room, where Hughes was lying in bed. "Sit up," Kaiser implored. "We want to talk about winning the war."

"I am very tired," Hughes reportedly answered. "I haven't had any sleep. Besides, you're crazy."

Undeterred, Kaiser laid out his grandiose vision for the giant flying boats, which Hughes would design and Kaiser would build. Hughes thought the timetable sounded impossible, but Kaiser assured him that he'd accomplished miracles before. And as Hughes thought more about the deal, the more alluring it probably seemed. He'd been trying fruitlessly on his own to break into defense contracting, but this might be the ticket. Two days later, the news broke in papers across the nation that Kaiser and Hughes were joining forces to build the world's biggest aircraft. To signify the Hughes-Kaiser partnership, they would name it the HK-1 Hercules.

Now that Kaiser had a partner, the War Production Board didn't dare turn him down, for fear of inciting a public backlash. The newspapers, after all, had given the flying boat plenty of ink, and it was the sort of thing that captured the imagination of a citizenry eager to believe that good old American ingenuity could vanquish the Nazis. So the government authorized Kaiser and Hughes to build three flying boats.

A Flying White Elephant

There were, however, a few downsides to the deal. The contract was good for only two years, and as Kaiser had originally promised, they had to deliver the first of the three planes in less than a year. It was an insanely short deadline for a project of such an unparalleled scale, filled with so many unknowns. No one had ever built a two-hundred-ton plane, let alone tried to build one out of wood—another of the government's requirements, since officials didn't want to risk scarce aluminum on such a risky experiment. And they had a strict budget amounting to $215 million in today's dollars. As economist Eliot Janeway once put it, the situation was like telling Kaiser he could have a sandwich, as long as he baked his own bread and stole the meat. Aviation historian Charles Barton, whose 1982 book, *Howard Hughes and His Flying Boat,* is the most detailed history of the project, notes that Hughes himself was so worried by the challenges that a month or so before the agreement was finalized, he showed up in the middle of the night at a government official's hotel room, lamenting that the deadline was impossibly short.

To make things even more difficult, the two moguls' work styles were about as mismatched as could be. For all his flamboyant salesmanship, Kaiser also was a stolid workaholic with a no-nonsense attitude about deadlines, a trait which had helped him accomplish other similarly daunting projects. Hughes, in contrast, was doing the Lindy Hop on the precipice of sanity. He hadn't yet devolved into the reclusive, paranoid nudist of his later years, when he would subsist on a diet of narcotics and ice cream. But his quirks and fixations were already rampant. He once drafted a lengthy memo to his secretary detailing the alternative forms of punctuation that he wanted to be used in his will.

As Kaiser soon learned to his dismay, Hughes Aircraft was perhaps the most bizarrely run company in America. Hughes had amassed some of the best engineers and technicians in the business, but the owner still ran the operation as if its purpose were to produce a few flashy high-performance planes in which he could set speed records. And for all his rule-making fixations, Hughes couldn't be bothered with going through proper channels, adhering to regulations, or any of the things defense contractors are expected to do. (For example, he'd once contacted the Army Air Corps to let them know he was developing a revolutionary fighter-bomber, and then refused to let the brass in to see it.) Hughes had about as much interest in time management or information flow as he would later have in bathing and haircuts. Once, after Kaiser repeatedly tried without success to locate Hughes and get an update on the project, the worried industrialist was reduced to writing Hughes a letter. "Since my reputation is at stake as well as yours, I request that you immediately advise me by letter the actual schedule, number of man hours per day, and a chart showing how these planes are being completed," Kaiser pleaded. Hughes essentially ignored him. He could afford to, since Kaiser had unwisely signed an agreement that gave Hughes virtually complete control over the plane's engineering and construction.

Hughes didn't even come close to fulfilling the government contract. That his company actually managed to build even one flying boat in five years, however, is amazing, considering the project's mind-boggling difficulty. Just to house the flying boat's construction in Culver City on the edge of Los Angeles, Hughes had to build what probably was the largest wooden building ever, a structure eight stories high and the length of two and a half football fields. For the plane itself, Hughes opted to use Duramold, a process patented in the 1920s for laminating and molding thin sheets of plywood together, but never before used for anything but small aircraft. His workers had to develop new processes and equipment to shape each gigantic piece of plywood to exacting specifications. Keeping the plywood parts fastened together was another problem, until a subcontractor figured out how to glue the aircraft together using epoxy resins cured at high temperatures. (The pieces were held together temporarily by nails—eight tons of them—until the glue dried.) Hughes became so fascinated with wood that even when the metal shortage eased in 1943, he stubbornly refused to follow government officials' recommendations that he switch to aluminum.

Continually having to come up with such innovations ate up a lot of time—as did Hughes's increasingly disorderly mind and leadership style. He was an extreme micromanager who insisted on being consulted on every detail, no matter how small. But Hughes's mysterious schedule often paralyzed the project; he was absent from the plant for weeks or months at a time, and when he did show up, it was usually in the middle of the night. When Hughes was around to make decisions, they frequently turned out to be bizarre ones. For example, he inexplicably hired a manufacturing supervisor who had no experience either building airplanes or working with wood. And when an alarmed government official pointed out to Hughes that his specifications called for engines bigger and more powerful than anything in production, Hughes just said he would take responsibility for however things turned out.

In the spring of 1943, Hughes slipped away to Lake Mead, ostensibly to gather data on amphibious landings for the flying boat. There, he crashed his personal Sikorsky S-43 seaplane, suffering yet another head injury. His behavior became even more erratic. With the first plane due for delivery in November, the project was sinking into chaos. Hughes hired former airline executive Edward H. Bern to get things back on track, but he quit after four months, complaining to the government that Hughes continued his micromanaging, and would meet with Bern only between 10 p.m. and 2 a.m. When government officials paid Hughes Aircraft a visit to see how things were going, they came away disturbed. The government had assumed Hughes would employ tried-and-true wood-building technology to build the flying boat. Instead, he was experimenting with a radically new construction method. There was no way to know whether the glued joints in the plywood would withstand the stress of flight. The design had "an element of unreliability that is definitely scary for aircraft," the inspector warned in his report. In February 1944, another government report concluded that the overdue flying boat would be unable to carry enough cargo to justify its size, and belonged in the "white elephant class." Beyond that, the tide of the war had turned. Allied forces were preparing for a massive invasion of Europe, the success of which would render the flying boat irrelevant.

The War Production Board decided that it had had enough, and moved to cancel the flying-boat contract. At the last moment, a government official friendly with Hughes managed to convince President Franklin Roosevelt that it would be a waste not to finish it. In March 1944, the government tore up the three-plane deal with Hughes and Kaiser, and gave Hughes alone a new contract for a single plane, which was renamed the H-4.

The Costliest Minute in Aviation History

The flying boat was still unfinished when Europe was liberated in May 1945, and Hughes was rapidly going to pieces. His repeated head injuries apparently were taking a toll, and he was teetering on the verge of mental breakdown. To recuperate, he spent most of 1945 away from Hughes Aircraft, shuttling between hotel rooms in Las Vegas, Reno, and Palm Springs, carrying his belongings in cardboard boxes tied with string, which he preferred to suitcases. Nevertheless, when Hughes finally returned to work in the fall, he continued to insist on moonlighting as a test pilot. In April 1946, he crashed a prototype for the F-11 reconnaissance plane into a house in Beverly Hills, suffering such severe injuries that he spent more than a month in the hospital. When he recovered, he agreed to pay the government $5 million in compensation if he ever crashed another defense project.

Meanwhile, the flying boat was inviting increasing scrutiny from Republican members of Congress, who were eager to expose any improprieties in war spending by the Democrats. Though Hughes hadn't made any money on the flying boat—in fact, he ended up spending the equivalent of $63 million in today's dollars to finish it—he nevertheless was summoned to Washington to testify before a Senate investigation led by Senator Ralph Owen Brewster of Maine. In August, amid the glare of klieg lights and whir of newsreel cameras, Hughes stood at the witness table and gave a performance whose transcript reads like an absurdist play by Samuel Beckett. He gave sarcastically officious answers to even the simplest of questions, when he wasn't demanding the opportunity to cross-examine Brewster about his ties to Pan American Airlines, a rival of Hughes-owned TWA. In a moment of candor, however, Hughes admitted that he was unsure whether the flying boat would actually ever fly. He added that if the project was judged a failure, he would probably leave the country and never return.

According to Barton, Hughes returned to California and for the next three months spent every night working on the flying boat, which had been moved, in pieces, to a dock on Terminal Island in Long Beach harbor. He sometimes brought his then girlfriend, actress Jean Peters, who sat and watched him supervise work on the flying boat's engines. As an executive, Hughes often was disinterested in details, but when it came to the precise location switches in the cockpit, he was fastidious to the point of mania. "Howard probably spent more time positioning controls and instruments than he did anything," an engineer on the project told

Barton. Finally, Hughes announced that he would begin testing in the harbor on November 1, 1947. Thousands of spectators gathered to gape at the silver behemoth as it was lowered into the water.

The next morning, Hughes invited reporters onto the plane with him as he took it for what he told them would be a series of taxi tests at a maximum speed of 40 mph. After the second run, he slowed to an idle and answered his guests' questions. Hughes insisted that the aircraft, which still had plenty of bugs, wasn't going to be ready for a flight test for months. Most of the reporters caught a boat ride back to shore to file their stories, while Hughes took one more taxi run.

To this day, it remains unclear whether Hughes was playing a sly joke on them all along, or whether his unstable mind was seized by an impulse, as he later suggested. Engineer David Grant, who served as Hughes's copilot, recalled in a 1987 interview that on the final test run, Hughes told him to lower the flying boat's flaps to 15 degrees—"that's takeoff position. He shoved the throttles forward and away we went." As the giant aircraft hit 95 mph, it suddenly left the water and rose about seventy feet into the air. Hughes flew for less than a minute, covering about a mile, before setting the plane down smoothly on the water.

In today's dollars, the adventure cost about $3.75 million per second.

Since the government had no use for the flying boat, Hughes brought it back to Terminal Island, where he had a special air-conditioned hangar built. He eventually bought it from the government for the equivalent of about $5 million in today's dollars, plus the title to another experimental aircraft. He spent another inflation-adjusted $9 million annually to maintain it in perfect working condition for the next three decades, until his death in 1976.

But Hughes never tried to fly the giant plane again, perhaps because he knew, even with his deteriorating mind, that it was unsafe. In his book, Barton quotes unnamed Hughes mechanics who recalled that the glued joints in the wings showed signs of damage from the stress of flight, as government naysayers had predicted. Instead, after Hughes's death, the aircraft became a tourist attraction, first in Long Beach and later in Oregon, with a mustachioed mannequin wearing a snap-brim hat taking Hughes's place at the controls.

After bowing out of the flying-boat project he'd conceived, Henry J. Kaiser, Hughes's former partner, went on to build an even bigger fortune in the aluminum, steel, and automobile industries. During the Korean War, he again built military cargo aircraft, though nothing as ambitious as the flying boat. Today, however, the only remnant of his business empire is Kaiser Permanente, the world's largest health maintenance organization.

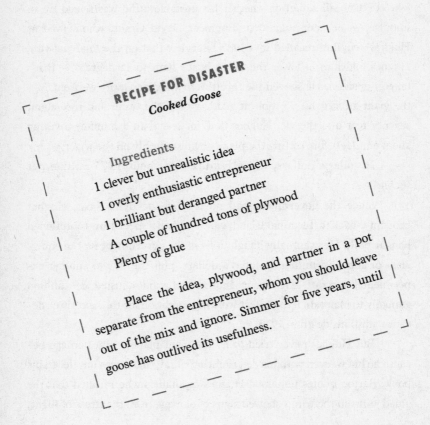

RECIPE FOR DISASTER

Cooked Goose

Ingredients

1 clever but unrealistic idea

1 overly enthusiastic entrepreneur

1 brilliant but deranged partner

A couple of hundred tons of plywood

Plenty of glue

Place the idea, plywood, and partner in a pot separate from the entrepreneur, whom you should leave out of the mix and ignore. Simmer for five years, until goose has outlived its usefulness.

The flying boat turned out to be little more than a curious historical footnote, except to provide a case study for today's would-be captains of industry about the limitations of thinking big—and about the necessity of giving careful thought to one's choice of partners. According to an April 2000 article in *Forest Products Journal,* however, the adhesive technology developed by Hughes's subcontractors to build the H-4 helped lead to the widespread use of plywood in the postwar construction industry. Thus, in a sense, people in suburbs across the nation have Hughes's madness to thank for their affordable houses.

GERMANY'S EVEN DUMBER IDEA

Kaiser and Hughes weren't the only ones who thought enormous transport aircraft might win the war for their side.

German aircraft maker Willy Messerschmitt took a different—and ultimately even more disastrous—approach. The Gigant ("giant" in German), an enormous tow glider, was conceived to rush German tanks and troops across the English Channel during the planned invasion of Great Britain. But with a 92-foot-long fuselage and 180-foot wingspan, the glider weighed more than twelve tons, so heavy that even a trio of fighters wasn't able to tow it.

Stymied, the Germans converted the design into a powered aircraft with six engines, but by the time it was finished in 1942, the invasion plans had been put on permanent hold. As it turned out, the lumbering Gigants, which could attain only half the airspeed of Allied interceptors, were easy targets in the air. Sixteen Gigants were sent to deliver supplies to besieged German forces in Tunisia the same month they were delivered. All but two were shot down in a single day.

the 1955 dodge la femme

*In the 1950s, Dodge saw a pink car with a matching um-
brella and lipstick case as the way to a woman's heart.
But that was only the worst of the automotive industry's
efforts to woo a misunderstood market segment.*

TODAY, THE IDEA of designing products to suit women consumers
is so ingrained, so ubiquitous, in popular culture that Hollywood actually
has used it as the premise for a cornball romantic comedy. In the 2000 film
What Women Want, a chauvinistic male advertising executive, played by
Mel Gibson, suddenly finds himself endowed with the ability to hear what
women around him are thinking. It's too bad that executives at the Dodge
division of Chrysler in the spring of 1955 didn't have that sort of miracu-
lous cross-gender mind-reading ability. If so, they might have reconsid-
ered the Dodge La Femme, a two-door sedan that its maker touted as
"in mood and manner, a distinctive car for the discriminating modern
woman."

Distinctive, it certainly was. The 1955 La Femme had a two-tone
exterior of pink—technically, "heather rose"—and white, with a matching rosebud-patterned interior. Even the steering column was pink. But
the vehicle, gaudy as it was, was just part of the deal. Dodge also threw in
an assortment of "special feminine accessories"—from clothes to a lipstick case, all in matching colors.

"I believe you will agree that this unusual car has great appeal to women," a Dodge sales manager boasted in a letter to dealers that he surely came to regret, given the La Femme's dismal fate in the marketplace. When Dodge discontinued the La Femme after just two seasons, division president M. C. Patterson claimed to have sold 2,500 of them, though years later, company historians would put the number at between 300 and 1,500.

"Not too surprising, even back in the mid-'50s, we didn't sell too many of them," Chrysler vice president for marketing and communications Arthur Liebler told the Reuters news agency several decades later. "I guess we just didn't get it at the time."

While the car that one critic ridiculed as "La Fiasco" quickly vanished from the marketplace, the Dodge La Femme has earned a lasting, albeit dubious, place in automotive history. It wasn't actually "the first car ever exclusively designed for the woman motorist," as Dodge proclaimed it to be. But it was quite possibly the most exquisitely tacky styling faux pas ever made, so perfectly cloying that even a satiric kitschmeister such as filmmaker John Waters would have been hard pressed to make it up. More important, the La Femme became the perfect symbol for many years' worth of ham-handed, patronizing-to-the-point-of-being-silly attempts by the boys in Detroit to woo female customers, who now make up 52 percent of the $85 billion U.S. new-car market. Despite their vast numbers, until recently women were about as inscrutable to car executives as the Style Network might be to the typical ESPN viewer.

But in a small but significant way, the La Femme's over-the-top ridiculousness may have helped the car industry eventually to see the light. Today, in addition to prompting eye rolling and smirks when it is mentioned, Dodge's gaily colored bit of gaucherie helps inspire a new generation of auto designers to create cars that are better suited for female drivers, by providing a blueprint for what *not* to do.

A Short History of Automotive Ms.-Marketing

The painfully chichi pastel La Femme wasn't an isolated marketing miscue, but rather the result of a paradox that the automobile industry has struggled with since its beginnings. The rough-hewn male tinkerers and mechanics in grimy overalls who invented the horseless carriage in the late 19th century undoubtedly were dumbfounded by the enthusiasm with which Victorian women took to the new form of transportation that freed them from the confines of the home. (One of the most avid early drivers was author Edith Wharton, who so enjoyed her first automobile ride in 1903 that she purchased her own Panhard-Levassor, the first car with an engine between the front wheels.) Nevertheless, as cars grew into a major industry, alpha males dominated the executive suites and design studios, and produced virile-looking cars to appeal to the male customers they presumed controlled the family bank account. What ruled for decades were massive, powerful engines, sweeping sharp-lined hoods with unsubtle phallic overtones, and colors as somber as the neckties in corporate boardrooms.

But as historian Virginia Scharff details in her 1999 book, *Taking the Wheel: Women and the Coming of the Motor Age,* carmakers soon discovered that their focus on machismo hurt the bottom line. Husbands might pay for the car, but more and more it was their wives who were driving them, and women had a major say in deciding what model to buy. Carmakers grudgingly added what they saw as female-friendly features to their designs. During the 1920s, for example, most manufacturers switched to enclosed passenger compartments with roofs and windows, a change widely attributed to the perception that women disliked having their hairstyles messed up by the wind. Ford began advertising in *Ladies' Home Journal,* with copy that promoted the automobile as a convenience more valuable than even the garbage disposal or electric clothes dryer, because it not only made running errands easier, but allowed women "to call upon friends and share pleasantly their companionship."

In the 1950s postwar economy, when prosperity and profits depended on continually jacking up consumption, car manufacturers renewed their efforts to convince married couples to trade up to flashier, more expensive models—or better yet, to buy a second car for the lady of the house. Detroit's marketing men, who may not have been too familiar with what their wives actually did all day while they were at work, apparently figured that convenience and time-saving practicality, such as the ability to shop for groceries during the day, or to pick up the kids from school on a rainy afternoon, weren't enough sales motivation. Instead, they hit upon high fashion to lure glamour-starved housewives—or at least, the ones in their imaginations—to drag their husbands to the showroom.

Decades later, a 1997 exhibit at New York's Fashion Institute of Technology would showcase some of their ploys. In 1952, for example, Ford dealers offered a free Motor Mates coat that enabled a female driver to coordinate her attire with the upholstery of her Crown Victoria sedan. General Motors tried to boost sales by commissioning haute couture designers such as Hubert de Givenchy, Elizabeth Arden, and Jacques Fath to create gowns that complemented various Cadillac models. Chrysler wasn't to be outdone. In 1954, the glossy women's magazine *Vogue* depicted cars as fashion accessories, with a photo spread of models in Dior and Madame Klari gowns inside a Dodge Royal sedan, and another model in a sweater-and-skirt ensemble lounging inside a Pontiac Catalina, which the caption described as "fashioned to win a lady's favor."

At car shows in the early 1950s, several manufacturers took the idea a bit further, and displayed experimental "fem show cars" with colors and fashion-oriented details designed to lure women buyers. The Pontiac division of General Motors, for example, put bright pink upholstery in a concept version of its Parisienne two-door sedan. At the 1954 auto shows in Chicago and New York, Chrysler unveiled a pair of his-and-hers concept vehicles—the bronze-and-black Le Comte for men, and the cream-and-pink La Comtesse for women. Beneath its platinum-colored brocatelle seat inserts and other dainty flourishes, the La Comtesse was just a basic

Chrysler Imperial sedan, just like its manly counterpart. But enough spectators were curious that Chrysler decided to have its Dodge division actually produce a similar car.

To create the La Femme, Dodge designers took the Dodge Custom Royal Lancer two-door hardtop—already a bit of an automotive fashion plate, with its lower, wider body, bubbled-out wraparound windshield, and ample chrome—and glamorized it with frilly flourishes. Du Pont's recently developed nonchalking white pigment, which made pastel car colors possible, enabled them to give the exterior its two-tone pink-and-white paint job. The wheel covers were pink as well. The interior featured more pink—pink fabric upholstery with a design of tiny roses, matching pink vinyl trim, and a pink-and-black dashboard with a pink steering column and white steering wheel. The scant bit of disharmony was burgundy carpeting on the floor, perhaps out of recognition that a grimy pink carpet would look a bit too much like strawberry ice cream dripped onto a sidewalk.

Two special compartments were built into the backs of the front seats to store the color-coordinated fashion accessories that propelled the La Femme over the top in terms of preciousness. In a 2000 article for *Forward: The American Heritage of Daimler-Chrysler,* writer Rick Trentacosta inventories the ensemble. It included a pink vinyl shoulder bag, a pink calfskin-trimmed makeup compact, a pink-and-gold lipstick holder, a pink-and-gold art deco–style cigarette lighter, a gold case designed to accommodate twelve unfiltered cigarettes, a wine-colored change purse, and a vanity mirror. In the event of inclement weather, the stylish La Femme owner could don a plastic rosebud-patterned rain cape and a wide-brimmed rain hat, and carry a rosebud-patterned plastic umbrella. According to Trentacosta, Dodge also planned to throw in what the promotional literature described as "dainty rain boots." Apparently, though, someone at Dodge eventually realized that fitting individual car owners' feet would be a big headache, and the automaker quietly dropped that accessory.

For 1956, Dodge switched from pink and white to two shades of purple ("regal orchid" and "misty orchid" in the promotional literature). This time around, the carmaker ditched some of the accessories—the cigarette case, lighter, makeup case, and lipstick—but continued to offer the raincoat and hat.

If the color scheme didn't create a sufficiently glamorous ambience, the La Femme offered another peculiar option that was available on a few other high-end Chrysler cars as well—a special "Highway Hi-Fi" record player, mounted under the dash. Developed by CBS Laboratories for the carmaker, the device had a special bump-resistant tone arm, designed to keep the needle in the grooves of specially constructed thirty-minute-long records that spun at a superslow 16 rpm. Besides the fact that the turntable wouldn't play regular 45s or LPs, the system had another inconvenient flaw—in order to change the musical program, a driver had to pull over, stop the car, and queue up a new disc before resuming the trip.

The Lady of the House Goes Drag Racing

All that might have added up to the ideal vehicle for, say, Liberace (especially if Dodge had added a few sequins and an under-dash piano), but the intended audience was decidedly unimpressed, judging by how few La Femmes were sold. Dodge moved roughly twenty-five gender-neutral Royal Custom Lancers for each La Femme that it managed to peddle. When the La Femme was discontinued in the fall of 1956, Chrysler president Patterson theorized that the automaker had focused a bit too heavily on pleasing women, and ignored their husbands' tastes. "La Femme was definitely a two-car proposition," he told United Press International. "It was so feminine [that] a he-man would be embarrassed to drive it—rather impractical for an automobile."

Still, he admitted: "It's tough to sell [to a woman]. You never know what she'll go for. Sometimes it's the little things that interest her—the appointments, the dashboard."

In the 1950s, Detroit didn't yet grasp the importance of using surveys and focus groups to determine what sort of design and features would appeal to its audience, and the La Femme's design and marketing reflected that blithe ignorance. "It was obvious that the Chrysler marketing guys never bothered to actually *ask* women what they wanted in a car," *Auto Week* writer Bill Siuru has opined.

Some argue that the La Femme bombed largely because it was based upon an already obsolete view of gender roles. "By the Fifties, it was too late to bury Rosie the Riveter," Stanford University historian Joseph Corn, author of *Yesterday's Tomorrows: Past Visions of the American Future,* explained in a 2001 article in *Forbes FYI.* "Some social shift had already occurred."

It didn't help that the La Femme wasn't really a car designed from the chassis up for women, but rather, the vehicular equivalent of Charles Atlas in drag. Under the hood, it still sported a powerful V-8 engine, with far more horsepower than a 1950s housewife would ever need to rush over to the local supermarket in pursuit of some TV dinners. In the second and final model year, Dodge gave the car even more muscle under the hood, which might have come in handy if the lady of the house got the urge to stop on the way home from the garden club and challenge the local teenage delinquents to a little street racing. But that scenario wasn't much more bizarrely nonsensical than the fantasy conjured up by Dodge in its promotional literature, in which an Audrey Hepburn look-alike in matching raingear gazes beatifically into the distance as a uniformed chauffeur ushers her into the La Femme's passenger seat. None of the publicity images showed a woman actually behind the wheel. In a sense, that was oddly appropriate, since Dodge was selling a rose-colored fantasy of femininity that existed primarily in male automobile executives' minds.

No More Tea Parties!

Even after the La Femme flopped, Detroit inexplicably continued courting female customers in the same clumsy fashion. In 1962, Chrysler provided its dealers with Elizabeth Arden Imperial Travel Cases, specially designed to match the Chrysler Imperial sedan, and suggested that they offer them to women whose husbands were still leaning toward buying Cadillacs or Lincolns. In 1964, Studebaker's driver manual included an ostensibly gal-friendly insert entitled "Going Steady with Studie," which advised women who got flat tires to "put on some fresh lipstick, fluff up your hairdo, stand in a safe spot off the road, wave and look helpless and feminine." A few years later, Ford experimented with a special-edition "passionate pink" Mustang. As recently as the mid-1980s, General Motors' Buick division reportedly advised dealers to host tea parties for prospective women customers, until a group of female managers at GM suggested that some might find the inducement insulting.

By the early 1990s, it finally began to dawn upon car companies that they were taking the wrong approach. They realized the need to study the female market to find out what it wanted. For those in Detroit who clung to gender stereotypes, the findings were a bit unsettling. When Dodge designers gave the La Femme its pink paint scheme, for example, they apparently took for granted that affluent housewives would want to own a car in a traditionally feminine hue. But as a study published in *American Demographics* in 2002 details, when it comes to cars, women tend to pick exactly the same colors—blue, silver, and black—as men. As it turns out, men are more interested in a car's appearance, while women gravitate toward cars that are safe, durable, and functional. More effort in recent years has gone into designing vehicles whose interiors suit women drivers' slightly different ergonomic needs. Sometimes these efforts have evoked the old silliness—male Lexus engineers, for example, reportedly glued fake nails on their fingers to help them design more female-friendly door handles. Increasing female representation in the industry—by the mid-1990s, a quarter of Ford's design professionals were women—undoubtedly helped things along.

Today, the few remaining La Femmes still draw curious stares at antique car shows. In 2000, the *Detroit News* reported that one fetched $17,000 at an auction. Meanwhile, automakers have progressed dramatically in their efforts to develop the female-friendly car. In the spring of 2004—not quite a half century after the La Femme made its debut—Volvo, the Swedish carmaker now owned by Ford, unveiled a female-oriented car prototype that's a startling contrast to its pastel primogenitor. In developing the YCC ("Your Concept Car"), Volvo not only surveyed female drivers to see what attributes they most desired, but actually assigned a mostly female team of designers to create the car. The result is a vehicle that is more practical than flashy—a gas-electric hybrid engine, a Teflon-like silver-gray finish designed to repel dirt, rubber bumpers to protect against scratches in parking lots, flip-up rear seats for stowing grocery bags, a deep compartment in the center console for storing purses

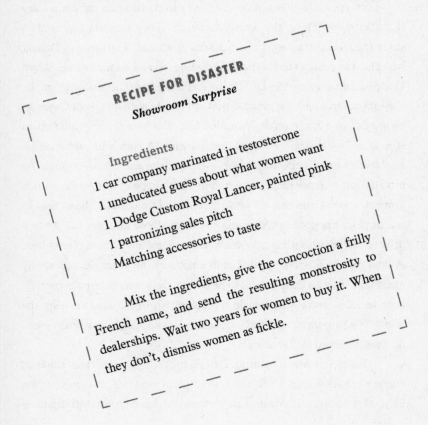

RECIPE FOR DISASTER
Showroom Surprise

Ingredients

1 car company marinated in testosterone
1 uneducated guess about what women want
1 Dodge Custom Royal Lancer, painted pink
1 patronizing sales pitch
Matching accessories to taste

Mix the ingredients, give the concoction a frilly French name, and send the resulting monstrosity to dealerships. Wait two years for women to buy it. When they don't, dismiss women as fickle.

or knapsacks, and indented headrests to accommodate occupants with ponytails. But like its unsuccessful pastel progenitor, even the YCC is not without its froufrou flourishes—swappable seat pads and carpeting that allow an owner to redecorate the interior from an embroidered flower pattern to funky-retro shag, as suits her mood.

WHY CAN'T A WOMAN BE MORE LIKE A MAN?

Starting in the 1970s, cars were subjected to federally mandated crash tests, which employed dummies carefully designed to simulate the effects of collisions on passengers. Or at least male passengers, anyway.

The requirements could originally be met with a dummy that was five foot eight and 170 pounds—about the size of the average man. But research showed that passengers who were even slightly smaller were more likely to suffer injuries, because air bags and other safety equipment weren't designed with them in mind. As a result, the crash-dummy family was enlarged to include a five-foot-tall, 100-pound replica of a female adult, complete with vinyl breasts.

the lingering reek of "smell-o-vision"

Sound revolutionized motion pictures, but the tortured effort to bring smell to the silver screen proved that some things are best left to the imagination.

IN SATIRIC DIRECTOR John Waters's 1981 film *Polyester,* Divine, a three-hundred-pound transvestite, portrays a love-starved suburban housewife married to a porno theater proprietor, and aging former Hollywood heartthrob Tab Hunter plays her malevolent paramour. But despite the perversity of the casting, and a script filled with jokes about subjects ranging from macramé to foot fetishism, the film became best known for an even more bizarre gag. *Polyester* was the facetious debut of "Odorama," in which moviegoers were handed scratch-and-sniff cards, and numbers were flashed on the screen to signal them when to smell appropriate odors ranging from "new car" to dirty tennis shoes. The film's prologue takes place in the laboratory of the technology's purported inventor, "Dr. Arnold Quackenshaw," who explains in a thick Teutonic accent that "through this nose come some of life's most rewarding sensations . . . however, you may experience some odors that will shock you. This film's producers believe that today's audiences are mature enough to know that some things just plain stink!"

It's a safe bet, however, that relatively few of the people who rent the DVD reissue of *Polyester* today even realize that Waters's fragrant humor parodied an actual cinematic phenomenon. In 1960, a romantic who-dunit entitled *Scent of Mystery* featured a dubious innovation billed as "Glorious Smell-O-Vision," in which a "smell brain" device pumped thirty different scents—wine, freshly baked bread, pipe tobacco, a salty ocean breeze—through a network of tiny tubes to movie viewers' seats. The gadgetry was the masterwork of Hans Laube, touted in publicity accounts as a "world famed osmologist," or smell expert, from Switzerland, who collaborated with flamboyant, gimmick-loving Hollywood producer Michael Todd Jr. on one of the most outlandish projects in movie history. "First they moved (1895)! Then they talked (1927)! "Now they smell!" the ads proclaimed.

While *Scent of Mystery* wasn't the first attempt to employ aromas in filmmaking, it was by far the most technologically intricate. Beyond that, it was the first—and apparently the only—motion picture that relied upon smells as integral devices in the plot. The history-making nature of Smell-O-Vision aside, audiences and movie critics were unimpressed, and *Scent of Mystery* quickly evaporated at the box office. Today it's remembered, if at all, as a bit of trivia on movie-buff Web sites. Yet Laube and Todd's attempt to lead moviegoers by their noses presaged a postmodern culture in which the manipulation of scents would become a powerful tool in shaping consumer behavior, in which synthetic aromas would become so ubiquitous that some would begin to fear them as environmental hazards.

So Real It Made Audiences Queasy

Almost since the invention of the motion picture, filmmakers have sought to exploit other senses in addition to sight, in an effort to create a more compelling experience for audiences. Some tricks, such the THX system that provides high-quality sound in theaters, have been successful. Others, such as "Sensurround"—a violent motion-simulating technology featured in the 1974 film *Earthquake*—ended up joining the list of cinematic gimmicks that fell flat.

The sense of smell, in particular, has tempted filmmakers for a long time, and with good reason. The olfactory neurons in the nasal cavity, which detect chemical components of aromas, and the brain's olfactory bulb—a clump of cells that somehow identifies nerve impulses as being caused by jasmine rather than rose petals—are capable of sensing and distinguishing about ten thousand different scents. Research has shown that scents are capable of stimulating physiological responses before people even realize what they're smelling, and as a result they often have powerful, primitive emotional associations. It was no accident that ancient Greek festivals such as the Eleusinian mysteries were replete with potent smells, such as burning incense and flowers. In the 19th century, stage dramatists sometimes used aromas as special effects in plays. They scattered pine needles to suggest the odor of a forest, or cooked food in the theater to simulate the aroma of a restaurant onstage.

The use of smells in the movie industry, in fact, actually preceded the introduction of sound. In 1916, proprietors of the Family Theater in Forest City, Pennsylvania, dipped cotton wool in rose oil and put it in front of an electric fan during a newsreel about the Rose Bowl game. Similarly, in 1929, a Boston theater put lilac oil in the ventilating system to get audiences in the mood for *Lilac Time,* a love story about a British aviator and a French woman during World War I. That same year, when *The Broadway Melody,* one of the first Hollywood musicals, premiered in New York, perfume was sprayed from the ceiling.

In the early 1940s, Hollywood experimented with using compressed air to force various artificial scents through air-conditioning systems. In 1943, a theater in Detroit showed *The Sea Hawk,* a pirate swashbuckler starring Errol Flynn, with aromas such as the smell of tar from a sailing ship to add ambience. Also on the bill was *Boom Town,* a drama in which each character was given a distinctive scent—tobacco for Clark Gable, a pine scent for Spencer Tracy, and "My Sin" perfume for sexy actress Hedy Lamarr.

There were two obvious shortcomings to early attempts at olfactory filmmaking. Since they were added to existing movies, they were an offense against film aesthetics, a distraction from what the director had intended audiences to focus upon. Beyond that, the clouds of perfume that accumulated in theaters created a problem. The human nose, which has only so many smell receptors, has difficulty transitioning to a new smell until it is cleared of the molecules that triggered a previous scent. The result was a phenomenon called "olfactory fatigue," in which the sense of smell gradually stops working, like a smoker who no longer notices the acrid stink of his cigarette. (Films with smells would work a lot better if audiences were rabbits, which depend upon smell to avoid predators and possess nostrils equipped with skin flaps, which restrict the volume of molecules they can take in with a sniff.)

Enter Hans Laube with what seemed like a solution. A tall, gray-haired Swiss native who affected owlishly severe dark eyeglasses, Laube's background is a bit mysterious—media coverage of his work identifies him variously as a professor, an advertising executive, an electrical engineer, and "an expert in osmology, the science of odors." By one account, sometime prior to World War II, he invented a method for cleaning the air in large auditoriums, which became widely used throughout Europe. That success somehow led him to his fascination with reversing the process, and putting odors of his choosing back into rooms. He developed an artificial scent-delivery process, in which chemicals were transmitted through a network of pipes connected to individual seats in the theater, so that the timing and amount of aroma could be more carefully regulated. With a colleague, Robert Barth, Laube produced a thirty-five-minute "smell-o-drama" movie, *Mein Traum*—in English, *My Dream*—for the 1940 world's fair in New York. The projectionist operated a control board with dials that allowed him to release thirty-two different odors, including roses, coconut, tar, hay, and peaches.

Laube's invention, "which of course is a secret pending patents, is said to have produced odors as quickly and easily as the soundtrack of a film produces sound," a newspaper reported in 1943. "The scientists maintain that with few exceptions, almost any smell can be produced and sent out to the audience, and furthermore, any theater equipped for sound can handle the odors, which are synchronized with the action of the picture just as the sound is." The *New York Times* was a bit more reserved, noting that audiences thought the film's simulated bacon aroma didn't quite seem real, but that the incense was on the mark.

Laube returned to the United States in 1944 intending to market a version of his smell-producing technology to the nascent medium of television. Laube claimed that he could produce five hundred different scents with a small, inexpensive gadget that could be installed inside a TV set. A 1946 United Press account of Laube's demonstration of "Scentovision" in a New York hotel suite depicted him as laconic and wary about revealing too much about his invention. Nevertheless, the correspondent came away impressed: "Laube has one view of a circus at work which gives off such realistic odors that his audience almost always lets out a yell and runs for the window."

In 1955, Laube set up his apparatus at the Cinerama-Warner Theatre at Forty-seventh and Broadway in Manhattan. He filmed a ten-minute pilot film, with seventeen different odors, to show to test audiences. Nevertheless, for reasons lost to history, the television industry passed on Laube's invention. The inventor also approached supermarkets with the idea of projecting slides of oranges, smoked ham, and chocolate pie, accompanied by the appropriate scents, as a way to entice shoppers. But that, too, proved fruitless.

The Sweet Smell of Excess

Laube finally found a patron in Michael Todd Jr., the son of flamboyant Broadway and Hollywood producer Michael Todd. The elder Todd, who today is best remembered as one of Elizabeth Taylor's husbands, had put on a series of successful musical spectaculars at the same world's fair at which Laube first exhibited his experimental smell movie. A decade and a half later, Todd and his collaborator-son were looking at gimmicks that might make Todd's outrageous wide-screen epic, *Around the World in 80 Days,* even more spectacular. Smells were an intriguing possibility, and the Todds looked at several different setups. Ultimately, they opted not to include aromas in the 1956 film—a wise choice, since *80 Days* already had enough pizzazz to become a box-office smash and win an Oscar for Best Picture. But after the elder Todd died in a 1958 plane crash, the younger Todd—who'd inherited his father's penchant for the outrageous—decided to take a chance on Laube's technology. He signed the Swiss inventor to a movie deal, one proviso being that "Scentovision" be redubbed "Smell-O-Vision." When asked why he didn't change the name to something more dignified, Todd Jr. was bemused. "I don't understand how you can be 'dignified' about a process that introduces smells into a theater" was his reply.

Todd Jr.'s wonderfully tacky, Walter Winchell–esque plays on words ("I hope it's the kind of picture they call a scentsation!") made great copy for newspapers, and before a cast had been hired, *Scent* was already generating hype. Syndicated columnist Earl Wilson, for example, gushed that Smell-O-Vision "can produce anything from skunk to perfume, and remove it instantly."

Meanwhile, Todd provided Laube with use of the Todd Cinestage Theatre in Chicago as a laboratory so he could perfect the patented process. The core of Laube's process was his "smell brain"—actually, an assortment of perfume containers linked in a belt, which in turn was wound around a motorized supply reel. As the movie footage began to roll, markers on it cued the brain. The containers, apparently arranged in the order that the scents would be used in the film, whirred into position. At the right moment, needles pierced membranes on the bottom of the appropriate container and drew off perfume. Electric fans mixed the perfume with air, which was then pumped through a mile's worth of tubing that stretched to vents under each and every seat in the theater. At the end of the movie, the belt would be rewound and the containers refilled.

Laube added other nuances in an effort to prevent the smells from clashing or mixing together, as had happened with other scent-producing gadgets. The special perfumes were mixed without the chemicals normally added to make a scent last longer. Between two clashing aromas—for example, garlic and the delicate smell of lilacs—he would squirt a neutralizing chemical designed to revive audiences' nostrils. Laube saw Smell-O-Vision as having certain aesthetic limitations. He theorized that heavy drama wouldn't mix well emotionally with odors, but that lighter fare could be enhanced by the right aroma. Wisely, Todd agreed, and scheduled Smell-O-Vision to debut in a tongue-in-cheek whodunit, *Scent of Mystery,* instead of, say, a biblical epic or historical costume drama that would have resulted in an even more embarrassing fiasco. *Scent*'s plot centers around a photographer, played by British actor Denholm Elliott, on vacation in Spain when he stumbles upon a plot to murder a beautiful American heiress played by Todd Jr.'s stepmother, Elizabeth Taylor, in a surprise cameo appearance. With the help of a brandy-sipping cab driver, portrayed by screen legend Peter Lorre, Elliott embarks on a wild chase across the picturesque Spanish countryside to thwart the crime.

For someone who was building a movie around a gimmick, Todd was remarkably conscientious. To direct, he hired Jack Cardiff, who'd won an Oscar for his cinematography on the 1947 film *Black Narcissus,* and spent the summer of 1959 shooting at 149 different locations in Spain.

While Todd Jr. was in Italy working on the film's musical score, the entertainment press broke the story that *Scent* had competition. Soon after, Walter Reade Jr., owner of a small theater chain and film distribution company, confirmed at a news conference—scented, of course—that he was releasing *his* smell-enhanced film, *Behind the Great Wall,* in early December, two months before *Scent*'s planned premiere. Todd Jr. had been laboring for several years to generate hype for *Scent;* Reade's project smelled suspiciously like an effort to capitalize on that publicity spadework. He'd taken an existing Italian-made travelogue and added "AromaRama," which basically pumped perfumes into the theater's air-conditioning system in a fashion virtually identical to the one used to scent *The Sea Hawk* and *Boom*

Town back in the 1940s. To make matters worse, Reade boasted that AromaRama could be installed in a theater for just $7,500—about a third of what it cost to put in Smell-O-Vision. "This contest may well hang on who has the best set of smells," *Newsweek* reported.

Unfortunately for Reade, the pump didn't work any better in 1959 than it had years before. The high point of the production came during the opening minutes, in which TV newsman Chet Huntley cut an orange and the accompanying aroma was strong and realistic. But after that, the perfumes lingered in the air and mixed together. "The odors that follow are neither clear nor pleasurable," sniffed *New York Times* critic Bosley Crowther. *Great Wall* and AromaRama quickly disappeared.

But *Scent* still faced the difficult task of living up to the expectations that Todd Jr. had so artfully created for Smell-O-Vision. The technology was billed as far more precise and realistic than any of the previous attempts at olfactory filmmaking, and some, such as *New York Times* writer Richard Nason, thought it might actually represent a genuine advance in cinema, the way that early, crude attempts to add sound had eventually been followed by the synchronized sound track.

Scent opened in three specially equipped theaters in New York, Chicago, and Los Angeles in February 1960. Some of the olfactory effects clearly had been included to demonstrate the new technology's capabilities. A view of a monastery's rose garden, predictably, was accompanied by a floral scent. When wine casks rolled down a hill and smashed against a wall, the apparatus produced the odor of grape juice. Additionally, director Cardiff had included a number of "whiff gags," such as a scene in which Elliott and Lorre appear to be drinking coffee, but Lorre's cup gives off the smell of brandy—leading Elliott to chastise him about the need to keep a clear head. Beyond that, though, *Scent* was the first film in which aromas actually were integral to the story, providing pivotal clues to the audience. The killer is identified, for example, by the smell of his pipe tobacco, and in turn, the mysterious heiress by her perfume.

But despite Laube's years of laborious effort, on opening night Smell-O-Vision didn't work as intended. According to *Variety*, moviegoers in the balcony complained that the aromas reached them a few seconds after the action on the screen, and were accompanied by a distracting hissing sound. Crowther, the *New York Times* critic, complained that the aromas were too faint, so that "patrons sit there sniffling and snuffling like a lot of bird dogs, trying hard to catch the scent." He caustically suggested that Todd Jr. pump laughing gas into the audience instead, since the film's acting and script seemed to him nearly as sparse as the aromas.

Despite the care Laube had taken in designing his system, the audience apparently was still afflicted with the same olfactory fatigue that had doomed AromaRama—though, perhaps because of the delivery method, they perceived it as an absence rather than excess. As Todd recalled years later in an interview with Roy Frumkes of *Films in Review* magazine, Todd Jr.'s press agent, Bill Doll, finally suggested that the Smell-O-Vision pump be reversed after each scent. "It sucked air back so that there was no overhang on the previous smell," Todd Jr. explained to Frumkes. "Otherwise it just sort of drifted in between smells. It wasn't overpowering, but just enough not to make the clearest delineation." With that small adjustment, Todd claimed, Smell-O-Vision worked just fine.

But it was too late. Negative reviews and word of mouth had already doomed the film to oblivion. (Quipped comedian Henny Youngman: "I didn't understand the film—I had a cold.") Todd Jr. shelved plans for installing Smell-O-Vision in one hundred theaters around the world, and the film eventually was rereleased as *Holiday in Spain,* minus the odors. As a British newspaper, the *Daily Telegraph*, noted, "the film acquired a baffling, almost surreal quality, since there was no reason why, for example, a loaf of bread should be lifted from the oven and thrust into the camera for what seemed to be an unconscionably long time."

With the failure of *Scent,* Laube, Smell-O-Vision's inventor, quietly disappeared. Todd Jr.'s Hollywood career similarly petered out. He announced plans to make two more films—a sci-fi picture, *The Creature from the Bronx,* and *Bumpkin's Holiday,* in which the action was to consist of a man riding on a bus, with no spoken dialogue or subtitles. Neither film was made, and Todd went nearly another two decades before producing another. Strangely, the olfactory auteur's swan song was a painfully serious cinematic version of suicidal poetess Sylvia Plath's autobiographical novel, *The Bell Jar.*

Nevertheless, the notion of "smellies," as some had called them, was as stubbornly persistent as the aroma of cat urine on a carpet. In 1981, independent filmmaker John Waters parodied the idea in *Polyester* with Odorama scratch-and-sniff cards, and Waters's gag was copied by makers of the 2003 animated film *Rugrats Go Wild,* who claimed it was an "homage" to him. Laube and Todd Jr.'s film was revived briefly in the mid-1980s, when the MTV cable network aired it in conjunction with a convenience-store-chain promotion that offered scratch-and-sniff cards.

In 2000, Hong Kong director Ip Kam-Hung released *Lavender,* a fantasy romance in which an aromatherapy shop owner falls in love with an injured angel who has tumbled onto her balcony. To add to the film's ambience, producers reportedly spent $1 million to purchase special devices that would pump flowery scents into the air-conditioning systems at theaters. Ip told the *South China Morning Post* that he got the inspiration from Internet accounts of previous odor-enhanced films. Ip, mercifully, chose to forgo the gimmick in a subsequent film, 2004's *Elixir of Love,* which focused on the romantic travails of a princess afflicted with intolerable body odor.

But while success has eluded *Scent*'s cinematic imitators, another of Laube's underlying notions—that synthetic aromas could be used to influence consumers—has become a postmodern paradigm. Today, manufacturers of an astonishing variety of products imbue them with artificial fragrances—from chamomile-scented carpeting and rosebush sofas to wristwatches and mobile phones that smell faintly like coffee. Some doctors have blamed synthetic aromas for exacerbating patients' hay fever, and a small but vociferous segment of the population have protested that the continual barrage of simulated scents may be having harmful effects on their immune systems. In the late 1990s, a high-tech company even developed a system called iSmell for transmitting aromas via the Internet. Perhaps fortunately for the olfactory-fatigued among us, the technology never made it to market.

OTHER DOOMED INNOVATIONS

Smell-O-Vision was just one of many outlandish gambits tried over the years in the movie industry. Among the others:

- **CinemaScope.** *The Robe,* a ponderous 1953 religious epic, was the first film to use special lenses, one on the camera and another

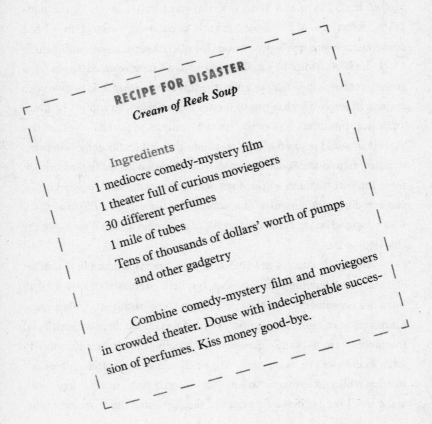

RECIPE FOR DISASTER
Cream of Reek Soup

Ingredients
1 mediocre comedy-mystery film
1 theater full of curious moviegoers
30 different perfumes
1 mile of tubes
Tens of thousands of dollars' worth of pumps
and other gadgetry

Combine comedy-mystery film and moviegoers in crowded theater. Douse with indecipherable succession of perfumes. Kiss money good-bye.

on the projector, that squeezed a wide-angle camera image down to 35mm size and then expanded it again on a gigantic screen that was two and a half times as long as it was tall. The action was supposed to be more vivid; instead, it was grotesquely distorted. Director Fritz Lang once joked that it was fit only for photographing snakes or funerals.

- **Cinemagic.** An attempt to exploit the hype around 3-D. In the 1959 film *The Angry Red Planet,* producer Sid Pink added a filter to the projector, which was supposed to make the screen image seem surrealistically distorted. Instead, it was simply hard to look at.

- **Percepto.** B-movie horror director William Castle, who never saw a cheesy gimmick he didn't like, tried to put some electricity into his 1959 film *The Tingler* by rigging a few seats in the theater to give unsuspecting patrons a mild shock.

- **Hallucinogenic Hypno-Vision.** Ads for the 1964 film *The Thrill Killers* (also known as *The Maniacs Are Loose)* claimed that it featured a hypnotic effect, which would supposedly fool audiences into thinking the crazed killers were running around in the theater.

- **Sensurround.** The 1974 film *Earthquake* and 1977's *Rollercoaster* used low-frequency sound to create the illusion of violent movement. And you thought that footage of Shelley Winters swimming underwater in *The Poseidon Adventure* was nauseating?

CONVENIENCE ISN'T ALWAYS ENOUGH

the paper dress

In the mid-1960s, ordinary housewives and the fashion elite thrilled to the notion of cheap, disposable garments. The fad lasted about as long as the clothes themselves.

ON AN OTHERWISE unremarkable afternoon in July 1966 in the town of Great Bend, Kansas, downtown pedestrians undoubtedly were puzzled by the sight of a woman frantically using big strips of masking tape to patch tears in her chic-looking red bandanna-print shift.

"It was me wearing my new paper dress," lamented a columnist for the women's pages of the local *Daily Tribune*. "Of course, I had to show it off and elaborate on how wonderful I thought it was and how it would probably revolutionize the clothing industry. Then things began to happen." When she went out after lunch to shoot a photograph for the paper, a rip developed in one of the dress's side seams. Then she inadvertently spilled a few drops of water on the dress, which exacerbated the damage. "Before I knew, the friction of my arms rubbing against the fabric made it come apart," she wrote. "So I ended the day wearing a series of patches and masking tape. I was lucky that no one dropped a match on me. I'd certainly hate to be caught out in the rain in one of those dresses."

But our bedraggled correspondent wasn't alone in her predicament. For a brief period from 1966 to 1968, countless women across

America excitedly donned similarly flimsy, poorly fitting, and not particularly comfortable disposable paper attire in an ill-conceived effort to be stylishly modern. One paper-dress maker alone, West Asheville, North Carolina–based Mars Manufacturing, reportedly churned out one hundred thousand dresses each week. Department stores set up boutiques devoted to paper fashion, and Manhattan trendsetters and small-town society matrons alike flocked to paper-dress balls. Designers such as Dior and Halston created haute couture for the upper-crustiest of clients, while the less affluent could make do with the paper dress offered by General Mills for $1 plus a box top from Betty Crocker instant au gratin potatoes. *Life* magazine, then a definitive voice in popular tastes, ran a photo spread on disposable fashion, and happily announced that "this is the year of the paper dress that can be worn and then just tossed in the wastebasket." Only a worried wool merchant, perhaps, would have disputed the conclusion that paper dresses were the first wave of a wonderful new disposable future, in which humans would enter the world swathed in paper and ultimately leave it the same way.

But then, with the same spectacular suddenness with which it had emerged, the paper dress fad fizzled and vanished. Today, the last few remaining specimens of 1960s paper dresses linger in eBay advertisements, thrift-store inventories, and museum collections, and we are left to ponder a massive, paradigm-shifting trend that, as it turned out, never actually happened. Nevertheless, paper dresses were also something more than just another deluded bit of 1960s silliness, like Day-Glo vinyl go-go boots or Nehru jackets. They became an extreme symbol of a mass-consumption culture tied inexorably to planned obsolescence, in which prosperity depended upon people's continual willingness to toss aside yesterday's prized possessions and acquire new ones. And although paper dresses ultimately flopped, the notion of inexpensive, ephemeral fashion eventually resurfaced—albeit in somewhat less fragile form—and became a staple at shopping malls across the land.

Radiation Suits at the Junior Miss Pageant

With the exception of Aztec, Maya, and Inca weavers in the pre-Columbian Americas who fashioned garments from palm leaves, most people throughout history would probably have seen throwaway clothing as lunacy. From the togas of ancient Romans to Victorian matrons' billowing skirts, clothing was made of materials prized for durability—wool, cotton, silk, leather—as well as appearance. But washing, ironing, and mending all those durable garments was hard work, which usually fell to women. To solve that problem, Edward Bellamy, author of the 1888 utopian novel "Looking Backward: 2000–1887," envisioned the stylish liberated woman of the millennium as clad in disposable, recyclable paper trousers, which would reinforce equality by freeing females from the drudgery of hand laundering.

Bellamy may have been the first to dream up disposable clothing for women, but it took three-quarters of a century for his idea to resonate. After World War II, manufacturers began to make products such as teabags and polishing cloths from synthetic fibers that were bonded together rather than woven. (According to legend, the idea dates back to ancient camel drivers in the Middle East, who stuffed tufts of unwoven wool between their sandals and the soles of their feet, creating a primitive version of the Dr. Scholl's gel innersole.) In the mid-1950s, Wisconsin-based paper products manufacturer Kimberly-Clark developed a new wood-based fabric, K-200, at the behest of the Atomic Energy Commission, which wanted overalls that could be used once and thrown away to avoid contamination. *Paper, Film and Foil Converter,* an industry journal, predicted that "garments made of K-200 will some day become an important factor in the nation's clothing industry."

Kimberly-Clark design consultant Vera de Give touted the idea of using K-200 to make dresses. "I expect to see the time when a woman can buy a fashionable dress for a mere nothing and throw it away after one wearing," she told a newspaper interviewer in 1956. That same year, Dr. Dorothy Lyle of the National Institute of Dry Cleaning displayed a knitted paper dress at the American Home Economics Association convention at Kansas City.

Kimberly-Clark continued to explore the idea of making paper dresses for years. In 1965, for example, a company magazine featured a disposable wedding dress, an evening frock, and a "futuristic" gown that Chicago designers had created from bolts of Kaycel, another paper-based fabric that today is used in the caps worn in hospital operating rooms.

But competitor Scott Paper beat Kimberly-Clark to the punch. In the spring of 1966, on the national telecast of the Junior Miss Pageant, the paper company unveiled its sleeveless shift paper dress, with the choice of either a bandanna print or a geometric op-art design. The revolutionary disposable garment could be had for a mere $1.25, plus a coupon clipped from the packaging of Scott's Colorful Explosions line of paper towels, napkins, and bathroom tissue.

It was a whimsical promotional gimmick, but the response was startling. From March to August, Scott received five hundred thousand mail coupons for paper dresses. National magazines and small-town newspapers alike scrambled to run articles about what they eagerly proclaimed to be the next big fashion fad. "Paper clips, a ruler and an eraser are not exactly the tools of a Christian Dior, but nowadays they will do in a pinch, or more readily, in a tear," proclaimed a typical example in a suburban Philadelphia newspaper in April 1966. "The latest gimmick in the fast-paced world of fashion is the paper dress, which probably will develop into a throw-away wardrobe."

But Will It Outlast the Frug?

According to a 1991 essay by fashion historian Alexandra Palmer, Scott was taken aback, since it had no real ambitions of branching out into fashion. But others quickly jumped on the opportunity. North Carolina's Mars Manufacturing rushed in with its line of "Throwaway Clothes," with op-art, paisley, and paint-your-own designs, in addition to a space age silver-foil shift made from a fabric used to insulate astronauts' spacesuits. That summer, Mars shipped 120,000 dresses to JC Penney, Sears, and other middlebrow department stores across America. Moda-Mia, a division of Rayette-Fabrege, soon unveiled its own line of $2 Mexican-print shifts in sleeved and sleeveless styles.

By fall, bizarrely, the fad had migrated upstream from coupon-clipping middle-American housewives to the urban fashion elites. Chic emporiums such as I. Magnin and Neiman Marcus opened their own paper dress boutiques, stocked with items such as New York designer Elisa Daggs's "wastebasket dress," which used a petticoat to mimic the shape of a waste receptacle. In October, at a charity ball in Hartford, Connecticut, to benefit the Wadsworth Atheneum Museum, society swells eschewed evening gowns in favor of paper dresses. An Associated Press correspondent depicted the event as "a nationally important test to determine whether non-woven paper wrapped around a pretty package doing the frug, the swim or the monkey could long endure." Model Peggy Moffitt reportedly stole the evening in a creation by Los Angeles designer Rudi Gernreich—a see-through vinyl dress with paper polka dots obscuring the critical areas.

A paper-napkin manufacturer's publicity ploy had inadvertently tapped into the mother lode of the mid-1960s zeitgeist. It fit perfectly into the pop art movement led by Andy Warhol and others, which embraced modern mass-production methods and techniques borrowed from comic books and advertising, and celebrated ordinary objects as irony-tinged objets d'art. And after all, what could be more ironic than a $100 designer version of the same flimsy, mass-produced garment that could be had for $1.25 and a coupon cut from a bathroom tissue package? Warhol himself created a dress emblazoned with Campbell's soup cans, a reference to his own pop art painting. (A surviving copy recently was offered for sale on the Internet for $3,700.) Graphic artist Harry Gordon used his paper dresses as wearable canvases, emblazoning them with cryptic images such as an eye, a rocket taking off, or a Buddhist peace gesture. The novelty of paper as a haute couture material fascinated European designers such as

Paco Rabanne, who probably found it easier to work with nonwoven fabric than with the metal dresses that he had to use pliers and a blowtorch to create.

Some of the elite, of course, still sneered. "I am sure that the elegant rich, the tasteful tastemakers, will not throw away that kind of money on such wasteful nonsense," fashion designer Oleg Cassini wrote in a 1967 newspaper column. "Rather, you will notice attention seekers, theatrical sorts, and those who rush to latch on to the latest fad."

But that was lost upon the housewives in Des Moines and Walla Walla. To the masses, paper dresses were something different—an invention that made the hippest fashion standard accessible to every would-be fashion maven within driving distance of a supermarket. Before long, women's clubs in small towns and cities were holding their own paper dress balls—albeit, usually without see-through attire. For less formal soirees, Hallmark offered a complete party package—paper cups, plates, and a matching dress for the hostess.

The paper industry, meanwhile, foresaw a profitably bright future for the disposable wardrobe—not just dresses, but swimsuits and even men's attire. Ronald Bard, vice president of Mars Manufacturing, boldly told *Life* in November 1966 that "Five years from now, 75 percent of the nation will be wearing disposable clothing." He dreamed of paper football jerseys, graduation gowns, children's wear, even disposable undershorts for traveling salesmen. "In paper, you are limited only by your imagination," he explained. *Fortune* magazine touted paper as the fabric of the future, cheaper than conventional textiles. Trans World Airlines experimented with paper uniforms for its flight attendants. The U.S. Army even began testing paper underwear for soldiers. *American Home* looked to paper pillowcases and even furniture as "fun" furnishings that "can be bought on impulse without the usual lasting commitment."

Amid that chorus of upbeat forecasts of a paper-clad future, a few downsides of paper dresses—ultimately critical ones—were being overlooked. Most of the American women buying paper dresses had never worn one before, and some had only seen them on TV. As they quickly discovered, disposable fashion wasn't necessarily very comfortable. "They didn't move well, they were uncomfortable when you wore them, and they billowed out when you sat down," Ellen Shanley, curator of costumes at the Fashion Institute of Technology Museum, told *Newsday* in 1999. And as our newspaperwoman in Kansas discovered, they also were prone to sudden disintegration. *Consumer Reports* derided the original Scott Paper Caper dress's quality, noting that it "is rather sloppily made; the 'fabric' is not very strong; and the printed color has a tendency to rub off when it gets damp."

Paper dress wearers also often found themselves feeling nervous at parties, out of fear that a chance encounter with a Benson & Hedges 100 could turn them into a fashionista flambé. The Los Angeles City Fire Department briefly banned the sale of paper dresses in late 1966, until a department chemist determined that they were no more flammable than other garments. In truth, paper dresses were probably safer than cotton or nylon, since most were treated with a flame-retardant finish.

But there was a catch. As the chief of the U.S. Public Health Service's injury-control program warned in a newspaper interview, the flame-retardant chemicals were rendered ineffective if the garment was washed or dry-cleaned. To be on the safe side, paper dresses could be worn only once—unless, perhaps, the wearer had the same blithe disregard for personal hygiene that she had for sartorial convention. *Life* discovered that limitation when it tested paper dresses' durability by somehow convincing a woman to wear one every day for a month while she did housework. Though the fabric didn't shred, she complained afterward that "I like a dress I can wash."

As those drawbacks started to sink in, sales of paper dresses plummeted as quickly as they had risen. In a sense, the paper dress was a victim of its own success. As fashion writer Angela Taylor noted in 1969, the garment became popular so quickly that companies, in their rush to meet the unexpected demand, didn't have any time to perfect the materials or manufacturing process. Presumably, some of those problems might have been corrected over time. But the ambience of the pop culture was changing as well. Disposable clothing was the sort of ultramodern convenience that fit with a sunny, optimistic view of technological progress. By the late 1960s, consumers' optimism was being supplanted by environmental awareness and fears of a future ravaged by waste, pollution, and thoughtless overconsumption. The ad copy touting the garments' quick obsolescence— "Won't last forever. Who cares? Wear it for kicks, then give it to the air"—no longer sounded so cool. Mars Manufacturing, the major maker

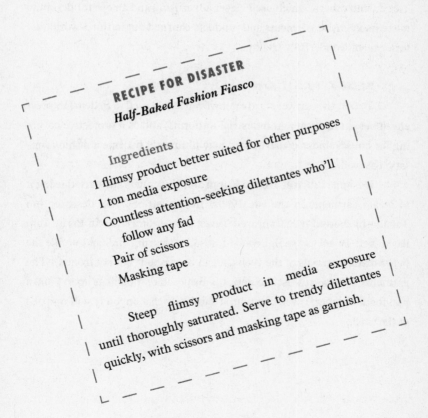

RECIPE FOR DISASTER

Half-Baked Fashion Fiasco

Ingredients

1 flimsy product better suited for other purposes
1 ton media exposure
Countless attention-seeking dilettantes who'll follow any fad
Pair of scissors
Masking tape

Steep flimsy product in media exposure until thoroughly saturated. Serve to trendy dilettantes quickly, with scissors and masking tape as garnish.

of paper dresses, soon switched to marketing them as a novelty promotional item. It produced dresses promoting Richard Nixon's 1968 presidential campaign, and once churned out a special order of forty thousand dresses designed to look like the Yellow Pages.

Though the paper dress flopped, nonwoven fabrics themselves have turned out to be a more enduring success. Paper dress makers such as Mars found a less glamorous but profitable niche, making disposable gowns and other garments for the hospital industry. Moreover, the concept of disposable fashion for the masses eventually showed a similar resilience. The 1990s saw the rise of retailers such as the Gap, Old Navy, Target, and others, which used clever advertising and an eye for design to make inexpensive garments and products churned out in third-world factories seem wonderfully trendy.

FEDEX FASHION

Tyvek, the soft yet sturdy nonwoven fabric used in Federal Express envelopes, in medical and industrial uniforms, and as a protective covering for houses under construction, may ultimately become a fashion sensation as well.

Designers such as Donna Karan and Vivienne Tam started using it to create garments in the late 1990s. In the fall of 2004, designer Jun Takahashi showed paint-smeared Tyvek dresses at a show in Paris. Tam has touted Tyvek as "so lightweight, it's like wearing air," and unlike the paper dress materials of the 1960s, it can be washed (but not ironed). The garments are also at least theoretically disposable, though at up to $300 a pop for a designer Tyvek creation, it's unlikely that anybody will toss one in the trash.

the u.s. psychic friends program

*The federal government dabbled in paranormal espio-
nage for decades, using clairvoyants for everything from
spotting enemy subs to "reading" documents on Nikita
Khrushchev's desk. And for fun, they bent spoons.*

IN THE EARLY 1970s, U.S. intelligence officials learned that the
Soviet Union was apparently trying to add a strange new weapon to its
arsenal—a Russian psychic named Nina Kulagina. Film footage of the
Russian woman, seen in Moscow by westerners, showed her moving com-
pass needles and small, light objects without touching them. Skeptics
would later suspect that she was using concealed magnets, but no matter.
A then-classified July 1972 Defense Intelligence Agency report explained
in breathless detail, Kulagina—whom the Soviets supposedly kept in top
secret seclusion—did even more impressive tricks for Soviet military researchers. She was said to be able to stare at a raw egg in a glass case six
feet away and, through the power of her spirit aura, separate the yolk from
the white portion. She also reportedly possessed the mental ability to
cause a frog's heart to stop—and then to start it beating again, at will.
When it came to that feat, "the military implications . . . if true, are extremely important," the document's author emphasized.

The classified report also described other parts of a far-ranging
Soviet effort to exploit "psi," the term used by believers in paranormal

mental powers, in which the Kremlin was investing an amount equivalent to nearly $100 million in today's dollars. For example, the Soviets were eager to master something called the Apport Technique. "When fully developed, this technique would make possible the abduction of actual objects, including documents, in enemy territory and then transfer to [Soviet] territory," the report proclaimed breathlessly. "Then they could be returned without the enemy [the U.S.] being aware of this temporary abduction." They were also trying to develop a capability in astral projection—specifically, how to project a "luminous cloud" of energy that would, at a distance, materialize to form a human hand, which they might use to disable U.S. weapons or communications equipment, or even "to produce instant death in military or civilian officials."

Had common sense prevailed, Pentagon and CIA honchos might have breathed a sigh of relief—or perhaps burst into spontaneous hysterics—at revelations that suggested the Kremlin's brain trust had pickled itself in vodka. Instead of developing better missiles or submarines or space-based weapons, the Ruskies were wasting precious time, money, and scientific talent on what might have been promising script premises for *The Outer Limits* or *The Twilight Zone*. But that would have been too easy. Instead, U.S. officials took seriously the prospect of falling behind in an ethereal arms race. They quickly moved to counter the Soviets by developing their own cadre of psychic soldiers and spies. The secret U.S. effort, conducted by a succession of government agencies under a variety of code names—Scangate, Gondola Wish, Grill Flame, and finally Stargate—continued for the next two decades and actually outlived the Soviet Union itself. In the process, the program defied repeated attempts by skeptical scientists and budget watchers to terminate it, in part because of congressional patrons' fascination with the paranormal. Even though no bona fide supernatural warfare techniques or extrasensory spying capabilities resulted from the psychic espionage program, in the end it did prove conclusively the power of one phenomenon—the human mind's amazing ability to become utterly, stubbornly enthralled with an idea, no matter how nonsensical it turns out to be.

"From the Incredible to the Outrageously Incredible"

In fairness, the government's pursuit of paranormal powers probably doesn't rank as the wackiest top secret project ever—that honor probably belongs to "Acoustic Kitty," the CIA's ill-fated 1960s scheme to use a cat equipped with a listening device and transmitter to spy on the Soviets. (Unfortunately, the feline agent was run over by a car instead.) And unlike, say, "Curveball," the Iraqi defector whose revelations about what turned out to be nonexistent mobile biological weapons labs helped make the case for the 2003 invasion of Iraq, the psychic corps didn't have any significant consequences in terms of U.S. national security. In truth, the 1970s effort wasn't even the first U.S. attempt to wage paranormal espionage. As former North Carolina congressman Charlie Rose (not to be confused with the TV host of the same name) told the *Charlotte Observer*, he once attended a CIA briefing on Capitol Hill at which he was introduced to a psychic who had attempted to spy on former Soviet leader Nikita Khrushchev, who was premier from 1958 to 1964. The man claimed that he had projected himself inside the Kremlin so that he could peruse documents on Khrushchev's desk. Unfortunately, the psychic "couldn't read Russian, and it didn't do him much good," the congressman explained.

But the psychic espionage effort that stretched from the 1970s to the mid-1990s definitely was the most determined and prolonged government exploration of phenomena that, in the words of a 1988 report by the National Research Council, "range from the incredible to the outrageously incredible."

It began in the summer of 1972, when officials from the Central Intelligence Agency went to California to meet with H. E. Puthoff, a former navy officer and government intelligence employee who had moved on to the Stanford Research Institute, a private think tank. Puthoff was investigating a type of clairvoyance known as "remote viewing," in which a person with psychic powers attempts to visualize something that isn't possible to perceive with normal senses—a place he or she has never visited, an object hidden from view, the location and activities of a distant person. Puthoff's research subject was a painter named Ingo Swann, whom Puthoff said had the ability to see inside pieces of machinery in the lab. By Puthoff's account, the CIA men tested Swann by quizzing him about the contents of a small box. Swann reportedly said that it contained something that looked like a leaf, except that it moved. Apparently, that was close enough to the correct answer—a small moth—for the CIA. In October of that year, the agency gave the SRI a $50,000 contract to pursue more research.

The research team recruited more subjects who claimed to have psychic abilities, and during the next fifteen years it conducted some twenty-six thousand experimental trials. One such experiment took place in July 1974 at the SRI in Palo Alto, California. A psychic was given the coordinates of a nuclear weapons research facility in Kazakhstan, then a part of the Soviet Union, and asked to use his remote viewing powers. The subject described a road through a river gorge leading to a series of low, cramped one-story buildings partially dug into the ground, with a five-hundred-foot antenna and an outdoor pool for underwater testing. He mentioned the proximity of a nearby village, but said the closest rail line was about sixty miles to the north. It was a strikingly vivid description of a place he had never actually seen.

Unfortunately, it was pretty much all wrong, except for the subject's mention of a rail-mounted crane on the site. Over the years, paranormal proponents have pointed to the crane as evidence that remote viewing does sometimes produce results. To a CIA official who evaluated the experiment, however, that one bit of semiaccurate information was the result of the subject making enough guesses that he finally got something right. As the official noted in his report, at times the psychic seemed to be influenced by suggestions from the experimenters, while at other points he became evasively vague. When researchers challenged a detail, he wrote, "the subject replies with, 'I'll come back to that,' but he never does." The CIA man concluded that the experiment had been unsuccessful.

Uri Geller, the Israeli nightclub performer famed for his mental spoon-bending act, claimed in a 1999 essay for the *Jerusalem Post* that he was recruited to be a subject in the CIA program. In Geller's version of events, he went beyond remote viewing and began to channel voices from the spirit world before quitting the program when the CIA asked him to use his mental powers to stop a pig's heart in an experiment, as Soviet psychic Kulagina had supposedly done with a frog. (If Geller is to be believed, you at least have to give the CIA credit for trying to outdo the Soviets in tormenting animals.)

It's unclear whether the CIA became disenchanted with the psychics' lack of success, or whether the agency—already embarrassed by a congressional investigation of its flirtations with LSD and assassination plots against foreign leaders—decided it didn't need another potentially embarrassing project. Either way, in the summer of 1975, the CIA quietly terminated its support for the psychic research project.

Saffron Robes and Spoon Bending

But the Pentagon wasn't ready to give up on the prospect of its own spoon-bending brigade. Initially the air force, and later the Defense Intelligence Agency, took over the funding for the SRI's research. The army also set up a remote-viewing unit, based at Fort Meade, Maryland, in a numberless building formerly used as a mess hall. "Detachment G," as it was known, included both soldiers and civilian employees believed to possess paranormal abilities. It was "kind of like *Men in Black*," one participant, retired U.S. Army major Paul Smith, explained to CBS News in 2002. "They say, you know, 'If we tell you about this program, you have to basically pretend like you don't exist anymore.' "

While Detachment G's members didn't have to wear uniforms like the rest of the army, they showed up for work early and drilled—in their case, by playing guessing games with cards, or by sitting in a room and trying to visualize the location of another unit member who'd left the premises. As one member later recalled, remote-viewing efforts usually resulted in a jumble of vague details: "You may get the colors red and yellow, smell food, hear traffic sounds, and get the impression of a clown—and it ends up being McDonald's."

Under military control, the psychic project expanded its scope. In addition to studying participants' extrasensory abilities, the program added a counterintelligence element to its mission, to find out if the USSR or other adversaries were developing paranormal espionage or warfare capabilities. (Despite such efforts, U.S. officials never stumbled upon the true irony of the situation—that the Soviets' paranormal obsession had been motivated by fear, after a false report that U.S. submarine crews were using telepathy to communicate under the Arctic ice cap.) The Defense Intelligence Agency also set up an operations component. A half dozen psychics—known in intelligence circles as "the Naturals"—were made available to any government agency that wanted to put them to use.

Participants in the effort have claimed that their success rate was better than what detractors give them credit for. In his 2002 memoir, *The Stargate Chronicles,* army psychic Joseph McMoneagle claims to have used remote viewing in 1978 to identify a structure in the Soviet Union as a secret factory where a giant submarine, previously unknown to U.S. intelligence, was being built. (To his chagrin, he writes, National Security Council officials discounted his vision as "a lucky guess.") One former military remote viewer, the army's Paul Smith, told a newspaper interviewer that in May 1987, he visualized the Iraqi bombing of the USS *Stark* in the Persian Gulf, which killed thirty-seven Americans. Smith said he filed a report two days before the attack, but that no action was taken.

But other attempts to use psychic intelligence proved fruitless. When U.S. Army brigadier general James L. Dozier was kidnapped by Italian terrorists in 1981, the army tried to use remote viewing to find him.

According to a 1988 *Washington Post* account, a seer dressed in "flowing saffron-colored robes" arrived in Padua, Italy, and had a State Department official take him to the apartment from which Dozier had been kidnapped so he could get a "reading" of where Dozier was being held. Eventually, Dozier was rescued without any paranormal assistance. In 1986, *Time* later reported, military psychics tried to pinpoint Libyan dictator Muammar Gadhafi's location before U.S. warplanes attacked the country, but were unsuccessful. *ABC News Nightline* would later report that the psychic spies were employed in about five hundred different intelligence operations over the years, but that the clairvoyants came up with useful information in less than a dozen instances.

The program gradually began to deteriorate, one participant later complained to *Newsweek,* after the army began letting "any old kook" into the psychic corps. One psychic quit the project after he became convinced that there was a Martian colony hidden beneath the New Mexico desert. And military brass irked the psychics by treating them at times as if they were a Vegas magic act. One general, for example, reportedly tried to see if he could get participants to bend spoons.

Meanwhile, the research part of the project continued until 1986. Typically, a researcher would sit and look at a picture of, say, an Indian temple, clipped from *National Geographic,* while at another location, a psychic would try to visualize and describe the image. The psychic's description was then given to a third person acting as a judge, who was also given the temple picture and four other photos of similar locales. If the judge decided that the psychic's description most closely resembled the picture of the temple, the test was scored as a successful "hit."

Scoring a hit, of course, didn't necessarily prove that the remote viewer's powers were real. Psychologist Ray Hyman of the University of Oregon, who later evaluated the research for the government, pointed out in a 1996 article for the magazine *Skeptical Inquirer* that it had some obvious flaws. Even if the subjects managed to score a higher proportion of hits than the 20 percent that mere chance would dictate, the work didn't necessarily prove that remote viewing was real, because researchers lacked a theoretical model that would explain how it worked. Without being able to measure the results against such an explanation, "any glitch in the data can be used as evidence for 'Psi' [paranormal abilities]," Hyman wrote.

In 1988, a National Research Council study threw cold water on the military's interest in the paranormal, concluding that such techniques were "scientifically unsupported." The NRC report also discounted other army attempts to explore the New Agey frontiers of human potential, such as a study in which marksmen were instructed to hum "Mary Had a Little Lamb" while they shot, to test what effect such a cognitive distraction would have on their accuracy.

After that, military officials tried to terminate the program. But like some wraith from the spirit world, it refused to die. As the *Washington Post* later reported, it was kept alive at the insistence of a handful of U.S. senators, who were still worried that a paranormal powers gap might open up between the U.S. and the Soviets. The psychic effort "didn't make any more or less sense than a variety of programs we conducted in the intelligence arena," C. Richard D'Amato, a staffer on the Senate Appropriations Subcommittee on Defense, told the *Post*. "I would say that if the Russians hadn't had such a big program, we wouldn't [have kept it alive]."

Finally, in 1994, the military convinced Congress to transfer the program back to the CIA, which had started it more than two decades before. The CIA, in turn, hired the American Institutes for Research, a nonprofit behavioral and social-science research organization, to evaluate it. The AIR's September 1995 report concluded that the information produced by the government psychics was too "vague and ambiguous" to be of any value, and that there was no compelling reason to continue the project any longer. By then, the CIA had already shut down the program.

If Only They'd Recruited Dionne Warwick

Though newspaper and magazine journalists had uncovered bits and pieces of the government's paranormal research over the years, it wasn't until November 1995 that *ABC News Nightline* revealed the lengths to which the government had gone in its failed effort. Host Ted Koppel's opening teaser—"Psychic spies: cold war whimsy or secret weapon?"— gave a none-too-subtle hint of the derision that many in Washington (and elsewhere) felt. Democratic senator Tom Harkin of Iowa ridiculed it as "the Pentagon's Psychic Friends" program, a mocking comparison to the pay-per-minute telephone fortune-tellers touted in late-night television infomercials hosted by singer Dionne Warwick.

Yet the media and political elite's view didn't necessarily reflect that of the public at large, which seemed to be more fascinated than outraged to discover a real government program that seemed like something out of *The X-Files,* the paranormal detective TV series that in the mid-1990s was at the peak of its popularity. (Nearly three out of five Americans believe in extrasensory perception, according to a 2002 CBS News poll.) While the mainstream media took a lighthearted approach to its coverage, the psychic spy story caught fire on what was then the media frontier—discussion groups and pages on the still-new medium of the World Wide Web, and the late-night talk radio program hosted by Art Bell, a mysterious figure who broadcast from a trailer in the southwestern desert. Bell's insomniac audience was fascinated with conspiracy theories about secret government involvement in paranormal phenomena, and remote viewing fit the bill perfectly. Edward Dames, a retired army major who had been involved in the military psychic intelligence effort, became a frequent guest on Bell's show.

Some former government psychics took the demise of the program hard. In a 1996 interview with *Psychology Today,* for example, one former government remote viewer described the experience of using extrasensory perception as a "morphine flow" that the brain learns to crave. Even after the experiments ended, he claimed to be unable to sleep without the television blaring to drown out the images that continually bombarded his mind. But others made the best of their newfound notoriety, writing memoirs about their experiences and hitting the college lecture trail. One alumnus started a company, Remote Viewing Technologies, which teaches remote viewing techniques to paying clients. (A five-seminar package can be had for $3,195, according to the company Web site.)

And just as it's difficult to disprove the existence of psychic phenomena, it's impossible to rule out the possibility that the government won't someday resume its explorations of the paranormal. Or maybe it already has. After the terror attacks of September 11, 2001, several high-profile psychics told *New York* magazine that they had been contacted by federal agencies and asked to help in predicting future attacks.

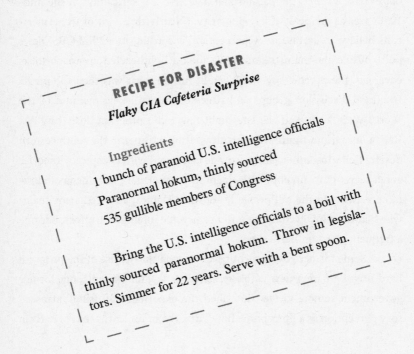

RECIPE FOR DISASTER
Flaky CIA Cafeteria Surprise

Ingredients
1 bunch of paranoid U.S. intelligence officials
Paranormal hokum, thinly sourced
535 gullible members of Congress

Bring the U.S. intelligence officials to a boil with thinly sourced paranormal hokum. Throw in legislators. Simmer for 22 years. Serve with a bent spoon.

ACTUALLY, THE PRESIDENT SAID, "I BURIED PAUL"

In October 1990, a U.S. Senate aide wrote to then secretary of defense Richard Cheney to warn him of a possible breach of national security. A researcher in reversed-speech therapy—that is, the notion that the subconscious mind slips backward words into a person's speech—had obtained tapes of speeches by then president George H. W. Bush, Secretary of State James Baker III, and Cheney. When the tapes were played in reverse, the researcher reported, the word "Simone" was audible in all three. "I mention this in case it is a code word that should not be in the national interest to be known," the aide wrote. A Pentagon spokesman later told the Associated Press that Cheney knew of no such code word.

the 1967 jimi hendrix–monkees concert tour

*Perhaps the greatest rock guitarist ever, his flamboyant
fusion of blues, psychedelia, and sex changed popular music. But to the prepubescent fans of a fictional TV pop
group, he was boh–ring!*

THE SCENE WAS Forest Hills, New York, on a night in July 1967,
and Jimi Hendrix, perhaps the greatest guitarist in rock history, was onstage with his band, the Experience. Not quite twenty-five years old, he
was fresh from his now-legendary performance at the Monterey Pop Festival, at which he climaxed his guitar pyrotechnics by lighting his instrument on fire. Hendrix was resplendent in his lush Afro hairstyle and the
ultracool gaze that before long would grace untold millions of album covers, T-shirts, and black-light posters in bedrooms across the land. Playing
a Fender Stratocaster in his unorthodox upside-down style, he let fly with
one of the otherworldly riffs that, even decades later, other guitarists still
struggle to imitate. The amplifiers exploded in a startling cacophony of
feedback, interspersed with rapid-fire bursts of melodic lines, as if the
instrument itself were writhing and squealing in pleasure at his touch. But
Hendrix wasn't content just to be a virtuoso. He was a master showman,
and an erotic bad boy to boot. He caressed the Stratocaster against his
loins and poked it with pelvic thrusts. At an opportune point in the music,

he raised the instrument to his face, suggestively nuzzled the strings with his lips and tongue, and kept playing with his teeth.

It might have been a moment that a middle-aged devotee of today's classic rock radio stations might dream about having a time machine to revisit. Or maybe not, because there was one problem: Hendrix was just the opening act. As he performed his wizardry, the crowd erupted—not in ecstatic, transcendent "like . . . wow, man!" glee, but with the whiny impatience of a bunch of eight- to eleven-year-old girls—which, in fact, they were. Squeaky prepubescent voices kept chanting for the headliners they had come to see.

"We want Davy!"

"Enough with the psychedelic, already!"

"We want the *Monkees!*"

Finally, a frustrated Hendrix stopped playing and threw down his guitar. Flipping his middle finger at the crowd and uttering an obscenity, he angrily stomped offstage.

To anyone even vaguely knowledgeable about rock, the notion of Jimi Hendrix as the opening act for the Monkees seems so utterly incomprehensible that one half expects it to be an urban myth, akin to the old rumors that Paul McCartney had died and been replaced in the Beatles by a look-alike, or that shock rocker Alice Cooper had played one of the kids in the TV sitcom *Leave It to Beaver*. Hendrix, after all, was the innovator who infused the blues with psychedelic pyrotechnics, bridging the distance between the Mississippi Delta and Haight-Ashbury. The Monkees— David Jones, Micky Dolenz, Mike Nesmith, and Peter Tork—were a pop group created to star in a TV sitcom. Recruited for their appearance and acting skills rather than musicianship, in concert they found it challenging just to approximate the simple melodies and innocuous lyrics of their hit singles, which actually had been written and performed on the records by industry pros.

"The whole thing was a disaster," admitted the tour's promoter, *American Bandstand* host Dick Clark, years later in an interview with a

Hendrix fan magazine. Hendrix's drummer, Mitch Mitchell, concurs. "[The Monkees] were a nice bunch of chaps and all that, even though we thought they couldn't play," he wrote in *Jimi Hendrix: Inside the Experience,* a 1990 memoir. ". . . But God, did their audience hate us."

How, and why, this unlikely pairing came to be remains one of the largely forgotten chapters of 1960s rock lore. The peculiar truth about the brief convergence of Hendrix and the Monkees is that despite the gaping disparity in their artistic stature, each possessed something the other wanted. The Monkees longed to be more than a comedy act—they harbored hopes of evolving into an actual rock group, of being taken seriously by an older, hipper audience. Hendrix, conversely, was eager for the sort of commercial breakthrough that too often eluded radically original, paradigm-shifting artists. And while their brief tour together was a spectacular fiasco, in subtle ways it did help both the Monkees and Hendrix achieve what they were seeking—and in the process, may have altered the history of rock.

"Are You Out of Your [Expletive] Mind?"

Musically, the difference between the "Prefab Four," as some derisively dubbed the Monkees, and the wizard of the wah-wah pedal was vast. Eric Lefcowitz, author of the group's definitive 1985 history, *The Monkees Tale,* described it as the equivalent of "soda pop versus psilocybin." But the disparity between their respective paths to fame was just as jarring. Hendrix, a Seattle native, was a self-taught virtuoso who honed his skills on the road as a humble backup player for Little Richard, the Isley Brothers, and others. He was playing in a bohemian nightclub in Greenwich Village for $15 a night, and in ill health from malnutrition, when he was discovered by Chas Chandler, bassist for the British rock group the Animals. Chandler convinced him to move to England, where his flamboyant fusion of blues and psychedelic rock might find a more sophisticated audience, with Chandler as his producer-adviser.

The Monkees, by contrast, were created by a pair of Hollywood producers, Bob Rafelson and Bert Schneider, who advertised in *Daily Variety* for "folk & rock musicians and singers." They selected the four finalists by analyzing their screen tests with one of the era's primitive computers. It was Hollywood television's attempt to capitalize on the popularity of the Beatles, with a thirty-minute sitcom about a similarly free-spirited rock group that affected the hipster look—shaggy coiffures and sideburns, turtlenecks and love beads—minus most of the implied rebellion. Only two of the members, the guitar-and-banjo-playing Tork and guitarist Nesmith, actually knew how to play instruments at the start. But that wasn't a problem for pop music publisher and producer Don Kirshner, who was hired to create music for them. Songs such as "Last Train to Clarksville," their first hit single, were composed by Kirshner's crew of professional songsmiths in New York, and were recorded by various studio musicians (including drummer Buddy Miles, who later played in Hendrix's Band of Gypsys.) The sound was a workmanlike facsimile of mid-1960s rock, but with lyrics devoid of any of the usual coded references to drugs, sex, racial tensions, or Vietnam (though Dolenz has written that "Clarksville" actually is about a soldier going off to war). The music initially served mostly as a way of hyping the TV show. On the program, musical sequences were used as breaks between playful gags and footage of slapstick antics, often speeded up to make it seem manic.

Unless one was an aesthetic purist, that wasn't all necessarily bad. As a TV show, it wasn't deep, but it was remarkably unconventional for its time, with nonlinear story lines, herky-jerky editing, and unorthodox camera shots—sort of the sitcom equivalent of avant-garde European cinema. (A cynic might note that the show's creators also none-too-subtly imitated the style of Richard Lester, who directed the Beatles' hit films *A Hard Day's Night* and *Help!*) And while they weren't much as musicians, as actors the Monkees were funny enough to win an Emmy Award for comedy. The group's fans included psychedelic guru Timothy Leary, who saw subtle subversiveness in their comedy, and Beatle John Lennon, who considered them rock's version of the Marx Brothers.

Nevertheless, the true genius of their act was not in their music or acting, but in the marketing of their wholesome, fun version of rebellion. As Tork noted in a 1988 interview with *Guitar World* magazine, the group was designed "not to scare the living daylights out of Mama."

But the Monkees longed to be something more. They hung out on the fringe of the Sunset Strip–Laurel Canyon counterculture scene, and knew many of the serious young hipsters who were revolutionizing music. (Tork, for example, had tried out for the Monkees at the suggestion of guitarist Stephen Stills, a friend who himself didn't make the cut, reportedly in part because of his already receding hairline.) The Monkees achieved astonishing commercial success—their single "I'm a Believer" sold 10 million copies worldwide, and at one point in early 1967, they had the top two albums on the U.S. charts. But the lads were chagrined because, as Lefcowitz notes, the rumors grew increasingly louder that the records were actually the work of others. (According to his book, the group's members didn't even learn of the existence of their top-selling second album, *More of the Monkees,* until they happened upon it in a record shop after its release.) By spring 1967, after an angry group meeting with Kirshner in which Nesmith reportedly put his fist through a wall, the TV show's producers agreed to allow the quartet creative control. They rushed into the studio and hammered out their first real album, *Headquarters.* The rock press, who had previously savaged the group, gave it surprisingly positive reviews. But the Monkees were cursed by bad timing. Their modest effort was overshadowed by the release the following week of the Beatles' *Sgt. Pepper's Lonely Hearts Club Band,* a masterpiece whose innovative recording techniques and eloquently insightful lyrics changed rock music forever.

Still, the Monkees hoped that their upcoming summer tour would establish them as a serious rock group. They planned to pull out all the creative stops—from frequent costume changes and their trademark clowning, to the first special-effects light show ever used in a rock concert. In June 1967, as the preparations were being completed, Tork and

Dolenz went to the Monterey Pop Festival to groove on the cutting-edge music and generate some publicity by being seen. Dolenz was clad in an antelope-hide suit, which he had made especially for the occasion, and a feathered headdress which he borrowed from the studio's costume department. At the concert, they saw an act that Dolenz had once caught at Café Au Go-Go in Greenwich Village—back when Hendrix used the stage name Jimmy James. "Hey, that's the guy that plays guitar with his teeth!" Dolenz exclaimed. That night, Hendrix went even further. He closed his set with a cover of the Troggs' "Wild Thing," altering it with bursts of feedback and wild improvised melodic lines, and then suddenly placed his guitar on the ground, soaked it with lighter fluid, and set it afire.

Dolenz was blown away, as much by the stunt as by Hendrix's playing. When he got back to Los Angeles, he lobbied the tour's promoter, Dick Clark, to hire the Jimi Hendrix Experience, which also included drummer Mitchell and bassist Noel Redding, as an opening act. "The Monkees was very theatrical in my eyes and so was the Jimi Hendrix Experience," Dolenz recalled in his 1993 memoir, *I'm a Believer.* "It would make the perfect union." Clark reluctantly agreed: "Anybody could have seen that it was not a compatible coupling. [The Monkees] were in the driver seat—that's what they wanted—and the deal was made." Tork even invited Hendrix to stay at his Laurel Canyon home.

One might expect that Hendrix's British business manager, Michael Jeffery, would have laughed at the offer of an opening gig with the Monkees. Instead, he readily accepted. Jeffery, by various accounts, didn't really grasp Hendrix's artistic stature—after Hendrix's sensational guitar-wrecking performance at Monterey, for example, Jeffery's response was to chastise the guitarist for breaking a microphone. Instead, Jeffery focused, perhaps myopically, on the bottom line. Even after Hendrix's hallucinogenic anthem "Purple Haze" climbed the English pop charts in early 1967, Hendrix and his band still appeared as the opening act on an English tour with Cat Stevens, hunky crooner Engelbert Humperdinck, and the Walker Brothers, a band of teen heartthrobs (who, like the Monkees, didn't actually play on some of their hit records). Hendrix had turned the gigs to his advantage, upstaging the other acts by writhing around so lasciviously with his guitar that the British press began hyping him as a new rock sex symbol. To Jeffery, the Monkees must have seemed like even better exposure—at that moment, after all, they were the hottest American act around, with hordes of screaming fans across the land. The fact that the Monkees' audience was largely prepubescent children seems to have eluded him.

Jeffery called Hendrix and his bandmates, who were in Los Angeles at the time, with what he thought was great news. As drummer Mitchell would later recall, the musicians initially thought Jeffery was putting them on. When they realized he wasn't, Chas Chandler, who was traveling with the group, was irate. "Are you out of your [expletive] mind?" he screamed into the phone, by one account. Hendrix, who was sitting nearby and listening, was aghast. He'd tolerated opening for lesser talents before— "The people who come to hear Engelbert sing 'Please Release Me' may not dig me, but that's not tragic," he once cheerfully rationalized—but this was the pits. Adding to the embarrassment, he now had to open for a group he'd already reviled as "dishwater" in an interview with the British publication *Melody Maker*. "I really hate somebody like that for making it big," Hendrix had complained. "You can't knock anybody for making it, but people like the Monkees?"

There was no time to object. Hendrix and his mates had to hop on a plane and rush back across the country, where the Monkees tour was about to embark.

Lollipops Versus LSD

For Hendrix, who was accustomed to driving long hours to play in small clubs, the Monkees' life of luxury had to be a shock. The Prefab Four played sports arenas and had their own DC-6 airliner, with the band's name emblazoned across the fuselage, staffed by attendants whose uniforms also bore the official Monkees logo.

Considering Hendrix's distaste for the Monkees' music and resentment of what he saw as their undeserved fame, he and his bandmates hit it off fairly well with the Prefab Four. It helped that the Monkees were refreshingly unpretentious about their humble abilities. "Peter Tork could play banjo, Mike Nesmith could play guitar, Micky Dolenz was one hell of a nice guy, and Davy Jones was extremely short," Mitchell recalled in his book. Tork carried a copy of the *I Ching* with him, and he and Hendrix had some talks about Eastern mysticism. "We had a lot of fun on the plane and between shows with Jimi," Tork recalled in Glenn A. Baker's 1986 book, *Monkeemania*. "He taught me how to play guitar vibrato one day."

But the Monkees' fans were an insurmountable problem. The tour opened at the Coliseum in Jacksonville, Florida, where organizers made the mistake of having another band open the show so that the Jimi Hendrix Experience came on just before the Monkees were to appear. In his early career Hendrix undoubtedly had played for some tough audiences in seedy roadhouses, but this was something new—row after row of elementary-school-age girls and their parents. Less than halfway through the first number, the impatient preteenyboppers were already screaming for him to yield the stage to their idols.

"We could have been Tom and Jerry on stage," drummer Mitchell would recall. "They didn't care."

It was the first of seven concerts in as many nights, and things only got worse. Hendrix's twenty- to twenty-five-minute sets drew crowd reactions that Hendrix biographer Harry Shapiro describes as "from muted to hostile." When Hendrix launched into "Foxy Lady," one of his signature tunes, the Monkees fans mocked him by chanting "Foxy Davy!" over his singing.

The parents were an even bigger problem, Dolenz recalled in his memoir. "They were probably not too crazy about having to sit through a 'godawful' Monkees concert anyway, much less see this black guy in a psychedelic DayGlo blouse, playing music from hell."

It all quickly got to Hendrix. Increasingly depressed and sullen, he would turn his back to the audience and play sloppy, breakneck renditions of his songs. He complained that his guitar was malfunctioning. Sometimes he would refuse to sing, compelling Redding and Mitchell to cover for him. The band drank and toked themselves into oblivion on the inevitable red-eye flight to the next show. As Redding recalled in his memoir, "This led to some awkward moments, as the tour was very straight." The bassist once amused himself by giving one of the Monkees a dose of amyl nitrite, a heart medication that when snorted causes a brief but intensely disorienting rush, just before takeoff.

Such fun aside, by the time the tour had returned to Forest Hills, New York, on July 14 for the first of three shows, the situation had deteriorated to a crisis point. Hendrix's producer-adviser Chas Chandler, who forced himself to attend the first show, saw the Experience struggle through a thirty-minute set in which Hendrix not only was subjected to the usual "We want the Monkees!" chants, but suffered the additional indignity of splitting his pants.

Hendrix's management quarreled about what to do. In Chandler's version, he wanted to pull Hendrix off the tour immediately, but Jeffery was concerned about being sued by tour promoter Dick Clark. Chandler then decided to take matters in his own hands. He called Clark, whom he'd gotten to know when the Animals played on another Clark tour. "Chas met me in the hotel and said, 'What are we going to do? This is not a compatible combining of talents,' " Clark recalled years later. "And I'm like, 'I think your client's going to get very sick—and we'll have to announce that he can't make it.' And that was the arrangement that we made."

The final show, on July 16, was the nadir. In Joe Smith's 1988 book *Off the Record: An Oral History of Pop Music,* Nesmith recalled the moment: "[Hendrix] was in a middle of a number. He threw his guitar down, flipped everyone the bird, said '[Expletive] you,' and walked off the stage.

I was standing with Micky Dolenz, and I turned to Micky and said, 'Good for him.' "

"They're Replacing Me with Mickey Mouse!"

Instead of explaining Hendrix's departure with a feigned illness, Chandler came up with a more ingenious solution. With the help of a journalist covering the tour, he spread the fictitious story that Hendrix had been fired from the tour as the result of pressure from the Daughters of the American Revolution, which supposedly was outraged over parents' complaints that the guitarist's act was too obscene for their kids to see. To pump up the hoax, a Hendrix publicist actually wrote letters of outrage, supposedly from irate parents, and sent them to Forest Hills Stadium's management and Warner Brothers Records. Hendrix himself played along, giving a bitter phone interview with a British rock publication, the *New Musical Express*. "We got screams and good reaction and some kids even rushed the stage," he insisted. "Some parents who brought their young kids complained that our act was vulgar. We decided it was just the wrong audience. I think they're replacing me with Mickey Mouse."

Newspapers eagerly ran with the story, without checking to see if it was true, and what should have been a debacle actually turned into a publicity plus for Hendrix. In America as well as England, the guitar virtuoso who'd burned his guitar at Monterey now was a racy, counterculture sex symbol, certified by the seal of disapproval as too edgy and dangerous for squares to handle. As Redding put it in his memoir, "Getting thrown off the Monkees tour was as good as not being invited to the White House, as far as credibility went."

Hendrix's failure to connect with the Monkees' fan base also freed him from further commercial pressure to appease mainstream tastes. Instead, despite being plagued by management and money squabbles and drug abuse, he pursued his avant-garde muse on a wild ride from psychedelic rock to blues to pop, to the borders of jazz fusion. It was a trip, tragically, that would be cut short. Despite his humiliating experience on the Monkees tour, Hendrix didn't nurture a grudge against the Prefab Four themselves. In September 1970, he even attended a party in London for Mike Nesmith. It was the last social appearance he would make before his death a few weeks later as the result of an accidental overdose of sleeping pills.

The Monkees, meanwhile, continued to chafe at their public image as an ersatz rock band. As Hendrix biographer David Henderson has written, Hendrix's departure from the tour compelled Tork to confront his own misgivings about the Monkees' lightweight pop and clowning, which eventually led him to be the first to quit the group. When the TV show was canceled in the spring of 1968, the band's members actually seemed relieved. They subsequently released *Head,* an arty, experimental movie made with the help of their former TV producer Rafelson and his then-obscure writer-actor pal Jack Nicholson, which was intended to explode their cutesy image once and for all. Perhaps one of the most difficult-to-watch films ever made—in one scene, for example, the Monkees are portrayed as dandruff being combed out of actor Victor Mature's hair—*Head* was savaged by critics and became a box-office flop. Nevertheless, the Monkees unwittingly made another, more significant contribution to 1960s cinema. Rafelson used $300,000 of his profits from their TV show to help finance a low-budget epic about two ex–drug dealers riding motorcycles on an ultimately fatal existential quest. *Easy Rider* became a huge hit and helped launch an era of breathtaking creativity on the big screen.

"We were on TV playing a band and then wanted to become a band," Dolenz explained years later in a newspaper interview. "It's a bit like Leonard Nimoy really becoming a Vulcan."

But they can't be faulted for having tried. And in time, the Monkees actually achieved lasting notoriety, albeit of a humbler sort. Unlike Jimi Hendrix, they never got close to ascending to the pantheon of the guitar gods. But in the minds of millions, they remained the same shaggy-haired free spirits, a fond reminder of a time when the younger half of the baby-boom generation still had its naïveté and illusions. In the mid-1990s, three of the former Monkees went on a 30th-anniversary reunion tour, and proved as zany and lovable as ever.

OTHER UNFORTUNATE PAIRINGS

- **Bruce Springsteen and Anne Murray, 1974.** Lightweight folk-singer Murray, who had a few Top 40 radio hits, made the mistake of hiring a then largely unknown Springsteen to open a New York concert, not realizing how badly she would be upstaged by the high-energy rocker. It was the last show that the Boss didn't headline.

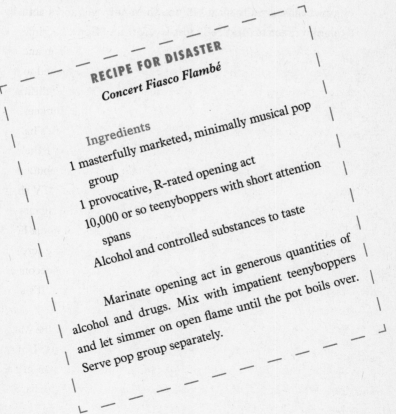

RECIPE FOR DISASTER
Concert Fiasco Flambé

Ingredients
1 masterfully marketed, minimally musical pop group
1 provocative, R-rated opening act
10,000 or so teenyboppers with short attention spans
Alcohol and controlled substances to taste

Marinate opening act in generous quantities of alcohol and drugs. Mix with impatient teenyboppers and let simmer on open flame until the pot boils over. Serve pop group separately.

- **Madonna and the Beastie Boys, 1985.** The white rappers, known for their irreverent humor as well as their inventive sampling, were booed by the Material Girl's fifteen-year-old fans at Madison Square Garden. By one account, the Beasties' Adam Yauch responded by jumping atop one of the speakers, grabbing his crotch, and spewing graphic insults at the crowd.

- **Smash Mouth and 'NSYNC, 2002.** Squeaky-clean harmonizers 'NSYNC and caustic Smash Mouth, whose songs deal with topics such as getting evicted and being threatened by a baseball bat–wielding girlfriend, were an incongruous pairing. But the two bands actually hit it off. Smash Mouth even did a thrashy punk version of 'NSYNC's lost-love lament "Gone."

the cleveland indians' ten-cent beer night

Lagging attendance. Latent hostility. Limitless lager. Add them up, and you get the most ill-conceived sports promotion in American history—and a pivot point in the new temperance movement.

EVEN AFTER IT was over—after the naked revelers were corralled, the makeshift weapons confiscated, and the injured coaches, athletes, umpires, and drunken spectators carted off to have their wounds mended—the management of the 1974 Cleveland Indians *still* thought Ten-Cent Beer Night had been a pretty good idea, maybe because no one actually died. But when the history of misguided American sports promotions is finally written, it's going to be hard to top the Indians' now-fabled debacle, even if you include the team's free-deodorant giveaway during one particular Mother's Day game.

That June 4, 1974, baseball promotion featuring the Indians and the Texas Rangers began as a well-intentioned effort to lure a crowd to Cleveland's seventy-eight-thousand-seat Municipal Stadium, which was averaging an anemic eight thousand fans per home game that fateful year. But make no mistake, from the very start this was an absolute *Hindenburg* of an idea—grandiose, ill-conceived, and with a potential for explosion that should have been obvious. To fill its usually empty stadium, the team's management deliberately assembled all of the essential ingredients for the kind of disaster familiar to those who have studied fan violence in sporting cultures around the world: frustrated fans of a hardscrabble team, simmering resentment of the opposing players, and alcohol. Lots and lots of alcohol. The echoes of that single game gone wild continue today in many ways, including stricter guidelines for serving alcohol at stadium events of all kinds, and a federally mandated nationwide minimum drinking age of twenty-one.

But Ten-Cent Beer Night wasn't just an isolated example of poor judgment and planning. When you consider the strange times in which it occurred and the long, beer-fueled history of baseball, there seems a weird inevitability to the moment when, in the game's second inning, a stout and apparently drunken woman kicked off the festivities by making her way from the grandstands into the Indians' on-deck circle. There, she lifted her shirt—the literal flash point for an evening of ribald revelry that, inning by inning, slid inexorably toward mayhem. But then, in Vietnam-era America, substance abuse, casual sexuality, and violence were always a potent mix.

Beer and Baseball: A Love Story

As relationships go, the one between beer and baseball is particularly long and profound. This should surprise no one, given that today the sport includes a Milwaukee team named the Brewers that plays in a stadium named after Miller Beer, and other landmark stadiums bear the names Busch and Coors. Television viewers have grown accustomed to the kind of full-saturation sponsorship deals that, during one recent American League Championship Series, introduced them to the "Budweiser Starting Lineup," aerial coverage by the *Bud One* blimp, and long, loving shots of play against the backdrop of red-and-white Anheuser-Busch stadium billboards—accommodations to one of Major League Baseball's most loyal sponsors. The November 1, 2004, World Series issue of *Sports Illustrated* was dominated by beer advertising, including a back cover and a special insert from Miller. But there was a frothy presence in the editorial material as well, including a full-page photo of Boston's David Ortiz swinging for Fenway's right-field fence, beyond which a gargantuan Budweiser sign glowed like a neon sunrise above the upper deck.

But those are just modern examples of baseball's beery culture. How intertwined are baseball and beer sales in the history of the sport? Go back, way back. When Christopher Von der Ahe, owner of the St. Louis Browns, bought the city's Sportsman's Park in 1880, he objected to a plan to cover the grandstands to protect the crowd from the hot sun. "Chris kicked like a mule about that project," recalled one sportswriter. "He argued that the fans wouldn't get as thirsty in the covered stands. But he finally compromised . . . with the understanding that there would be sizeable bleachers where the sun could get in its thirst-producing licks."

In 1881, a group of renegade team owners started their own league after getting fed up with the National League's efforts to screen out the "common element" by forbidding Sunday games, keeping prices high, and banning alcohol in the grandstands. The renegade owners started the American Association, though detractors (and some proponents) referred to it as "the Beer and Whiskey League" because of the owners' willingness to mix baseball and alcohol. The new league, which lasted from 1882 until 1891, ushered in what baseball historian David Nemec called "the most vibrant and freewheeling time in baseball history," and it's no wonder. The league had more than its share of teams fielded by beer makers, including brewers Henry von der Horts of Baltimore, Frank Fehr of Louisville, and John Hauck of Cincinnati. The American Association's motto might well have been "Don't hit the stands without a lager in your hand."

"The formula was simple, borrowed from an 1870s Burke's Beer ad featuring ballplayers Cap Anson and Buck Ewing," wrote Patrick Hruby in a 2003 story in the *Washington Times*. "Men like baseball. Men like beer. Wouldn't they stand to enjoy—and pay for—some combination of the two?"

The new league lasted only a decade, but its popularity was not lost on the National League. The surviving league absorbed some of the American Association's clubs and concluded that, as long as beer flowed like a revenue stream, maybe having the common element in the grandstands wasn't such a bad thing. Big-league beer drinking resumed, and except for a few dicey years during Prohibition, the stadium taps have remained open ever since in synergistic splendor, mostly without incident. By the year 2000, experts estimated that the average major-league team was grossing more than $5 million per year on beer sales alone.

Even so, beer and baseball usually aren't enough to ensure large crowds, especially for the less talented teams. Team owners have long relied on giveaways and promotional gimmicks to put butts in seats. Fireworks Nights are usually a good draw. Ladies' Day was an early favorite, followed by cap, poster, and bobble-head doll giveaways. (Ball and bat giveaways proved problematic, as fans sometimes turned those into projectiles and weapons when things got ugly.) The hopeless Washington Senators once staged "Pantyhose Night," offering free pantyhose to every woman who bought a ticket, prompting the authors of one trivia compendium to declare that promotion "the ultimate degradation of the national pastime."

The notion of using cheap beer as a lure—ten ounces for a dime—seemed, at the time, just a natural extension of that tried-and-true promotional formula. "The media didn't seem the least bit put off by the prospect," noted Bob Dyer in his 2003 book *Cleveland Sports Legends: The 20 Most Glorious and Gut-Wrenching Moments of All Time.* "In his pre-game story in the *Cleveland Press,* baseball writer Jim Braham gleefully proclaimed, 'Rinse your stein and get in line. Billy the Kid [then Rangers manager Billy Martin] and his Texas gang are in town and it's ten-cent beer night at the ballpark.' " Indians management's only concession to the evening's potential volatility was its decision to increase the size of the thirty-two-member stadium security force to forty-eight. It's just a guess, but that security force probably was not trained for tactical response.

Some say cheap-beer night was the brainchild of then Indians president Alva "Teddy" Bonda, who believed cutting-edge promotion was the key to building attendance. He was, after all, the visionary who orchestrated stunts for opening day in 1974 that involved a human cannonball and a tightrope walker traversing the field from one of the stadium's roofs to the other. But understandably, after things went bad, no one in the Indians organization ever stepped up to take full credit for an idea that ultimately was complicated by dark psychocultural subtexts, including everything from a White House scandal to Cleveland's persistent struggle to transcend its reputation for Rust Belt grime and midwestern dowdiness.

The city entered the disorienting final days of the wounded Nixon administration already in a foul mood. Cleveland's Cuyahoga River was so polluted that even the sludge worms were dying. Four years before Ten-Cent Beer Night, the city had become the laughingstock of the nation when the river actually caught fire, making Cleveland both the poster city of the fledgling environmental movement and a national punch line. (Q: What's the difference between Cleveland and the *Titanic?* A: Cleveland has a better orchestra.) The 1970s were the decade in which Cleveland's mayor unwittingly caught his hair on fire with a blowtorch while touring a construction site, making unwanted headlines; the same mayor's wife made even more headlines when she snubbed a White House invitation from Pat Nixon in order to keep her regular bowling date; and the local school board president was arrested for mooning. Critics had dubbed Municipal Stadium, which sat along the shores of Lake Erie, "the Mistake on the Lake," but that phrase had evolved into a slogan often applied to Cleveland itself. The hapless Indians seemed a perfect metaphor for a city with a self-esteem problem.

Adding to the foul civic mood was the lingering animosity from a nasty brawl between the Indians and the Rangers during a game in Arlington, Texas, less than a week before. What had begun with a hard slide in the fourth inning was followed by a knockdown pitch in the eighth, which then escalated into a couple of thrown forearms along the first-base line, followed by a bench-clearing brawl. By the time the teams moved their hostile rivalry to Cleveland six days later, the city was generally pissed and ready to party. And, by coincidence, the first game of that home series against the dreaded Rangers was being heavily promoted as a cheap-beer extravaganza. Some reports note that the moon that night was full.

"The Golden Age of Outdoor Partying"

Most Major League Baseball teams at the time considered the million-fans-a-year threshold a benchmark of franchise success, but it had been fourteen seasons since the Indians had drawn a million fans. The 1974 season was likely to continue that streak. According to Dyer, author of *Cleveland Sports Legends,* average yearly attendance at Indians games during the previous three seasons was about 611,000. So on one level, the Ten-Cent Beer Night promotion worked like a charm. The Indians drew a paid crowd of 25,134 for that game, more than three times the average attendance that season. Even before the gate success of the first beer night, the team's optimistic management had scheduled three more beer nights for later in the season.

While that may seem boneheaded, consider the times. America in 1974 was a far wetter place than it is today. Mothers Against Drunk Driving (MADD) did not yet exist. Betty Ford was four years from disclosing her addiction to alcohol and prescription drugs. Nancy Reagan was six years from launching the "Just say no" mantra that would become the hallmark of her tenure as first lady. In 1974, it was still more or less okay to get stinking drunk in public, and many of the finest baseball players of the day were role models in that regard. (Mickey Mantle, who was inducted into baseball's Hall of Fame in 1974, later did a stint in the Betty Ford Center and died in 1995 after alcohol-related cirrhosis, hepatitis C, and cancer ravaged his liver and spread throughout his body.) If drinking then led to a spur-of-the-moment decision to doff your clothes and run naked in public, so be it. Such moments were chronicled in the media as a harmless and good-humored trend called "streaking."

While the on-deck breast flasher was a catalyst for what came later, there were hints early on that this would be a game for the record books. The drinking started well before game time, and Rangers manager Billy Martin was booed vigorously when he was introduced before the game. He responded by tipping his cap and blowing kisses to the Cleveland fans. Even before the first notes of "The Star-Spangled Banner," Dyer noted, at least one fistfight broke out between a vendor and a fan. Firecrackers began going off before the first pitch. Plus, by the time the woman lifted her shirt, the visiting Rangers had a lead over the luckless Tribe.

Jerry M. Lewis, a sociology professor at Ohio's Kent State University who has studied fan violence, believes "the real problem wasn't so much the beer, but that so many people had access to the field because that's where the beer trucks were." Those trucks, loaded with Stroh's finest, were parked behind the outfield fence, and beer was being dispensed from them, giving fans unusually convenient field-level access.

In the fourth inning, the Rangers' designated hitter stroked his second home run of the game. As he circled the bases, a naked man sprinted from the stands and slid into second base. Not to be outdone, the next inning a father and son ran into the outfield, dropped their pants, and mooned the crowd.

By the sixth inning, though, the frat-house kegger giddiness was curdling. A few fans threw objects onto the field after a disputed call and were warned not to do so by the stadium's public-address announcer. Others ran onto the field and were subdued by cops, setting a mindless us-versus-them tone that went well beyond the competing teams.

By the seventh, relief pitchers in the Rangers' bullpen were being bombarded by firecrackers so often that the home-plate umpire ordered them all into the dugout for their protection. At one point, a group of fans began tearing chunks of padding off the left-field wall to keep as souvenirs. The groups of trespassers—mostly male—grew larger and soon were roaming the field at will, all of them certainly drunk, some of them naked. The antics overshadowed what was actually a dramatic comeback by the Indians, who'd been down 5–1 in the sixth inning but had tied it by the ninth.

That's when Ten-Cent Beer Night reached its full potential.

"Gradually, the streaking, showboating, and taunting gave way to sheer violence," wrote Dyer. "Fights raged in the stands all evening, but direct combat didn't spread to the field until the ninth, when one guy climbed over the outfield wall, ran up behind Texas right fielder Jeff Burroughs, and grabbed his cap." When Burroughs tried to retrieve it, he fell.

Seeing his player go down, and not certain what had happened, Billy Martin—no slouch when it came to ill-considered behavior—grabbed a bat and led his team into the fray. After they arrived to help their downed right fielder, they found themselves surrounded by hundreds of Cleveland fans. According to various reports, some were carrying chains, knives, and pieces of broken stadium seats. To the Rangers rescue came . . . the Indians. Also carrying bats.

Combat began and lasted about ten minutes, turning Municipal Stadium into what one sportswriter later dubbed "the Beirut of ballparks." At least one player was hit in the head by a steel folding chair thrown from the stands, and the injured home plate umpire later referred to the beery horde by using many colorful expletives, as well as the phrase "pack of animals." The Cleveland police, apparently alerted to the unfolding riot by an off-duty sergeant working stadium detail, showed up in force somewhat after the fact with twenty cars from the tactical and impact units. The final box score:

- at least nine arrests for disorderly conduct;
- at least sixty thousand cups of beer served;
- an officially recorded 9–0 Indian loss after the umpire declared the game a forfeit.

"Team owners and league commissioners have been forced to take long soul-searching looks at what they have created," wrote Ron Fimrite in a post–beer riot article called "Take Me Out to the Brawl Game" in the June 17, 1974, issue of *Sports Illustrated*. "They must begin to wonder if it is even possible now, in an age of free expression and at a time when violent action and reaction are everyday facts of life, to assemble large numbers of people in one place, excite them, and expect them to behave themselves."

That's not to say everyone was soul-searching. Indians management was pleased enough with the outcome to persist with plans for additional 10¢ beer promotions later in the 1974 season. It was left to then American League president Lee MacPhail to convince them otherwise, and to add the following incisive analysis: "There was no question that beer played a great part in the affair."

Looking back, Ten-Cent Beer Night clearly was a turning point. "Historians will inevitably trace the fall of the Golden Age of Outdoor Partying to the twilight hours of June 4, 1974," wrote Jamie Kitman in a 1986 story about baseball's new family image, published in the *Nation*. "Since that fateful night in Cleveland, owners around the country have turned off the spigots." Mobile beer vendors were eliminated at many major-league parks, and many now limit those who trek to concession stands to only two beers at a time. Some parks now ban beer sales during the later innings, an especially onerous restriction during extra-inning games. Noted Kitman: "Experiencing tomorrow's hangover today, even the most good-natured fan gets cranky." There was even talk of banning alcohol sales entirely at some venues, a dramatic proposal that perhaps led *Sports Illustrated,* in its 50th-anniversary issue in 2004, to rank Ten-Cent Beer Night as number eight on its list of ten "Dumbest Sports Moments." (Boxer Mike Tyson's decision to bite off chunks of Evander Holyfield's ears was listed as number six.)

Such restrictions didn't stop all alcohol-related sports stupidity. In 2002, a bare-chested father and his teenage son rushed from the stands at the Chicago White Sox' Comiskey Park and attacked Kansas City first-base coach Tom Gamboa. In 2004, a brawl erupted at a National Basketball Association game in suburban Detroit after the Indiana Pacers' Ron Artest went after an unruly fan who pelted him with a cup of ice. But those are isolated incidents rather than the kind of carefully orchestrated, embarrassingly predictable beer brawl that was Ten-Cent Beer Night. For the most part, sports have worked hard to erase the stain.

While not directly related to the events of that summer evening in 1974, antialcohol sentiments rippled throughout the culture in the years and decades that followed. Mothers Against Drunk Driving was founded in 1980, the year that individual alcohol consumption in America peaked, and a federal law signed by President Ronald Reagan in 1984 raised the legal drinking age in all states to twenty-one. The new temperance movement spearheaded by Betty Ford and Nancy Reagan lasted through the 1980s and 1990s, and into the new millennium.

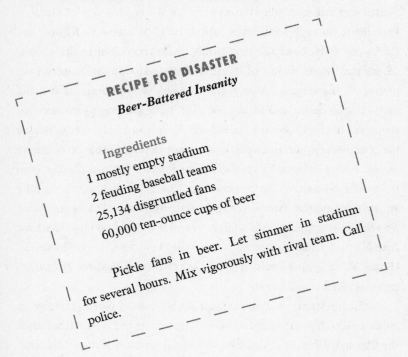

RECIPE FOR DISASTER
Beer-Battered Insanity

Ingredients
1 mostly empty stadium
2 feuding baseball teams
25,134 disgruntled fans
60,000 ten-ounce cups of beer

Pickle fans in beer. Let simmer in stadium for several hours. Mix vigorously with rival team. Call police.

But if you're waiting for a total ban on beer sales at baseball stadiums, better plan for a long wait. "Beer sponsorship is such a big-dollar component," sports sociologist Richard Lapchick told a newspaper sportswriter in 2003. "It's hard to imagine a professional league banning its sale." Besides, in an age when increasingly fast and extreme sports have conditioned fans for a constant adreno-rush of action, it's harder still to imagine watching nine innings of baseball without at least a little help.

BROADCASTING THE BRAWL

As Ten-Cent Beer Night descended into madness and savagery, the honor of broadcasting the unfolding events fell to radio announcers Joe Tait and Herb Score. The transcript of their comments, reproduced in Bob Dyer's *Cleveland Sports Legends*, has a *Hindenburg*ian oh-the-humanity flavor, but with hints of World Wrestling Federation nuttiness. Some abridged highlights:

Tait: *Tom Hilgendorf has been hit on the head. Hilgy is in definite pain. He's bent over, holding his head. Somebody hit Hilgendorf on the head, and he's going to be assisted back to the dugout. Aw, this is absolute tragedy. Absolute tragedy . . . And I'll be perfectly honest with you: I just don't know what to say.*

Score: *I don't think this game will continue, Joe. . . . The unbelievable thing is people keep jumping out of the stands after they see what's going on!*

Tait: *Well, that just shows you the complete lack of brainpower on the parts of some people. There's no way I'm going to run out onto the field if I see some baseball player waving a bat out there looking for somebody. This is tragic. . . . The whole thing has degenerated now into just—now we've got another fight going with fans and ballplayers. Hargrove has got some kid on the ground and he is really administering a beating. . . . Boy, Hargrove really wants a piece of him, and I don't blame him.*

Score: *Look at Duke Sims [the Texas backup catcher and a former Indian] down there going at it.*

Tait: *Yeah, Duke is in on it. Here we go again.*

Score: *I'm surprised that the police from the city of Cleveland haven't been called here, because we have the makings of a pretty good riot.*

Tait: *Well, the game, I really believe, Herb, now will be called. Slowly but surely the teams are getting back to their dugouts. The field, though, is just mobbed with people. And mob rule has taken over.*

Score: *They've stolen the bases.*

the sixty-story john hancock guillotine

If you're going to build a masterpiece of modern high-rise architecture, make sure the five-hundred-pound windows don't fall out during windstorms.

AS MUCH OF Boston slept on January 20, 1973, a nasty storm with winds gusting to 75 miles per hour raked the city's recently transformed skyline, including the sixty-story John Hancock Tower, a glass-sheathed architectural sensation that was almost finished after nearly a decade of corporate egomania, visionary design, public debate, engineering fiascoes, and nonstop controversy. The slow-motion disaster that began to unfold that night would reverberate for decades, reshaping the careers of some of the nation's finest architects, challenging long-held engineering assumptions, and, some say, redirecting the course of modern architecture.

That the building existed at all that night was a marvel. It had risen from the floor of the early American city like the monolith from *2001: A Space Odyssey,* and from the very beginning the icy prism—dramatic, elegant, enigmatic—had driven the locals wild. The giant John Hancock Mutual Life Insurance Company had decided to build its new headquarters on four compact acres across St. James Avenue from Copley Square, a hallowed public space to the city's residents as well as the site of historic Trinity Church, where Boston's establishment had worshiped since 1877. It also was next door to the venerable Copley Plaza Hotel, as well as near the Museum of Fine Arts, finished in 1876, and the Renaissance Revival Boston Public Library, completed in 1895.

The tower, by contrast, rose 790 feet from the street, and was covered from bottom to top by a shimmering 13.5-acre skin of 10,344 windows. Each pane was a double layer of mirrored glass measuring 4½ by 11½ feet and weighing five hundred pounds—a size that architect Henry Nichols Cobb of New York's I. M. Pei & Partners felt was needed to create the building's sleek surface. The new building was an exotic dancer among gray-haired crones; a diamond among squarish, hand-carved stones. The very idea of it rankled.

But there it stood in the wind-whipped city that night in 1973, defiant as it faced its first real structural test. Then, unexpectedly, one of the building's 10,344 eyes blinked as one massive window cracked and failed. That failure was quickly followed by another. Then another. Some windows shattered and sent showers of glass raining down. Others simply fell out and crashed onto the pavement. By the time the wind died down, dozens of the building's panes were damaged or destroyed. No one was dismembered that night, or during the many window failures that followed before the problem was finally solved. That's considered somewhat of a miracle today, especially since a single pane about half the size of the Hancock's windows fell from the 29th floor of a Chicago skyscraper and guillotined a young woman as she walked hand in hand with her toddler in 1999.

As it turns out, the falling-window problem wasn't even the most serious defect with the John Hancock Tower, though it's certainly the one that made it a laughingstock. It also was spectacular enough to earn it inclusion in *Business Week* magazine's list of eight "top technological blunders" of the 20th century, along with the 1940 collapse of the Tacoma Narrows Bridge (see Lesson #5) and the 1986 Soviet nuclear plant explosion at Chernobyl. And although today the building is widely regarded as a masterpiece of modern architecture, cherished even by many of its harshest critics from the 1960s and 1970s, it remains a gleaming sixty-story reminder that, no matter how bold the vision or bright the mind of the visionary, everyone needs to sweat the details.

Whose Is Bigger?

The story begins with Robert Slater, who in the mid-1960s was the aggressive, take-no-prisoners chairman of Boston-based Hancock. His company's chief rival, the carpetbagging New Jersey–based Prudential Insurance Company, had the audacity to christen a massive fifty-two-story building in 1965 that was just a few blocks from Hancock's existing headquarters. This profoundly irritated Slater, according to Carter Wiseman, author of a comprehensive account of the Hancock episode, "no matter that [the Prudential building, or 'Pru'] drew instant public derision for its graceless bulk." Slater resolved to build something bigger.

Comparative contests like this have played out since men's locker rooms were invented, but few have played out on this scale. Make of it what you will, but the first design developed in 1966 by Pei's firm—and enthusiastically endorsed by Slater—was a tall, cylindrical masonry shaft with two low-rise buildings clustered at its base. Edward J. Logue, head of the Boston Development Authority, also endorsed that initial design, saying: "If you don't understand a company wanting to go taller, you don't understand life."

But the company hesitated, and during the year that followed it reevaluated its space needs. Hancock eventually asked the architects to come up with a different plan, and due to scheduling and other concerns at the architectural firm, the project fell primarily to Cobb, one of Pei's partners and a Boston native. "We were never directed to make it taller than Prudential, but we understood in a fairly clear way that it should be," recalled Cobb, who set to work on September 15, 1967, to design what would become the tallest building in all of New England—sixty stories of pure, up-yours phallotecture.

Size wasn't the only consideration, of course. Years later, Cobb said he designed his building "to restore to Copley Square the dignity it had lost through the construction of the Prudential tower." He oriented the parallelogram structure on the property so that it showed one of its two slim surfaces to the square, and he ditched the masonry idea and went with a skin of solid glass that not only would reflect and honor the more traditional buildings around it, but would essentially blend with the sky and clouds overhead. He also designed vertical, off-center grooves in the building's small sides to create the illusion of less bulk.

The locals, still smarting from Hancock's choice of an upstart New York architect, weren't appeased. One critic called it "a monster." Even Logue, who'd endorsed giving the job to the Pei firm, called the Cobb design "an outrage," and the redevelopment design board of the city opposed its construction. The whining continued through the August 1968 groundbreaking, and it intensified after the ground beneath the nearby church and hotel began to shift during the digging of the foundation. But the criticism faded as the building rose. "Cobb's emphasis on proportion was paying off," wrote Wiseman in the 2001 revised edition of his Pei biography, *I. M. Pei: A Profile in American Architecture*. "The slab was indeed enormous, but its slim profile had incontestable grace, and because of its unconventional siting at an angle to the street, its impact on Copley Square was not nearly as oppressive as many had feared."

When the structure was finished and the windows were installed, the effect was complete. The Boston skyline had a sparkle it had never had before, a stunning and elegant counterpoint to the high-rise stump that was the Pru. The city also had an additional 2 million square feet of office space. Sixties radical Abbie Hoffman later stood on the steps of the nearby library and shook his fist at the gleaming representation of corporate might and said, "*There* is the enemy," but the building seemed destined to rise above even the tumultuous times in which it was spawned.

Then came the windstorm that began nudging the massive windows from the building's sparkling face. During the single night of that January storm in 1973, according to the *Boston Globe*'s Robert Campbell, at least sixty-five shattered and dropped "like sequins off a dress."

Public hearings and environmental-impact reports generally cover development issues such as traffic flow, noise, and congestion. Nowhere in nearly a decade of planning and public debate had anyone raised the possibility that razor-edged shards or unguided five-hundred-pound wings of glass could, from time to time, hurtle down on Boston's pedestrians and motorists. Concerned city officials roped off the streets and sidewalks surrounding the John Hancock Tower, and shattered and suspect windows were quickly replaced by inelegant sheets of plywood that eventually covered about one-third of the building's surface, earning the building the inglorious nickname "the Plywood Palace." The effect was about the same as adding orthodontia to the *Mona Lisa,* and the falling-windows fiasco quickly took its place among some of Boston's other bizarre disasters, including the Great Molasses Flood of 1919, when a sticky, thirty-foot-high wave of molasses from a North End distillery explosion killed 21 people and injured 150.

Replacing the defective double-pane windows with single-pane safety glass—a retrofit that cost the window maker more than $7 million and was completed in 1975—did not completely solve the problem. Nor did the installation of an electronic sensing system wired to each and every window that signaled any problems to a centralized alarm. Wooden canopies were built to cover the adjacent sidewalks, and city officials still had to barricade the sidewalks and surrounding streets any time winds aloft reached 45 miles per hour. In October 1977, *Newsweek* magazine reported that, for the previous three months, "two men with binoculars" had been posted in Copley Square between 6 a.m. and midnight each day to scan the tower constantly for windows that changed color, a telltale sign that the glass was cracking. At that point, the tower was losing about one replacement window each month. In 2003, Jack Connors, chairman of an advertising agency located on the tower's 39th floor, recalled to *Boston Globe* reporter Mark Feeney how one of those falling panes sliced through the rear window of his parked car.

As architects and engineers scrambled to figure out the window problem, they placed sensors all over the still-unopened John Hancock Tower to determine if the building's movement in the wind was the cause. It wasn't, because the problem turned out to be a manufacturing flaw with the windows themselves. But like most skyscrapers, the building *was* moving, and moving far more than it should have been, and in an unexpected way. The movement—a back-and-forth motion with a twist, which the *Globe*'s Robert Campbell described as a "cobra dance"—was particularly unsettling to anyone on its upper floors. The solution, developed by Cambridge engineer William LeMessurier, was a "tuned mass damper" that involved installing two three-hundred-ton weights at opposite ends of the 58th floor. Those sliding weights acted like an internal gyroscope, offsetting the building's motion every time it moved. Cost: $3 million.

While the world watched the tower's windows and snickered about motion sickness, though, a far more troubling problem with the building was being studied in private.

But the *Really* Bad News Is . . .

Reeling from the problems, Cobb, the architect, decided he needed to do some public-relations work. What the troubled Hancock needed, he thought, was the endorsement of the world's leading authority on highrise steel-frame buildings. He sought out Swiss engineer Bruno Thurlimann to evaluate the integrity of the structure and, presumably, testify to its safety.

In March 1975, about eighteen months before the tower was dedicated, Thurlimann flew from Zurich to Boston to deliver a verdict that no one could have predicted. He calculated that under "extreme and rare wind conditions" that were entirely possible during the building's lifespan, the whole thing might just fall over, and in the most bizarre way imaginable. The *Globe*'s Campbell, in a 1995 story that was part of his Pulitzer Prize–winning architecture coverage, used the metaphor of a book standing upright on a table. Imagine that you bumped the table and knocked over the book, but that instead of falling onto one of its wide, flat sides, the book fell onto its spine. That's what, theoretically, could happen to the John Hancock Tower.

"Nobody ever thinks of a long, thin building like the Hancock falling over in the long direction," Campbell wrote. "But no, said Thurlimann: The building was stiff enough in the flat direction. The danger was that it might collapse on a narrow edge."

Cobb and the engineers had no choice but to reinforce the nearly completed building from bottom to top with more than 1,500 tons of diagonal steel bracing. Cost: $5 million. Michael Flynn, a technical expert with the Pei firm, described the retrofit as being "like putting your socks on after your shoes," but considering the building's history to that point, what were they going to do?

By the time the John Hancock Tower was dedicated on September 29, 1976, it was four years behind schedule, and had cost at least $160 million, nearly twice the original estimate. "No building in our time has been so cursed," the *New York Times* once declared of the Hancock, and it's hard to disagree.

But the fallout didn't stop. The fortunes of the Pei firm nose-dived in the wake of the blunders. "It was a disaster," Pei told the *Washington Post* in 2003. "After John Hancock, I had to go abroad to find work. No one would talk to me." Cobb conceded years later that the project was "calamitous." He said the firm was "blacklisted" from corporate and development work for about seven years and "could have gone out of business" if not for projects in Asia and the Middle East.

The appetite for building delicate geometric skyscrapers was never quite the same, either. "If it was not exactly the last, best example of the Modernist skyscraper, it was at the very least a unique monument to that form," wrote Wiseman in his Pei biography. "After Hancock, architects of tall buildings (including Cobb) were forced to find other avenues of expression, manipulating their forms in ever more complex ways or embellishing them with mock-Classical details and 'hats' like the one Philip Johnson and John Burgee put on their headline-catching headquarters for AT&T in New York. Just as Mies van der Rohe had with the Seagram Building in New York brought one interpretation of the skyscraper to its logical conclusion, Cobb had, with Hancock, all but written *finis* to this building type as pure geometry."

Then something even more remarkable happened. Typically, a building that looks cool when it's first built begins to look dated over time, such as the futuristic concrete ballparks that sprouted like mushrooms in American cities during the same era. Some of those have already been demolished as hopelessly out of touch with the times. In the case of the John Hancock Tower, though, the building's elegant final form slowly began to eclipse its soiled reputation. The American Institute of Architects gave its creators a National Honor Award in 1977, and the same Boston Society of Architects that once derided the building design awarded it a medal for the best new work in the city and described it as "probably" the most beautiful contemporary tower in the U.S. In a 1994 *Boston Globe* poll, architects and historians rated the Hancock Boston's third best work of architecture, behind neighbors Trinity Church and the public library's McKim Building. The falling windows and other early problems became an asterisk in the recorded history of what's now considered an architectural treasure—and one that sold for a staggering $910 million in 2003.

That's not to say the problems are forgotten. Court files still bulge from the explosion of litigation triggered by the project, legal fallout from which continued until 1981. The final settlement agreement forbade the players from talking about its terms, though details eventually were released. In arguing why those terms and similar sealed agreements should be made public, attorney Barry LaPatner used language that might just as well apply to any failure, large or small:

"Good judgment is usually the result of experience. And experience is frequently the result of bad judgment. But to learn from the experience of others requires those who have the experience to share the knowledge with those who follow."

WINDOW-SHOPPING?

What to do with more than five thousand undamaged but unusable windowpanes measuring 4½ by 11½ feet and weighing five hundred pounds each?

According to Robert Campbell of the *Boston Globe,* the still-intact double-pane mirrored windows from the original tower design were sold for $100 each through bargain outlets in Hingham and Lynn, Massachusetts, as well as in Maine.

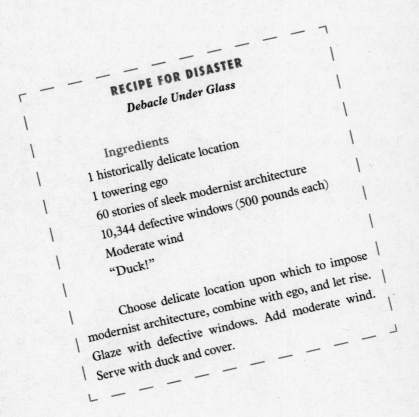

RECIPE FOR DISASTER
Debacle Under Glass

Ingredients
1 historically delicate location
1 towering ego
60 stories of sleek modernist architecture
10,344 defective windows (500 pounds each)
Moderate wind
"Duck!"

Choose delicate location upon which to impose modernist architecture, combine with ego, and let rise. Glaze with defective windows. Add moderate wind. Serve with duck and cover.

"Many are now tabletops, picture windows or greenhouses," he wrote. "As for the plywood [that replaced the broken and suspect windows], much of it went to the Boston Redevelopment Authority, where it was used to board up abandoned buildings. Life goes on."

male fashion's fabulous faux pas

The leisure suit is reviled as the ultimate icon of 1970s-era bad taste. But what was hyped as a harbinger of a male fashion revolution actually turned out to be just that, in a flammable double-knit way.

IT SPEAKS VOLUMES about the infamously kitschy reputation of the leisure suit that today, the garment's most prominent aficionados are Leisure Suit Larry, animated star of a series of tawdry computer games about a "pathetic loser" trying to pick up women, and North Korean dictator Kim Jong Il. In the case of the fictional Larry, his luminous pastel wardrobe is intended to be ludicrous. Kim, on the other hand, gets away with wearing leisure suits because the secretive "Dear Leader" seldom ventures out of an isolated, totalitarian police state where nobody dares smirk, for fear of ending up in a reeducation camp.

But let those of us in the free world not sneer too unreservedly. Put aside for a moment the point that by any reasonably refined aesthetic, leisure suits are, well, hideous. How else would one conceivably describe an ensemble fashioned from stiff double-knit polyester, usually in a startlingly bright hue or garish plaid, consisting of flared trousers and a matching four or five-button jacket with a winged collar in lieu of lapels? Throw in optional epaulets and large, buttoned breast pockets, and the result is a peculiar garment in which even the most debonair specimen of manhood would look like a habitual patron at the Loser's Lounge. (No wonder that comedian Steve Martin made the leisure suit the favored attire of the Festrunk brothers, those pair of "wild and crazy" sex-crazed eastern European émigré-rubes that he and Dan Aykroyd portrayed on *Saturday Night Live*.)

How easy it is to forget that for a brief, hallucinatory interlude in the mid-1970s, the leisure suit seemed like the hottest phenomenon *ever* in the history of the American menswear industry. In 1974, males across the United States spent the equivalent of $6.7 billion in today's dollars on leisure suits, and clamored for them so frantically that manufacturers couldn't keep up with the demand. In 1975, at one Manhattan men's store, 65 percent of the suits sold were of the leisure variety. In 1976, the high-water mark of the leisure suit's popularity, a single Chicago clothing store, Richman Brothers, sold seventy thousand of the garments. But the garment that now crowds thrift-store racks was more than just another short-lived fashion experiment gone awry, like the eight-buttoned neo-Edwardian look in the 1960s or voluminous parachute pants in the 1980s. Strange as it may seem, there was a time when the leisure suit was hailed as the most revolutionary development in men's attire since the waistcoat and breeches were supplanted by the business suit in the mid-1800s.

For generations, middle-class American males had struggled in vain with the intricacies of the Windsor knot, and meekly complied with the dictum that they needed one wardrobe for the office—tailored according to mysterious, niggling rules of propriety—and another set of clothes for the rest of their waking hours. As tacky as it might look to us today, to the man of the 1970s, the leisure suit offered permanent, necktie-free liberation from fashion faux pas. It was advertised as the first male attire that could be worn appropriately at virtually any occasion, from the boardroom to the nightclub dance floor.

"Can an executive wear at work what he wears at play?" a Macy's television commercial asked. "Can a lawyer meet with a client dressed like a client? Can a white-collar worker work with his collar open? Yes, thanks to the leisure suit revolution!"

Moreover, because of the limitations of the then-crude synthetic fabrics from which they were made—an expensive version didn't look that much different from a cheap one—leisure suits' popularity had the subtle effect of blurring the rank and class distinctions usually signified by one's tailoring. Some even saw them as evidence of an evolutionary change in corporate culture, away from rigid conformity and toward a more relaxed, convivial atmosphere. *New York Times* fashion critic Philip H. Dougherty boldly proclaimed in 1975 that the leisure suit and its variations were "symbols of a new lifestyle and are with us for good, as far as some experts are concerned." In 1976, Chip Tolbert, an official of the Men's Fashion Association of America, a clothing industry group, went so far as to refer to the leisure suit itself as "a way of life." The leisure suit was so ubiquitous that toy maker Mattel updated Barbie's companion Ken by dressing him in a rakish white version. As fashion historian Valerie Steele has noted, leisure suits became "a middle-class spin-off of hippie clothing, part of the experimentation with men's wear and the breakdown of formality."

Conversely, to traditionalists of that era, the leisure suit was not so much laughable as a potentially cataclysmic threat to the status quo of men's fashion. Brooks Brothers president Frank Reilly told the *Washington Post* in 1977 that he found the 1970s leisure suit far more disturbing than the unkempt, denim-clad sixties counterculture's rejection of traditional fashion. "Everybody was going to buy one," he reflects with distaste, "because they were cheap. That was much scarier to me."

And of course, it didn't happen. After several years of astounding popularity, the leisure suit abruptly went from sartorial sensation to object of ridicule—an extraordinarily rare event in the normally glacially slow evolution of men's attire. But even though the leisure suit flopped, the notion behind it—that men felt constrained and uncomfortable in traditional business attire—did ultimately resonate within the American male psyche, leading belatedly to the sort of seismic cultural shift in the workplace that the leisure suit's adherents had predicted.

Splendor in Terry Cloth

To grasp the leisure suit's peculiar appeal, first consider the American male's traditionally uneasy relationship with his wardrobe. Men don't dare pay too much attention to fashion, for fear of being derided as foppish, narcissistic, and/or unsure of their sexual orientation. Yet paradoxically, for decades they've struggled to adhere to a business dress code as nonsensical, yet mind-bogglingly exacting, as the etiquette imposed by Louis XIV, who permitted counts to watch his morning toilette, but would allow only princes to hand a clean shirt to him. While some bosses such as IBM founder Thomas Watson saw the only acceptable attire as a blue suit, white shirt, somber tie, briefcase, and hat and exercised strict control over employees' sartorial options, most companies maintained an unspoken code, which was even more anxiety-inducing. That totally useless, impractical, and uncomfortable accessory, the necktie, has long been a particular source of neurosis, since research shows that the choice of pattern, color, and fabric is perceived by men as a subtle indication of a wearer's career and social status. Some men were so intimidated that they avoided buying clothes at all. For decades, about 80 percent of the menswear sold was purchased by women shopping for their mates, according to industry sources cited in a 2000 *Wall Street Journal* article. Even today, only about half of American males purchase their own attire.

But by the early 1970s, change was brewing. Corporate coat-and-tie-clad wage earners watched uneasily as hipsters in turtlenecks and bell-bottom jeans folded, spindled, and mutilated the rules of male dress. As writer and costume designer Ann Hollander observed in a 1974 article for the *New Republic*, wearing staid business attire no longer conferred "cozy anonymity," but instead "stamped one as a convinced follower of the old order." The sartorially oppressed felt even more uncomfortable, and grassroots resentment against the old rules began to emerge. But the tipping point may have been the Watergate scandal, in which an assortment of traditionally attired Nixon administration officials were paraded before the TV cameras and shown to be liars or worse. Public opinion research by John T. Malloy, a corporate fashion consultant and author of the *Dress for Success* manual, found that the credibility rating for someone in a conservatively cut gray suit and club tie plummeted from 81 percent in 1972 to just 57 percent in 1973, while the believability rating for a dandy in wide lapels and a colorful shirt rose from 28 percent to 62 percent. The timing was right for a new style that would cash in on those male corporate middle-class blues.

As it happened, the leisure suit had already been lingering on the experimental fringe of fashion for several decades. It evolved not from the coat and tie but from the safari suit, a khaki ensemble with roomy pockets and epaulets that was worn by colonial troops in Africa and later popularized by American outdoorsmen such as President Theodore Roosevelt and author Ernest Hemingway. Another possible distant relation was the custom-made velvet "siren suit" worn by British prime minister Winston Churchill, a flamboyant but unorthodox clotheshorse, who stubbornly insisted on being comfortable *and* fashionable as he braved German rocket attacks during World War II. In postwar America, designers vainly coaxed men to try similarly adventurous attire in their off hours, such as a terry cloth one-piece "leisure suit" that a 1952 *New York Times* fashion spread touted as "suggested for TV sessions or around-the-house lounging." In 1964, a *Times* fashion review featured another leisure suit, this one a corduroy shirt and matching trousers for "at home wear." In 1968, one designer offered a short-sleeved version in plain cotton, and in 1969, another unveiled a jacket-and-pants combination made out of velvet.

While fashion aesthetes devised exotic costumes for men to luxuriate in during their leisure hours, though, their real-life customers actually had less and less opportunity to relax. As Juliet Schor notes in her 1991 book *The Overworked American,* by the late 1960s the hours that full-time workers spent on the job was starting a climb that continues today. By the early 1970s, clothing manufacturers finally had an epiphany: What the office drudge really needed was an outfit he could wear continuously, around the clock, in a variety of situations.

For that sort of marathon wear, the natural fibers used in early versions of the leisure suit simply wouldn't do, since they wrinkled and were too pricey for salaries ravaged by the stagnant Nixon-era economy. Technology, however, had an answer: double-knit polyester. The synthetic fabric was knitted together in loops, rather than woven in an interlocking pattern, using a revolutionary double-needle process that some predicted would make the loom obsolete. There was another advantage—it was cheaper to make suits, thanks to new automated manufacturing processes that fused seams with heat and pressure, reducing by half the amount of stitching required. A clothing maker could churn out a cheapo grade X suit on an assembly line in as little as an hour and a half, less than half the time required to make a higher-quality garment in wool.

Leisure Goes Legit

"You just gotta have a leisure suit!" exclaimed an ad by New Jersey–based mail-order clothing retailer Haband's, and indeed, men did. In 1974, they grabbed up the garments so quickly that manufacturers had trouble meeting the demand. Such immediate acceptance of a radically new style was almost unheard-of behavior by male consumers, and the investment firm Merrill Lynch even issued a bulletin for investors about the leisure suit's potential effect on the clothing market. According to a study conducted in the mid-1980s by department store merchandising consultants, only about 8 percent of American men are early adapters of fashion trends, while 50 percent are oblivious of fashion, buying new clothes when old garments wear out. However, as psychologists Craig Johnson and Brian Mullen wrote in their 1990 book *The Psychology of Consumer Behavior,* fads, like mutant viruses, manage to propagate because they short-circuit the usual thinking process that precedes a purchase. So it was with the leisure suit, which tugged on the loose thread of conformity and ended up unraveling good taste.

By the summer of 1974, the *New York Times* was reporting that three main styles of leisure suits had emerged. The most popular was the "safari" suit, which had a winged collar, and sometimes epaulets and short sleeves. Another variation included the "battle jacket," which ended at the waist, reminiscent of the outfit that General Dwight D. Eisenhower wore during World War II. It could be worn with a necktie. Yet another was the shirt suit, a pajamalike outfit that vaguely evoked the wardrobe of Hugh Hefner, or perhaps certain third world dictators.

The leisure suit's popularity had overwhelmed the menswear market in small towns and cities across America, places that fashion trends usually reached slowly and sometimes bypassed altogether. In Lincoln, Nebraska, the *Evening Journal* concluded that "the leisure suit is where it's at." The *Newark (Ohio) Advocate* offered locals advice on what sort of shirt was acceptable to wear under their new leisure suits: "turtlenecks, open-neck solids, prints and crew necks, open shirts with ascots, even no shirt at all."

Only the bravest of Ohioans likely tried that last suggestion, but it hinted at the degree of sartorial anarchy that the leisure suit induced, as the style evolved from playfully flamboyant to outright garish. The garment came in colors seldom before seen in men's suits—mocha, peach, fire-engine red, pumpkin, forest green, sky blue. (Decades later, a vintage clothing store's Web site would struggle to describe one surviving specimen as "a shade of rust that is brown more than orange.") In 1976, Haggar unveiled a special bicentennial-edition leisure suit—white, with red and blue stitching, and a similarly patriotic belt.

By early 1975, the leisure style had become so pervasive that in New York, the Lord & Taylor University Club shop, traditionally devoted to the staid Ivy League look, had to confess that its top-selling item was a leisure suit. Even Max Evans, fashion director of tastemaker *Esquire* magazine, revealed that he was a fan of the style because it was "comfortable and usually in easy-care fabric."

Business Casual-ties

That's not to say the garish, unorthodox garment was without detractors. Makers of traditional men's clothing, for example, saw the leisure suit as a dire menace. If cheap polyester outfits became acceptable in both the workplace and social situations, it would take a huge chunk out of their profits. Additionally, since leisure suits were made of cheap synthetic material and fused together rather than stitched, they could be sold for much lower prices than regular suits made from woven wool. For example, an ensemble by Haggar, one of the major brands, could be had for $38.50 (about $140 in today's dollars). Haband's mail-order version, which came in a choice of camel, navy, brown, or light green, was available for $29.95. Even cheaper versions gradually flooded the market. No wonder that in a statement to investors, Jerome S. Gore, president of Hart Schaffner & Marx, once alluded to "that horrible situation called the leisure suit."

The leisure suit was also an affront to the etiquette sticklers at fancy restaurants and country clubs, who regarded wearers of the garment with the same horror that citizens of Rome reserved for the Visigoths. In New York, the dining rooms at the Hotel Pierre and the Regency permitted diners in leisure suits, but La Grenouille and "21" seated them only if they committed the fashion apostasy of donning neckties. Another upscale eatery, Lutece, actually posted a sign on its door: "Please! No Leisure Suits!" In 1977, a California court found in *Hales v. Ojai Valley Inn and Country Club*—a landmark case for leisure suit wearers—that a man had been discriminated against when he was refused service for wearing a leisure suit without a necktie. Women, the court noted, did not face similar restrictions—no matter how tacky their wardrobes.

What hurt the leisure suit was that corporate employers reacted negatively to the new style. In 1976, corporate fashion consultant Malloy surveyed forty managers in offices where employees wore leisure suits. Only one of the bosses was wearing a leisure suit himself. A resounding thirty-four of the remaining thirty-nine said they would be more likely to trust an important assignment to a man in a traditional suit. Fourteen said they would be less likely to promote a man who wore leisure suits. Malloy found that bosses considered leisure suits acceptable only if they were made of some material other than polyester, preferably in a solid color. A few companies—including, the *New York Times* reported, an unnamed department store that probably sold leisure suits—banned employees from wearing them at all. (The very name "leisure suit," which suggested that the garment inspired languor in workers, certainly didn't help.)

Nobody wanted to commit career suicide in the name of having a versatile wardrobe, especially in the sputtering economy of the mid-1970s. The leisure suit might have survived anyway as sportswear if it had delivered on the "hassle-free" comfort that manufacturer John Pomer touted in an ad. Instead, membership in the fashion avant-garde required putting up with double-knit polyester's tendency to trap moisture, rather than breathing as natural fibers did. On warm days, a leisure suit doubled as a portable sauna. "It had an especially bad reputation in Texas and the Southwest," synthetic fabric scientist Dmitry Gagarine told United Press International in 1983. And the material, especially in the cheaper suits, was so stiff that some wearers joked that they could stand their leisure suits up in a corner rather than hanging them in the closet. For all its coarse scratchiness, it wasn't particularly durable. "The double-knits were shiny and would snap and snag," Paul Apostol, director of woven markets for Celanese Fibers, told the *Wall Street Journal* in 1985. "It was tacky clothing."

By the summer of 1976, a little more than two years after the leisure suit had emerged as the hottest fad in fashion, it was starting to wane. In New York, sales slowed so abruptly that retailers were forced to offer 50 percent off on their inventory. That year, the clothing industry sold 6 million leisure suits, half as many as it had in 1975. By 1978, newspaper articles were speculating about what had killed the leisure suit. By the end of the decade, the hot trend among businessmen was well-tailored European-cut suits.

During the next two decades, the leisure suit evolved into such an object of ridicule that even companies that produced polyester disassociated themselves from it, to no avail. Polyester went from being the fabric of the future to a fashion no-no, causing a major shakeout of companies in the artificial-fibers industry. Eventually, synthetics made a comeback with the development of microfiber polyester, which bore a more plausible resemblance to wool.

Nevertheless, the leisure suit didn't go gently. From 1988 to 1997, die-hard aficionados held the International Leisure Suit Convention in Des Moines, Iowa, where they danced to music by the Bee Gees and the Village People, and held fashion shows on a runway lighted by Lava lamps. "When you wear a leisure suit you turn into a completely different person," convention founder Van Hardin explained to CNN in 1996. Even today, scores of old leisure suits are available from vintage clothing stores. That so many well-preserved specimens still exist probably isn't that much of a surprise, considering that the material from which they were made isn't biodegradable.

While the leisure suit has been relegated to its role as a kitsch icon, the notion behind it—that men felt uncomfortable in business attire—continues to resonate within the American male psyche. By the mid-1990s, some of the same casual-wear manufacturers who'd churned out leisure suits were getting a similar boost from the popularity of casual days at work, in which employers tried to improve morale by allowing male workers to dispense with coats and ties. This time around, however, corporations gravitated to the idea, because they saw dressing down as a way to eliminate hierarchical divisions and foster the "teamwork" concept that was the hot new corporate buzzword. In a survey taken by athletic shoe maker Converse in the late 1990s, nearly 80 percent of companies no longer had formal dress codes, and more than half specifically allowed casual clothes at the office. Whether the change really gave men more sartorial freedom is questionable, since the coat-and-tie requirement often was replaced by equally rigid but more complicated guidelines about what sort of casual clothes were acceptable.

As a result, the workplace often became an equally monotonous sea of long-sleeved buttoned-down denim shirts and tan or olive khaki trousers. Sportswear maker Levi Strauss actually established a toll-free number for employers who were uncertain about what sort of attire they should allow. Makers of traditional suits tried to dismiss the business casual look by derisively comparing it to the leisure suit—but eventually came to see it as an equally grave threat. They tried to deter the new style by publicizing a survey by an employment law firm in which 44 percent of companies saw an increase in lateness and absenteeism after they allowed casual dress, and 30 percent reported a rise in flirting. (In fairness, the same survey also showed that 40 percent of companies reported a rise in productivity when they went casual.) Nevertheless, as the 21st century began, the necktieless world that leisure suit designers had envisioned seemed to have arrived, albeit in a different form.

Meanwhile, Kim Jong Il continues to champion the leisure suit as determinedly as he's apparently pursuing development of his nuclear missile arsenal. He's said to reward the designers of his wardrobe with imported luxury automobiles and other perks when they come up with a new garment that particularly piques his atavistic sartorial sensibilities. As fashion critic Jess Cartner-Morley of the British newspaper the *Guardian* once noted, sardonically: "No one wears it with quite the flair that Kim does. Look at him: he's loving the camera. He knows he looks hot."

THE STYLE THAT WON'T DIE

Since the leisure suit's brief but intense popularity in the mid-1970s, designers have periodically tried to revive the garment. In 1986, designer Bill Robinson showed updated versions of the leisure suit at the

Men's Fashion Association fall press review in New York. In Paris in 1990, Paul Smith seized upon the leisure suit—which the *New York Times* described as "so out that it's in again"—as a way to rebel against fashion conventions, akin to the deliberately clashing colors in his models' other attire. More recently, unisex ensembles markedly similar to the classic leisure suit, but rendered in velour rather than scratchy double knit, have appeared in the designer lines of hip-hop stars such as OutKast, Snoop Dogg, and Nelly.

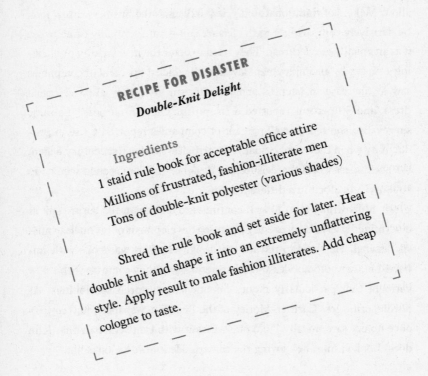

RECIPE FOR DISASTER
Double-Knit Delight

Ingredients
1 staid rule book for acceptable office attire
Millions of frustrated, fashion-illiterate men
Tons of double-knit polyester (various shades)

Shred the rule book and set aside for later. Heat double knit and shape it into an extremely unflattering style. Apply result to male fashion illiterates. Add cheap cologne to taste.

the abbreviated reign of "neon" leon spinks

The tragicomic heavyweight boxing champ was neither the first nor the last American sports hero to badly mismanage fame and fortune. But by rising higher and falling faster than most, he brought schadenfreude to the masses.

AMERICAN SPORTS GENERATE almost as many cautionary tales as heroes. For every athlete who converts his or her success in the sporting arena into success in the world beyond, there seems a corollary athlete whose most valuable contribution to society is to serve as a warning to others. But the dizzying rise and hurtling fall of boxer Leon Spinks may be the most exquisitely extreme reversal of fortune on record, a vivid chronicle of what can happen when short-term impulse trumps long-term planning. And in a strange way, Spinks's story has become a reassuring touchstone for everyone who works hard, lives responsibly—and doesn't have a chance of ever tasting the high life that Leon Spinks so blithely flushed down the toilet. The sad fact is, everyone feels a bit better about himself when an apparent superhuman turns out to be all too human.

No sporting pinnacle is higher than the singular title "heavyweight champion of the world," and few men ever grasped that title with as much drama as the upstart Spinks, who on February 15, 1978, snatched it from the still-formidable thirty-six-year-old Muhammad Ali after having fought professionally only seven times before. Spinks's accomplishment was so stunning that his victory not only led the sports section of the next day's *Los Angeles Times*, but was the banner-headlined lead story on the paper's front page as well. As a news event, the paper's editors deemed "Spinks Dethrones Ali" more newsworthy than other front-page stories that day, including President Jimmy Carter's efforts to end a nationwide coal strike, a national PTA report on television violence, and Israel's objections to the U.S. decision to sell fighter jets to Arab countries. The dominant photograph on the page was of a jubilant Spinks on his handlers' shoulders, his still-wrapped hands thrust into the Las Vegas night air, flashing the gap-toothed grin that would become his trademark. It was heady stuff for a twenty-four-year-old former marine who, along with his brother Michael, had risen from a St. Louis housing project to become a 1976 Olympic gold medalist less than two years before.

Within seven months of winning the heavyweight championship, though, the gregarious and hard-partying Spinks had burned through nearly all of the $350,000 he earned for the Ali fight, and apparently had a good start on the $3.8 million that he was promised for the rematch. He bought, and eventually wrecked, a fleet of cars that included a Corvette and a Cadillac, and clad himself in a designer wardrobe that included at least one mink coat, a double-breasted Christian Dior sport coat, and a gray felt derby with his initials embroidered in the sweatband—all of which helped earn him the nickname "Neon Leon." He mated abundantly, tipped extravagantly, chartered airplanes, and partnered with his investment counselor's father-in-law to back a struggling rock band you've still never heard of. During his brief reign and beyond, the champ was as much in the news for his traffic accidents and assorted run-ins with the law as he was for his stewardship of the most coveted title in sports.

Ali snatched that title back from Spinks the following September, but by then Spinks had already begun his sad slide into the Pantheon of Wobbly Gods—American sports heroes who had it all, but who managed their success with the restraint of a sailor on shore leave. Because Leon

Spinks's rags-to-riches-to-rags career arc is so extreme, and because his life stands in such stark contrast to the subsequent sports success stories of both his younger brother Michael and now his son Cory, he endures as the archetype for all of the one-hit wonder boys in American sports. After fighting against the odds for years, it took Spinks only seven months to recast himself as the great grinning Goofus of professional career management, and he remains the most memorable example of a man who paid a high price to live only for the moment.

Gods in the Chasm

The divide between promise and potential can be wide and deep, and into that chasm have fallen some of the finest athletes ever born. What lures them over the edge, in far too many cases, is the spoils of success—money, alcohol, drugs, and sex, but usually drugs and alcohol. For athletes whose fortunes rise and fall based on their body's ability to perform, celebrating their good fortune with substance abuse is like celebrating the goose's golden egg by roasting and eating the goose.

Their names are familiar to sports fans in much the same way as the names *Titanic* and *Challenger*. Houston McTear was one of the fastest sprinters ever to come out of an American high school, and his college and professional careers promised to rewrite the record books of track and field. Just three weeks after Spinks defeated Ali, McTear exploded onto the cover of the March 6, 1978, issue of *Sports Illustrated*. Cover line: "Off on a record tear: Sprint sensation Houston McTear." By the mid-1980s, though, the man who had once laid claim to being the world's fastest human was addicted to cocaine and sleeping on a tennis court in a public park. Micheal Ray Richardson was drafted by the New York Knicks in 1978, and the six-foot-five phenom was considered one of the finest point guards of his time, able to control a game with his scoring, playmaking, and defensive skills. On February 25, 1986, though, he tested positive for cocaine for the third time and became the first player to be banned from the NBA for drug use under a policy adopted three years before. Richardson recovered, but never again played in the NBA and spent the rest of his career playing in exile in Europe. Quarterback Todd Marinovich came out of high school touted as a future NFL Hall of Famer, but started partying hard during his college career at the University of Southern California. The NFL's Raiders made him their first-round draft pick in 1991, but by 1993, according to the *Los Angeles Times,* the team had cut him loose because of erratic alcohol- and drug-related behavior. He played guitar in a bar band for a while, and attempted comebacks in both the Canadian Football League and the Arena Football League—not easy when you're addicted to heroin, as Marinovich later said he was—but he eventually joined the other wobbly gods at the bottom of the chasm.

It's one thing to fall short of your potential, but quite another to reach it and then punt it away. None of those other athletes occupied the pinnacle that Leon Spinks did on February 15, 1978. The sport of boxing had not fully splintered into its often meaningless factions and federations, and Spinks stood astride the sporting world like a conquering hero. There was only one generally acknowledged heavyweight champion of the world, and suddenly, unexpectedly, Leon Spinks was it.

By most accounts, Spinks was a fun-loving and affable champion who was only looking for a good time, and who understood from the start that he'd been given a chance that few fighters ever got. (Archie Moore, for example, didn't get his first shot at the title until his 172nd pro fight.) But the seeds of Spinks's calamitous future were already sprouting. Recalling the early days of Spinks's boxing career, trainer Kenny Loehr told Wayne Coffey of the *New York Daily News* in 1997 that Spinks arrived for a rubdown the morning of his 1976 gold-medal Olympic bout against Cuba's Sixto Soria smelling like he'd drained a distillery the night before. "The smell could've knocked me out," Loehr said. Promoter Butch Lewis also told of Spinks's pre-Olympics training habits, which included relaxing behind a tree while other fighters did roadwork to build endurance, then splashing his face with water to create the illusion of sweat after his "workout."

"Leon Spinks had it all," recalled fabled sports columnist Jim Murray in 1987. "He was strong, quick, muscular, charismatic and he loved to fight." But, Murray added, Spinks "also loved to party. He thought he was strong enough to drink all night and fight all [day]. He almost could."

That wasn't just hyperbole. Spinks apparently adhered to his less-than-steely training discipline even as he stood on the threshold of fame. While Spinks was training for the first Ali fight, Lewis assigned an associate to sleep on a cot outside the door to Spinks's bedroom to keep the boxer out of trouble. Spinks got out anyway, climbing through his window and turning up later in a nearby tavern, where his handlers found him shooting pool. In an interview with Associated Press boxing writer Tim Dahlberg in 2004, Gene Kilroy, an Ali confidant, recalled an early-morning encounter with Spinks at a Las Vegas hotel not long before the two men were scheduled to climb into the ring for the first time. Kilroy and Ali were getting off a hotel elevator at 4:30 a.m. so Ali could go running at a nearby golf course. The elevator doors opened, and there stood Spinks, apparently drunk and with a woman on each arm.

"Champ! How's it going?" Kilroy recalled Spinks slurring.

Rather than working out, Ali headed straight for the hotel coffee shop. Kilroy recalled Ali's reaction: "I'm an Olympic champion, a two-time heavyweight champion, and I have to go through this for *him?*"

Ali paid dearly for that misjudgment. He entered the Las Vegas ring as an overwhelming favorite and with a twenty-seven-pound weight advantage over the Olympic light heavyweight gold medalist, and his strategy was to wear down the inexperienced Spinks in the early rounds. "But he never got tired," Ali told reporters in a postfight news conference. "He kept getting stronger." Spinks was aggressive throughout the fight, clearly in command through the first six rounds. Ali began to tire. Judges awarded Ali most of the middle rounds, but Spinks rallied in the final rounds and won on a split decision. Even Ali agreed that Spinks had won the fight.

"It was a win that deserved to be celebrated in style," wrote Sean

Davies of BBC Sport, who interviewed Spinks in 2004. "And on that count Spinks certainly didn't disappoint."

Leon's Biggest Crash

"Neon Leon" was born shortly thereafter, and his victory party lasted until the rematch. The new champ began making news from the moment of his ascension. Take, for example, one remarkable three-day stretch just a month after winning the title. In a single lost weekend in mid-March 1978, the new champion was stripped of his title by the World Boxing Council (for ignoring his contractual obligation to fight Ken Norton and opting instead for a lucrative rematch with Ali), sued by his Philadelphia landlord for failing to pay two months' rent, and arrested for driving without a license down a one-way street. It was one of five traffic arrests within four months of winning the title—this from a man who, in an elegant and rare quintuple negative, thus explained why he'd waited until he was twenty-four to get his driver's license: "I didn't see no point in getting no driver's license when I couldn't afford no car."

His traffic mishaps paled, though, compared to his most disastrous head-on collision. That came during the Ali rematch. Old habits die hard, and Spinks was so caught up in living the life of the champ that he never quite got around to preparing for the fast-approaching second fight, which was scheduled to be televised live from the Superdome in New Orleans.

Spinks may have been the only one who wasn't taking the rematch seriously. It was preceded by the kind of public acclaim normally reserved for papal visits. "Crowds lined the streets of the Crescent City for parades, stormed practice facilities during warm-ups and bought tens of thousands of tickets, filling the Superdome from the floor to the rafters," wrote *Times-Picayune* sportswriter Amalie Benjamin in a 2003 story about the 25th anniversary of the rematch. "The city was bursting at the seams in the days leading up to [the] fight."

Ali understood that nothing less than his boxing legacy was at stake in the rematch and trained hard. Spinks, on the other hand, approached the second bout like a reigning monarch who was guaranteed the heavy-weight title by circumstance of birth. He "lived his new life of fame and fortune to the fullest," Benjamin wrote. "In one of the many parades and motorcades the fighters participated in during the week leading up to the bout, Spinks—who arrived with a pre-'A Team' Mr. T as a bodyguard—gave the assembled crowd a little taste of his wild and uncontrollable side, though he denies the event ever occurred. As the fighter journeyed to his hotel room sitting atop a limousine, waving to the masses, he nonchalantly pulled a marijuana cigarette from his pocket and proceeded to light up."

On fight night, with television cameras and seventy thousand im-patient fans waiting for the fight to begin, Spinks somehow managed to disappear. He eventually turned up in his dressing room, but without his custom mouthpiece and other important equipment. Ali and Spinks barely touched one another in the early rounds, and Spinks's strategy during the fight was so disorganized that, according to a *Los Angeles Times* account at the time, one of his handlers, George Benton, quit in disgust in the 5th round and abandoned the fighter's corner. As Spinks tired, Ali pep-pered him with jabs and hooks that did little damage, but which won him points from the judges. The fight went the full fifteen rounds without a knockout or any real damage to either fighter, but in the end no one doubted that the ancient champion had outpointed his younger opponent. Wrote Jim Murray in a memorable postmatch column: "Never have so many paid so much for so little. Spinks got to be an instant millionaire with less expenditure of effort than a guy opening cab doors. It wasn't even a good workout for Ali, whose own skills have eroded, but not to the extent that he is in danger from a guy who stands there and waves at him all night like a guy on a dock [waving] at a passing ocean liner. Arum did not quote his source for the notion that Spinks trained for the fight the way Errol Flynn trained for a yacht trip. Maybe he just counted the bottles."

Arum described Spinks's brief championship reign as a "tragedy" and said the young man clearly "wasn't mature enough to accept the re-sponsibility of being the world heavyweight champion."

Promoter Lewis, who also handled the career of Spinks's brother, Michael, noted that Leon's younger sibling earned $30 million by the time his boxing career ended and retired, at age thirty, to a five-acre estate in Wilmington, Delaware. "I know I could have made Leon upwards of $50 million if he had disciplined himself and done the right things for four or five years," Lewis told Coffey of the *New York Daily News* in 1997.

Instead, Lewis and others watched Leon Spinks plummet from the pinnacle like a man riding a greased rocket to the chasm's bottom. He fought many more fights, forgettably, against mostly forgettable opponents. Three years after the Ali rematch, he got one last shot at the title he had once held, but he suffered a technical knockout at the hands of Larry Holmes in the third round. In subsequent bouts, quick knockouts became his trademark, but not in a good way. During a ten-month period in 1986 and 1987, Spinks was knocked out three times. His official declaration of bankruptcy came in 1986, to no one's surprise. In 1987, he was banned from boxing in Florida following a technical knockout after two minutes and ten seconds of the first round of a fight there. The following year, Connecticut banned him after a fight in which he remained conscious for only thirty-three seconds of the first round.

He retired for the first time in 1988, at age thirty-four, and promoter Butch Lewis helped Spinks get work as a $1,500-a-week greeter for a Chicago nightclub owned by football great Mike Ditka. Even that didn't work out; according to Coffey's account in the *New York Daily News*, Spinks couldn't even show up the required four days a week and eventually was fired. For a short period in the late 1980s, according to *People* magazine, Spinks was tending bar at Jovans in Bingham Farms, Michigan, where at the same time disgraced Tigers pitching ace turned racketeer Denny McClain entertained patrons by playing "Misty," "Yesterday," and other Ramada Inn–style staples on his synthesized keyboard. Jovans was, for a brief period, a sort of Fallen Angel Lounge.

Spinks's son Leon Calvin was shot to death in a gang-related incident in 1990, and the tragedy briefly sobered Spinks, though his parenting to that point had been spotty at best. Spinks and his then-wife Betty adopted the younger Leon's son, Leon III, but Spinks's slide eventually continued. He was featured—along with NFL washout Brian Bosworth, baseball great turned World Series goat Bill Buckner, and Mike Tyson rape victim Desiree Washington—in a 1994 *People Weekly* cover story titled "Where Are They Now?" He decided to unretire that year, but Spinks's final rounds didn't last long. He was knocked out in sixty-nine seconds of the first round of his comeback fight, and lost again in his final fight in 1995. That one left him with a check for $2,500 and a professional record of 25-17-3. Coffey, the *New York Daily News* reporter, found Spinks two years later working for minimum wage at a St. Louis temp agency called Labor World. Spinks apparently supplemented that income by appearing at autograph shows and as a celebrity presence at other events, though the wages weren't much better. In 2001, he turned up on the daily syndicated court show *Judge Mathis,* haggling over another boxer's alleged promise to pay Spinks $1,650 to attend his fight in New Orleans, where Spinks's roller-coaster descent first began.

America is nothing if not forgiving, though, especially since Spinks had an appealing naïveté for a heavyweight and has remained affable and philosophic throughout. "It would be one thing if he was a jerk," said one promoter of wrestling and ultimate-fighting shows who hoped to use Spinks for promotional work in the late 1990s. "But this is a guy who has never harmed anybody but himself."

One could argue, too, that Spinks's tragicomic career has had tonic effects on the culture. His monumental failures of judgment make everyone else's failures of judgment seem small by comparison, and, as loath as some may be to admit it, there's real psychosocial value to seeing a hero stumble.

In addition, many professional athletes these days prefer performance-*enhancing* drugs instead of the merely recreational ones, though the long-term effects of that preference may prove just as risky. Elite athletes in all sports today understand the importance of diet and training to peak performance. Think about it: When was the last time you saw any champion athlete spark up a joint in the middle of a parade in his honor? Surely that's progress.

You could certainly argue that Leon Spinks's impulsive seven-month reign as heavyweight wild child proved to be a great example for at least one person—his son Cory, a quiet and polite young man who became undisputed welterweight champion in 2003 but who, forever conscious of his father's squandered potential, achieved greatness with the sober work ethic of an Amish farmer.

His father wasn't around much when Cory was growing up on the tough streets of St. Louis, and his mother, Zadie Mae Calvin, and older brother Leon died too young. He and his father reconciled in recent years as the younger Spinks's boxing career took off, but to this day Cory carries himself like a man who knows how much he has to lose.

"It comes from all of the struggles I've been through and the people that I've lost," Cory Spinks told boxing writer Thomas Gerbasi in 2004. "I just want to do my best to make them proud even though they're not here. And I don't want to let myself down; plus, I have a little daughter, and I want her to not have to go through the same things I've been through."

HONORING THE PATRON SAINT OF IMPULSE

Johnny Knoxville, host of the popular MTV show *Jackass,* has made a career for himself by allowing jai alai players to rocket balls at his buttocks, putting live leeches on his face, and swimming in raw sewage. So when the time came to get a tattoo for his right shoulder, Knoxville chose an image that serves as an exquisite homage to the man who has become a patron saint of impulse and shortsightedness.

When a writer for the British Web zine Cinemas-Online.co.uk asked Knoxville about his unusual body art in 2004, the actor said that he'd gotten it ten days before in Austin, Texas, on a sudden whim. "I was sitting in a bar, thinking, 'I should get a tattoo of Leon Spinks on my arm!' "

Knoxville recalled. "I wrote, 'Get tattoo of Leon Spinks tomorrow on your left bicep.' And I woke up [the next day] and I thought, 'Wow! That's an awesome idea!'" Oddly, Knoxville isn't actually a Spinks aficionado. "That's the damnedest thing about it!" he said. "I just had a vision!"

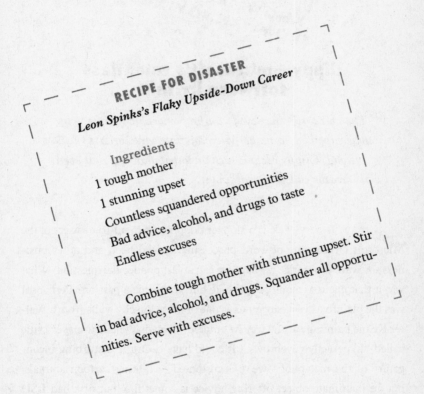

RECIPE FOR DISASTER
Leon Spinks's Flaky Upside-Down Career

Ingredients
1 tough mother
1 stunning upset
Countless squandered opportunities
Bad advice, alcohol, and drugs to taste
Endless excuses

Combine tough mother with stunning upset. Stir in bad advice, alcohol, and drugs. Squander all opportunities. Serve with excuses.

clippy — microsoft's relentless software irritant

The bizarre, bug-eyed anthropomorphic paper clip was supposed to make Microsoft software easier to use. Instead, Clippy became such an unpopular pest that even its creator ended up mocking it.

NOW THAT CLIPPY is no longer popping up to infuriate users of the Microsoft Office suite of word-processing, spreadsheet, and other business software programs, perhaps we can at last ponder the question, What was it that made so many people hate him with such a passion? Perhaps it was the plaintive eyes, enormous as one of those kitschy waifs from a Walter Keane painting, or the way he emoted with what one newspaper critic called "hyperactive eyebrows." It could have been the disturbing incongruity of the metaphor—we're accustomed to talking cartoon animals, but an inanimate object offering advice is something out of a bad LSD trip. Undoubtedly, Clippy's exquisitely bad timing was a factor. He seemed to have the knack for choosing moments when business users were in the midst of some particularly stressful, time-sensitive assignment to appear, uninvited, and breezily offer unsolicited advice on some basic function of the program. "It looks like you're writing a letter" was his exasperating mantra.

As Timothy Dyck of the computer publication *eWeek* put it, Clippy's main achievement was "leaving users of two generations of Microsoft Office products seriously bent out of shape." Financial analyst Michael Silver told CNET news in 2001: "It's probably the most annoying innovation Microsoft has added to [Microsoft Office] in years." The *Financial Times,* a British newspaper, opined: "This incessantly cheery figure may well be responsible for much of the anti-Microsoft sentiment prevalent among computer users."

But those comments don't convey the extent of the public backlash against Clippy, judging from the venomous venting on Internet discussion boards about "that annoying little [expletive] that pops up with irrelevant and unwanted suggestions," as one Office user described him. "It looks like you're trying to get work done," wrote another user, mocking Clippy's cheery tone. "Would you like me to hinder you in as many ways as possible?"

"Clippy the WD 97 Office Assistant Deserves to Die and be Tortured!!!!!" wrote yet another. Clippy was so widely and intensely disliked that ridiculing him became both a badge of cool and an art form. Haters swapped their favorite methods of permanently disabling the office assistant—"Clippicide" in Internet parlance—and devised computer games such as "Die, Clippy, Die!" in which the object was to shoot or blow up the character. They created Clippy parodies that offered advice on how to write a suicide note or file an antimonopoly lawsuit against Microsoft.

Indeed, Clippy is probably the most hated software feature in history. Computer users turned the cheery paper clip into such a virtual pariah that Microsoft itself ultimately joined in the mockery. When Microsoft released a new version of its Office software in 2001, it demoted the annoying animated character to being an optional feature that users didn't have to install, and then tried to ingratiate itself with customers by inviting them to an anti-Clippy Web site that Microsoft itself had created.

But Clippy's ignominious flop had a larger, lasting significance, because the irksome automaton was more than just a cartoon. He also was the most conspicuous and ubiquitous harbinger of the social interface, an evolutionary development in software that many in the mid-1990s believed would radically alter the way people used their computers, even more so than the point-and-click graphics of Mac and Windows had done. The bug-eyed paper clip presaged a potential future in which computers would behave less like machines and more like sentient beings with personalities, continually offering advice and guidance to users—and perhaps, as some skeptics feared, subtly monitoring and shaping their behavior in the process. But the widespread aversion to Clippy showed that computer users had ideas of their own.

Talking Globes and Surly Rodents

Before you dismiss Clippy as just another annoying bit of computer animation, consider that his lineage actually goes back nearly three centuries, to the Reverend Thomas Bayes. When the theologian-turned-statistician wasn't debating the motivation of divine acts or defending Isaac Newton's theory of differential calculus, he tried mathematically predicting the future, based upon past events and new observations. *An Essay Toward Solving a Problem in the Doctrine of Chances,* which was published after his death in 1761, introduced Bayes' theorem, a statistical version of soothsaying. Imagine, for example, having six coins in a bag, of which one is double headed. You take a coin from the bag and flip it four times, getting heads each time. Bayes' theorem enables you to calculate that there is a 76 percent chance that you've picked the double-headed coin. (As British journalist Simon Goodley explains, Bayesian thinking would also help you to figure out that the word "Amazon" on a Web page refers to the river rather than the retailer, based on previous references to the rain forest and South America.)

Bayes's ideas were widely used over the centuries. Religious skeptics used them to infer that the amount of evil in the universe made God's existence improbable. Business-school professors taught executives how to use them to predict the probable demand for their products. In the 1990s, software designers hit upon another application. A software program could employ Bayesian methods to figure out what a computer user might be trying to accomplish, based upon the steps that the person had followed up to that point, and intervene to offer him what probably was the appropriate assistance.

That breakthrough came along at a critical moment for computer and software makers. By the mid-1990s, despite the introduction of graphical interfaces that made computers vastly easier to use, only about a quarter of American households owned PCs, according to the National Science Foundation. Other studies found lingering unease and suspicion of them. A 1994 Gallup survey found that 59 percent of white-collar workers were reluctant to try new technology. Nearly a third of the workers— including four out of ten women—confessed to being outright afraid of the powerful, still-mysterious machines on their desks.

Seeing a threat to its growth, the industry searched for ways to help people get over their cyber-anxiety. Stanford University researchers' "Computers as Social Actors" theory seemed promising. CASA held that users instinctively treated computers as if they were people, not tools, and that they might feel more comfortable if a computer acted more human— particularly if its virtual personality was similar to the user's. As Microsoft manager Chris Pratley explained in a 2004 Web log essay: "The theory was that if you could provide an interface for the computer that expressed emotion and that you could interact with, you would be less likely to develop animosity toward your PC . . . and would actually be encouraged to learn and interact."

Thus, software designers wedded CASA with Bayesian probability to create social interfaces peopled by "agents" who would guide actual humans' efforts to use the software. Instead of making characters realistic, however, they gave them the exaggerated, childlike qualities of Saturday morning cartoon characters. (Intentionally or not, that fit theories of

Nobel Prize–winning behavior researcher Konrad Lorenz, who saw cuteness as a potent cue for behavior, and noted that people were nicer to animals whose physical features reminded them of human children.)

Microsoft's initial attempt at a social interface, "Bob," was developed under the supervision of Melinda Gates, a Microsoft executive who also happened to be the wife of company chairman and cofounder Bill Gates. It was released in early 1995. When installed on early versions of the Windows point-and-click user interface, it converted the Windows desktop into a house with ten rooms—including a family room, a study, and an attic—that a computer user could decorate in a variety of styles, ranging from medieval to postmodern. The furnishings were actually icons that opened various applications, such as a letter-writing program, a checkbook, a calendar, and an e-mail program. The interface featured a number of animated inhabitants whose personalities ranged, in the words of software historian Dan Rose, from "happily enthusiastic" to "downright obnoxious." Bob's cast included cartoon animals such as Hopper the stuffed blue bunny, Digger the worm, Blythe the firefly, Rover the dog, and Chaos the cat. The program also offered Orby, an anthropomorphic world globe, and a William Shakespeare caricature who spoke in flowery Elizabethan language. The most bizarre character was Scuzz, a surly rodent who took occasional bites of a package of rat poison, tormented Chaos the cat, and dismissed the other guides as "losers." (Oddly, there was no character named Bob.)

Bob had at least a few fans. *Wall Street Journal* technology critic Walter Mossberg lauded it as "a bold departure that attempts to give nontechnical people more control over their computers. . . . It's better than cursing at the screen and feeling stupid." Reviewer Jack Warner of the *Austin American-Statesman,* in contrast, noted acidly that "I tend to resent small dogs or birds crouching in the lower right corner of the monitor throwing incessant balloons full of advice onto the screen."

Bob had one telling technical flaw. Since the program still required Microsoft Windows to remain running as well, it taxed the then-puny amounts of memory available in PCs, which tended to slow down users' machines. Though Microsoft didn't release specific figures, sales were weak, and Bill Gates later described the product as "a commercial failure." By early 1996, industry journal *Information Week* reported, unsold copies of Bob languished in the bargain bin at one major software retailer.

The Jar Jar Binks of Word Processing

The Bob fiasco didn't end Microsoft's interest in making computers seem friendly. By the late 1990s, the company's flagship business software suite, Microsoft Office—which included word-processing, calendar, e-mail, contact-management, spreadsheet, and presentation-creating programs—was bulked up like a baseball player on Andro. Office was capable of so many different tasks that, as one Microsoft engineer estimated, people seldom used more than 10 to 15 percent of its features. Microsoft researchers continued to look for ways to guide Office users. According to Microsoft manager Pratley, they even considered a radical overhaul that would have made Office mimic a Web site, with a search engine enabling users to find commands by typing keywords.

Ultimately, however, they returned to the cartoon approach used unsuccessfully in Bob. According to a document on Microsoft's Web site, the full installation of Microsoft Office 97 actually offered a choice of nine different assistants, ranging from a cute dog to a robot. But most users apparently stuck with the default, a character named Clippit (whose name soon morphed into Clippy).

The Office assistant was clever—a bit too clever, as it turned out, for its own good. To make users more comfortable, Microsoft included natural language capabilities—that is, users could click Clippy and ask it questions in the form of ordinary sentences. But whatever goodwill that engendered was offset by the way Clippy continually interrupted users to offer them tips. The idea, according to Pratley's essay, was to have Clippy rescue users who "did the same dumb thing all the time," and ideally to introduce them to Office's powerful, potentially drudgery-saving features. "It looks like you're writing a letter," for example, was intended to guide them to new Word features that enabled users to format a document without relying on complicated tab commands.

The problem, Pratley noted, was that Clippy not only offered the suggestion for the first document in which a user typed "Dear" followed by a string of words, but also every time it saw that combination in a document thereafter. "Compounding things was that this tip did not have a way for the user to turn it off, and it was a little too persistent before giving up," he wrote. And many people, as it turned out, didn't want Clippy's help at all. Steven Pemberton of the National Research Institute for Mathematics and Computer Science in the Netherlands found that older users liked help from intelligent agents, while younger, more savvy ones—accustomed to solving problems on their own—found them annoying.

Clippy's looks and manner were another miscalculation. In retrospect, Pratley wrote in his Web log essay, the dog might have been a better choice as a default—"he was cute, and animated to be subservient and harmless, whereas Clippy was sassy and annoying." Computer journalist Peter Lewis likened him to Jar Jar Binks, a computer-generated character in the *Star Wars* films *The Phantom Menace* and *Attack of the Clones,* whom legions of hard-core fans of the series found insufferable. Nisha Dharna, a computer science student at Southern Illinois University, did a study in which sixty test subjects learning tasks on a computer received assistance from one of three animated intelligent agents—a genie, a spacecraft, or a human being. The group receiving assistance from the spacecraft showed the most anxiety, while the subjects getting help from the human being were the least nervous and made the fewest errors. Dharna inferred that Clippy might not have seemed so irritating if it had been designed to look more like a person.

In a recent paper on human-computer relationships, Boston University researcher Timothy W. Bickmore and the Massachusetts Institute of Technology's Rosalind W. Picard noted that Clippy's habits of barging in uninvited, offering advice that was often useless, and refusing to leave quickly actually made him less anthropomorphic. They concluded: "If this behavior were that of a human office assistant, then he would eventually be fired, or at least severely marginalized."

The unfortunate paper clip did become a trendsetter—though not the sort Microsoft had intended. Clippy became a prototype victim of the sort of Internet-speed savaging later directed at politicians and movie starlets. ZDNet.com, the computer news site, offered a tutorial on how to eradicate Clippy, and people who posted to Internet discussion boards trashed the agent. Clippy served as the inspiration for a vast number of online amateur satirists. One of the funniest created an imitation Clippy, which offered nonsensical interruptions such as "Your computer seems to be on" and "It is time to play a game—let's play hide and seek." To make matters worse, ZDNet.com reported in 2000 that a hacker had found a potential security hole in Clippy that would enable him to attack users' computers. Microsoft quickly issued a security patch, but by then the revelation had already added fuel to the anti-Clippy conflagration.

"Useless, Obsolete, and . . . Hideously Unattractive"

In April 2001, Microsoft exiled Clippy to the options selection in its latest release, Office XP, which had new, improved help features, such as smart tags and task panes, that Microsoft said made the assistant unneeded. But Clippy had been so gratingly conspicuous on millions of computer screens that Microsoft could hardly just abandon it quietly, the way that Ford had tried to slip the Edsel's cancellation into an obscure financial report in 1959. Paradoxically, though Clippy's purpose had been to make Microsoft Office simpler to use, *New York Times* computing writer John Markoff observed that the annoying paper clip had come to exemplify the software giant's overburdening of users with too many features.

So instead, Microsoft opted for one of the most bizarre—yet successful—promotional gambits in history. To hype its new Clippy-free release of Office, it joined disgruntled users of the old version in ridiculing the hated paper clip. According to the *Times,* Microsoft spent $500,000 attacking its own creation. The campaign began with a mocking press release, saying that the character was "quite down in the dumps" after becoming the victim of a layoff. Microsoft put banners on its corporate Web sites to direct customers to its own official Clippy-bashing Web site. The site included video clips of office workers denouncing him ("Next to Microsoft Bob, you are the most annoying thing in computer history!" one shouted), and a plaintive missive from the character himself, in which he admitted that he was "useless, obsolete, and I'm told, hideously unattractive." Microsoft invited visitors to vote in an online poll on what Clippy's new career should be.

The software maker even imitated the anti-Clippy games floating around the Web, offering visitors a chance to shoot simulated rubber bands, staples, and other office supplies at the despised animated character. Greg Shaw, a partner in the advertising and public relations firm that helped design the concept for Microsoft, explained to the Associated Press: "You can go up there and have fun taking out whatever range of emotions you've had about Clippy."

In late May 2001, not quite four years after Clippy's debut, Microsoft held a publicity event to promote Office XP at the Hammerstein Ballroom in New York. An actor dressed in a Clippy costume joined Microsoft chairman Bill Gates onstage, and to the crowd's amusement, interrupted Gates's speech. "XP stands for ex–paper clip," he complained, and chanted, "Bring back Clippy! Bring back Clippy!" as he was dragged offstage by a magnet. A slide show showed his new job prospects, portraying Clippy as a taxi driver and United Parcel Service delivery worker.

Some Office users were not amused. "In less time than it took [Microsoft] to put this web site together, they could have pulled the dumb clip out of their software," one engineer wrote in an e-mail to the CNET technology news Web site.

But more people seem to have appreciated Microsoft's surprising willingness to laugh at itself. In the first three weeks after the company's

Clippy-bashing Web site's launch, it drew 22 million visitors. Clippy may have failed in his intended function, but he turned out to be a useful device for viral marketing, the cutting-edge communication technique that aims to manipulate the audience into spreading the message about a product themselves, via word-of-mouth buzz. Every joke about the character being fired reminded consumers that a new, improved version of Office was available.

By the time Gates gave a 2005 interview to *Infoworld*, an industry publication, the Microsoft chieftain was actually spinning Clippy's demotion as an example of the company's efforts to improve the user experience, and calling it "one of the most exciting things we did."

RECIPE FOR DISASTER
Stewed Computer User

Ingredients

1 complicated package of business software
1 personal computer
1 office worker under deadline pressure
1 irksome animated character
Dollop of useless advice

Place office worker under deadline pressure, computer, and software in a small cubicle. Let simmer. Toss in irksome animated character. Add useless advice until the mixture reaches boiling point. Serve while steaming.

Meanwhile, Clippy lives on as a target for Internet satirists. At the Web site www.Neopoleon.com, for example, writer Rory Blyth imagined tracking down the pink-slipped character for an interview, and finding that he had become just another bitter ex-celebrity, who between swigs of booze and bites of cocktail wieners blamed his downfall on the public's fickle tastes: "You know, the work wasn't all that great, to tell you the truth. There were a few people who treated me real nice, but I remember a few times when I'd show up and see the user on the other side of the screen just start to turn purple. It's like they didn't even want me there, you know?"

BEYOND THE TALKING, BUG-EYED PAPER CLIP

Software designers remain enthralled by the notion of helping computer users by using animated agents—albeit much more realistic ones, rather than cartoon figures like Clippy. A recent paper by University of Tokyo researchers Mitsuru Ishizuka and Helmut Prendinger, for example, noted that "life-like characters are one of the most exciting technologies for human-computer interface applications."

But the paper also noted that building an agent realistic enough to connect effectively with computer users remains a tricky task, requiring careful attention to detail. For example, they wrote, "an agent that speaks with a cheerful voice without displaying a happy facial expression will seem awkward or even fake."

the y2k scare

*To nervous Americans on the eve of the 21st century, a
couple of missing digits in a computer program foretold
a looming techno-apocalypse. So a few entrepreneurs did
what they do best: turned fear into cash.*

YOU MAY HAVE been one of those people who woke up on the
morning of January 1, 2000, and flipped on the TV to discover that civilization had not disintegrated into chaos. You may even have felt a bit of
buyer's remorse. That $1,495 twelve-month supply of dried beans and
fruit, the $7,000 "survival dome" tent, the boxes of shotgun shells and
hundreds of rolls of toilet paper that you stashed in the basement—which
undoubtedly would have been prized commodities for barter, had the
apocalypse arrived as predicted—suddenly didn't seem like such wise
purchases after all. But you can take solace in this: You may have been
bamboozled by the prophets of doom, but you weren't alone.

Millions of other Americans were similarly convinced that their
computers' inability to distinguish between the years 2000 and 1900—a
software glitch that became known as the Y2K bug—would trigger a cataclysmic upheaval. A January 1999 Time/CNN poll reported that nearly
60 percent of Americans were "somewhat" to "very" concerned about
Y2K. An even more astonishing finding: one in ten Americans expected
Y2K to bring the end of the world as we know it—or "TEOTWAWKI,"

in the shorthand of the many Web sites and chat rooms devoted to contemplating modern, technologically dependent society's imminent destruction.

And it was hard *not* to contemplate the various scenarios that were supposed to play out because of the millennium bug. They were laid out in macabre detail by prophets of doom on Web sites, in high-priced videos, and in books with enervating titles such as *Time Bomb 2000, 101 Ways to Survive the Y2K Crisis, The Christian's Y2K Preparedness Handbook, Y2K=666,* and the like. Across the United States and Canada, according to the doomsayers, lights would dim as electricity generating plants and power grids stopped working. The air-traffic control system would go on the fritz, leaving jets circling in confusion. On the highways, drivers would suddenly lose control of their cars as their computerized steering and brakes failed. Phones and e-mail would stop working. In hospitals, medical devices would malfunction, and patients on life-support machines would flatline.

It would only get worse in the days and weeks that followed. The U.S. government would be unable to issue Social Security checks. Hordes of depositors would descend upon beleaguered banks, demanding their savings out of fear they would vanish. Financial markets would be thrown into chaos. With government unable to collect taxes to pay police officers' salaries, law enforcement would wither, and violent mobs and vigilantes would roam the streets. Eventually, President Bill Clinton would seize upon the chaos to declare martial law, suspend the U.S. Constitution, and appoint himself dictator. Alternatively, blue-helmeted United Nations troops would show up on American shores, and the Antichrist would arise, revealing that what we had assumed to be innocuous computer bar codes on credit cards and retail products was, in fact, the sign of the beast as prophesied by the book of Revelation. In retrospect, it all may sound a bit too much like the plot of a cheesy 1960s apocalyptic disaster thriller, lacking only that climactic scene when Charlton Heston discovers the

Statue of Liberty, half buried in sand. But at the time, to very many people, it seemed terrifyingly real.

And to more than a few, it also seemed like a sign from above. "The Big Party is coming to an end," millennium disaster prognosticator Don Boys warned in his 1999 book *Y2K*. "Man has gotten too big for his britches, and God is going to bring him down." Steve Farrar, author of the 1999 book *Spiritual Survival During the Y2K Crisis*, wrote that the more research he did on the impending technological disaster, "the more I saw the fingerprints of God."

Or rather, perhaps they were the fingerprints of economist Adam Smith's "invisible hand." In the latter part of the 1990s, stirring up such nightmares—and providing protection from the technological bogeyman—became a growth industry, putting many millions of dollars in the pockets of computer programmers, and spawning thousands of books, videos, and other products, and even real estate developments.

"Terminal Screens, Dark as a Villain's Heart"

Over the years, humans have imagined myriad potential causes for the destruction of civilization, including divine retribution, a collision with a comet, nuclear war, a viral epidemic, climate change, and annihilation by space aliens. Compared to most of these exotic doomsday scenarios, the Y2K software bug was utterly banal.

When computers became widespread in the 1950s and 1960s, they used punch cards rather than magnetic hard drives to store programs and data. To save space on the cards, programmers came up with an ingenious solution. They wrote programs that had computers recognize years as two-digit numbers, rather than as four-digit numbers. As early as 1960, computer pioneer Bob Bemer, the father of the ASCII coding system for text (and also the man responsible for the escape key) pointed out that the two-digit date had a drawback. If dates had only two digits, when the 21st century eventually rolled around, computers would mistake 01-01-00 for the first day of 1900, not 2000. That could conceivably lead to bizarre mistakes, such as an insurance company computer giving customers who sought refunds a check for one hundred years' worth of premium payments. Or it might cause the machines to simply stop functioning altogether. A 1984 book, *Computers in Crisis: How to Avert the Coming Worldwide Computer Systems Collapse* by Jerome T. and Marilyn J. Murray, sounded a similar warning. If government and business procrastinated about fixing the date problem, they wrote, "we may well expect widespread suspension of computer processing in the year 2000 and beyond, with many terminal screens as dark as a villain's heart."

Hardly anyone listened, because everyone expected that the mainframes and programs would be replaced long before they posed a potential problem. As it turned out, government agencies and businesses kept using the aging equipment long after it became obsolete, and partly out of habit, programmers kept using the two-digit shortcut into the 1980s. As one corporate executive told the *New York Times* in 1988, "The joke in computing circles is that every data processing manager, no matter how old they are, is saying they plan to retire early in 1999."

By the mid-1990s, companies and the government started to wake up to the problem. A 1996 survey showed that six of ten companies already had Y2K upgrades under way. Fixing the flaw usually wasn't that complicated, though it was arduous. Armies of programmers had to go through the old code, line by line, and rewrite all the portions with code using four-digit years. Then they had to fix whatever other bugs might crop up due to the changes. A New Jersey public utility company found an ingenious way to deal with the problem. The company set some of its computers' internal clocks back to 1972, a year when dates fell on the exact same days of the week as 2000.

As technicians probed computer systems, they discovered Y2K flaws that might have caused some serious problems if they had gone uncorrected. The New York Stock Exchange discovered glitches that might have caused trading to grind to a halt three days after the millennium began. The Internal Revenue Service discovered 175 glitches in its computer systems, including one that would have caused tax notices to go out with a due date of 2099. Southern California Edison discovered that sensors throughout its power grid might fail, causing small-scale blackouts in some parts of the region. (Beyond that, repair crews wouldn't be able to tell which lines were dead and which still had current coursing through them, possibly endangering their lives.) Ultimately, U.S. companies would spend $125 billion between 1997 and 2000 making sure such calamities didn't occur. The federal government would spend $8.5 billion.

But in many instances, it turned out that the Y2K bug didn't present a serious threat. Aircraft manufacturers, for example, found that planes wouldn't fall out of the sky, because crucial electronic systems on planes didn't depend on having accurate dates. Hospitals found that defibrillators and other lifesaving equipment would work, even if the devices registered the wrong date. The eight major U.S. telephone companies at the time conducted 1,700 tests of their systems in 1998 and 1999, and found only seven Y2K bugs, most of which were quickly fixed. The personal computers on office workers' desks were usually too new to contain Y2K bugs, and the older ones could usually be easily fixed. Thus, by the late 1990s, computing experts worked overtime to assure a nervous public that the world wasn't about to end. In December 1997, for example, *PC Week* writer Michael Surkan wrote that "in all but an exceedingly small number of cases, these date bugs will cause little (if any) real damage." A yearlong U.S. Senate investigation concluded in February 1999 that while not all Y2K problems had been fixed, "talk of the death of civilization, to borrow from Mark Twain, has been greatly exaggerated."

Lawn Sprinklers Gone Berserk!

But the reassuring voices of experts were drowned out by the shrill voices proclaiming that all hell was about to break loose. The mainstream media quickly glommed on to a story it had ignored for years. *Newsweek* was among the first to pour lighter fluid on public anxiety with a June

1997 article headlined "The Day the World Shuts Down," which started with a hypothetical scene in which New Year's Eve revelers can't leave a party because the elevator has been paralyzed by the Y2K bug, and hinted that prisons might disgorge inmates, bank vault doors might pop open, and computerized sprinkler systems might become confused and drench lawns in the middle of winter.

Business Week followed with a March 1998 cover story entitled "ZAP! How the Year 2000 Bug Will Hurt the Economy." It concluded that "the Y2K bug is shaping up to have a profoundly negative impact on the U.S. economy—starting almost immediately," and predicted that Y2K-related breakdowns would cause power blackouts, disruption of the financial system, and a sharp drop in economic growth. But even if companies debugged their old software, in *Business Week*'s gloomy scenario, the amount of technical talent and money diverted by the effort would put a major dent in productivity. "Think of it as a town threatened by a rising river," the article warned. "Every able-bodied person—no matter what their job—is put to work stacking sandbags, while economic activity in the rest of the town slows down." Not to be outdone, *Vanity Fair* published a January 1999 article entitled "The Y2K Nightmare," which painted a lurid picture of paralyzed cities and global riots.

TV evangelists eagerly embraced the idea of an impending catastrophe with similar fervor. The Reverend Jerry Falwell offered viewers a $25 videotape, *A Christian's Guide to the Millennium Bug,* on which he warned that the Y2K problem "may be God's instrument to shake this nation, to humble this nation," and that he intended to stock up on food, gasoline, and ammunition for his family. He warned in a January 1999 sermon that "the Y2K threat could wipe out everything we have attained materially, because when people can't communicate with one another, their distrust turns to violent acts of hostility and aggression."

The march toward the millennium conveniently coincided with the increasing popularity of the Internet, perhaps the ideal medium for promoting anxiety. Virtually anyone with access to an Internet-connected PC could create a Web page devoted to apocalyptic Y2K rumors, and by the late 1990s, it seemed as if they all had. Gary North, who proclaimed Y2K to be "the greatest problem that has ever faced western civilization," created www.garynorth.com, one of the most popular online portals for doomsday information. (North also marketed two-year subscriptions to a related financial newsletter for $225 apiece.) Another site, www.Y2KWatch.com, touted a preparedness plan that included advice on safe investments, discussed the possible benefits of propane fuel and gun ownership, and counseled the nervous to embrace fundamentalist Christian beliefs if they hadn't already.

Survivalist Pizza and Advice from Spock

At the top of the apocalyptic food chain were the firms and consultants hired by worried companies to fix their software. By 1998, programmers capable of debugging old software could command fees as high as $100 an hour—more than twice what they were usually paid. Software and hardware manufacturers slapped "Y2K Compliant" labels on their new products—even though, as one industry source explained to CNN, previous versions had often been Y2K compliant as well, so that customers were buying upgrades they didn't need.

Hollywood, not surprisingly, also tried to make a buck from impending doom. There were at least two exploitation movies with the same title, *Y2K*—one a low-budget cinematic thriller starring Louis Gossett Jr. in which the military discovers that a long-lost nuclear missile is about to go off due to the Y2K bug, and the other an NBC made-for-television movie staring Ken Olin, formerly the brooding yuppie dad on the 1980s series *thirtysomething*, as a computer genius out to save the world from a massive breakdown. (As an Internet Movie Database reviewer caustically summed up the latter film: "Not only does Y2K affect every single electronic component in the world, but it also affects everyone's brain!")

Almost invariably, Y2K prognosticators had a book or video for sale, and sometimes both. One example was Y2K expert Michael S. Hyatt, whose Web site, www.y2kprep.com, gave tips on buying two-way radios and offered an advice column ("What do I do if my spouse thinks Y2K is a bunch of hype?"). He also was the author of *Millennium Bug: How to Survive the Coming Chaos,* which reached number six on Amazon.com's bestseller list. Expert credentials weren't always necessary: A 1999 video called the *Y2k Family Survival Guide,* for example, featured Leonard Nimoy, of *Star Trek* fame, presenting the usual advice on amassing emergency supplies. Publishers churned out an estimated 2,500 books with Y2K themes. They included Susan Robinson's *Whatcha Gonna Do If the Grid Goes Down? Preparing Your Household for the Year 2000,* and 1999's *Catastrophic Cooking* by Carol Reid and David Harrington, a cookbook that promised to show readers how to prepare "tasty, nutritional, well balanced meals" in the midst of Y2K disruptions. (The book also included instructions for using tinfoil and an ordinary cardboard box to create a charcoal-heated oven capable of cooking food at up to 475 degrees.) Investment adviser David Steelsmith Elliot wrote the 1998 tome *Everyone's Guide to Making a Million Dollars on the Year 2000 Crash,* the original edition of which retailed for a hefty $44.95.

Y2K mania also created endless opportunities to peddle survival products. The Web site www.Y2KWatch.com, for example, advertised hydroponic gardening kits, "non-electric cooking solutions," and investment opportunities in gold and silver. A Utah-based company, Preparedness Resources, which sold twelve-month supplies of dehydrated food for $1,495, saw its sales rise 1,200 percent in 1999. Another of its hot items was a $225 kit containing a water purifier, flashlights, and tools. A Michigan entrepreneur seized upon Y2K as the perfect opportunity to market his invention—pizza slices in vacuum-sealed packages, intended to last for as long as two years without refrigeration or cooking. Some entrepreneurs developed entire communities, such as Prayer Lake in northwest Arkansas and God's Wilderness in rural Minnesota. The latter offered ten-acre lots complete with an eight-hundred-square-foot cabin, a drilled well, a stove, a shed, a greenhouse, and an outhouse, for $40,000.

An anxious public was also vulnerable to Y2K scams. In late 1999, one Southern California financial adviser put clients' money into various high-risk options deals, which essentially were wagers that the stock market would crash due to Y2K disruptions. The clients lost $6 million. Some were conned into buying $299 Y2K home survival kits, which contained an assortment of supplies—flares, flashlights, bandages, candles, Kool–Aid, Spam, and inexplicably, tongue depressors—that could have been purchased at the local store for $50.

Oops . . . Never Mind

As it turned out, Y2K did cause scattered computer breakdowns—the U.S. government briefly was cut off from its spy satellites, for example, due to a flawed software patch. But crucial utilities, communications, and power systems kept functioning. In the private sector, an *Information Week* survey determined that 30 percent of companies experienced Y2K glitches, though only about 4 percent were significant interruptions. *Philadelphia Daily News* columnist Sandy Grady picked "Y2K furor" as winner of the year's biggest loser award. "Planes didn't crash, nuclear missiles didn't fire, computers didn't melt. Headlines should have said: OOPS, NOTHING HAPPENED," Grady wrote. Even Falwell had to admit that the efforts to remedy the situation in government and private businesses had been "a job well done."

But Y2K mania had an inadvertent upside as well. Some analysts say the billions spent on Y2K software fixes helped ignite the economic boom of the late 1990s. On the other hand, as *InternetWeek* writer Tim Wilson noted in 2000, the millennium bug may also have played a role in the boom's eventual crash, since Y2K consultants found themselves out of work, and companies stopped spending so much on new computers and software. The temporary shortage of programming talent led companies to look overseas for help—stimulating the trend of "offshoring" high-tech jobs to countries such as India and creating anxiety among U.S. workers scared about their futures.

And nineteen months after the millennial false alarm, the nation was rocked by an actual cataclysm—the September 11, 2001, attacks on New York and Washington, D.C. The backup communications systems and disaster preparedness finally were put to the test. In a 2004 interview with American Radio Works, Clinton administration Y2K coordinator John Koskinen said Y2K-inspired backup systems enabled Wall Street to reopen for trading less than a week after September 11. Without them, "they never would have been able to do it in the time frame, with the confidence they had."

A study published in the *Journal of Psychology* in 2003 noted a curious phenomenon. Several years after Y2K, survey subjects now claimed that they had never really been that worried about the Y2K bug—a result markedly different from a survey conducted with a similar group before

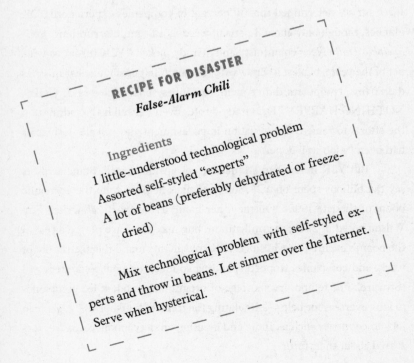

RECIPE FOR DISASTER
False-Alarm Chili

Ingredients
1 little-understood technological problem
Assorted self-styled "experts"
A lot of beans (preferably dehydrated or freeze-dried)

Mix technological problem with self-styled experts and throw in beans. Let simmer over the Internet. Serve when hysterical.

the ominous date. One possible explanation, the researchers concluded, was that "participants may have reported not being concerned about Y2K to avoid appearing foolish."

FROM CHAOS TO CLICHÉ

In December 2000, Yankelovich Partners surveyed one thousand Americans to learn what phrases "made them want to crunch something," as part of a promotion for the Snickers candy bar. The top ten answers, which scored too closely together to be listed in order, included "Y2K bug," "the millennium," and "The world is coming to an end." (Other irritating clichés that made the list: "Who let the dogs out?" "Is that your final answer?" and "Who won the election?")

the xfl's quick takedown

In a single season of televised T&A, backstage buffoonery, and second-rate football, the league launched by wrestling impresario Vince McMahon and NBC recorded the lowest prime-time ratings in network history.

ON THE SMALL screen, at least, the climactic game of the XFL's inaugural season might have seemed like a legitimate event in the big-money world of sports television. The championship "Million Dollar Game," hyped as the upstart league's Super Bowl equivalent, was played on April 21, 2001, in no less storied a stadium than the 92,516-seat Los Angeles Coliseum. The massive sports arena had been the stage for count-less culturally significant events, including two Olympiads, two Super Bowls, a World Series, John F. Kennedy's 1960 candidate acceptance speech, a 1987 Papal Mass, and sold-out concerts featuring the Rolling Stones and Bruce Springsteen. It's likely no coincidence that the XFL's visionaries—World Wrestling Entertainment (formerly World Wrestling Federation) chief executive Vince McMahon and NBC television sports czar Dick Ebersol—chose the coliseum for another reason: In 1967, it had been the site of the very first AFL-versus-NFL championship game, which later became known as the Super Bowl. From the beginning, the whole point of the XFL was not only to challenge the NFL head-on, but to go the established league one better.

The televised illusion seemed solid enough. Cameras panning the stadium recorded all of the requisite froth and glitter associated with prime-time TV sports—the competing teams in snazzy uniforms, the enthusiastic cheerleaders, overly exuberant fans, and aging sports icons offering color commentary. To give the game an extra whiff of legitimacy and a sense of history, the league owners even convinced the coliseum management to ignite the Olympic torch that had welcomed visitors to the Summer Games of 1932 and 1984.

But trying to divine reality from a television broadcast is a lot like watching an ancient stripper in a dark nightclub; look too closely and the illusion vanishes. What on television seemed a gathering of tightly packed and enthusiastic pro football fans was, in fact, an artfully produced exercise in futility. The competing teams, the Los Angeles Xtreme and the San Francisco Demons, were less a collection of elite athletes than a tribe of former jocks who, for the most part, had not had the right stuff for the NFL and were looking for a break. The cheerleaders, too, had a certain edginess that played neatly into the league's ham-fisted appeal to the desirable eighteen- to thirty-four-year-old male demographic; clearly some of the league's most telegenic booster girls had been surgically retrofitted, and some even relied on professional lap-dancing experience to inform their sideline spirit-boosting duties. If the cameras had pulled back far enough, viewers would have seen just how small a crowd of twenty-four thousand people can seem in an arena the size of the coliseum, and just how unenthusiastically the XFL had been greeted even in Los Angeles— a city that had lost both of its NFL teams six years before. Even the paying fans were less than enthusiastic, with one hoisting a hand-lettered sign that emphasized the letters NBC to attract the network camera operator's attention. It read: "No Body Cares."

Although no one knew it then, the Million Dollar Game was more than just the XFL's inaugural championship showdown. It was the last XFL game that would ever be played. After a year of high-decibel hyperbole and three months of actual play, the league touted as the next step in the evolution of American football—and pitched with unabashed appeal to what *American Demographics* magazine labeled "Guy Culture"—was just weeks away from the coroner's door, a victim of overreaching ambition, poor execution, and television ratings that essentially flatlined after the first half of the very first league game. To anyone not distracted by the cheerleaders and manufactured excitement, the Million Dollar Game was dead on arrival, with perhaps its most appropriate epitaph spoken weeks later by media buyer Bob Igiel to a reporter for *Mediaweek* magazine: "The XFL was an embarrassment for sports and for NBC. It was a complete waste of time."

On a brighter note, only a special kind of business can lose more than $70 million in just fifteen months. Surely that's some kind of record.

The Promise of Neanderthal Football

Vince McMahon, who first conjured the XFL illusion by announcing plans for the league in February 2000, came to that fateful crossroads in his life as both a man of admirable achievement and one searching for mainstream respectability. On the one hand, he was without question a staggeringly successful self-made sports entertainment entrepreneur. On the other, McMahon's fortune was derived from a decidedly lowbrow pursuit: professional wrestling. He was most viciously characterized by author Brett Forrest, who in his 2002 XFL autopsy report, *Long Bomb: How the XFL Became TV's Biggest Fiasco*, referred to the wrestling impresario as a "bumpkin billionaire" who'd made his fortune in a trade that "in many minds clung precariously to a rung one up from porn and cockfighting." The XFL, Forrest wrote, "wasn't just McMahon's attempt at expanding his wealth, influence, and empire, although it certainly was that. This was an exertion of another of his visions, that of sport's next step. If all went according to plan, no amount of criticism or envy could deny the achievement. The XFL was McMahon's shot at legitimacy."

But let's give credit where it's due. McMahon had built his World

Wrestling Entertainment Inc. from a foundation laid by his father, an old-time wrestling promoter. While not always successful during his early promotional efforts, the younger McMahon had staged several high-profile public spectacles, including Evel Knievel's comically aborted "jump" across Idaho's Snake River canyon in 1974. Beginning in the early 1980s, McMahon began packaging and marketing his pro wrestling shows as cheap programming for the then-decentralized cable TV industry and as pay-per-view television events, and he remade that old-fashioned form of sports entertainment into a modern and lucrative television spectacle. He even unselfishly played himself as a cartoonish villain ("Mr. McMahon") in many of his own scripted pro wrestling melodramas.

Goofy as they sometimes were, those seminude soap operas on steroids kept TV viewers tuning in with a potent mix of sexual tease, choreographed action-figure violence, and invented grudges. Researchers at Indiana University quantified the formula by studying fifty episodes of McMahon's wrestling shows from 1998, a year when the ratings for those shows increased by 50 percent from the year before. According to *Sex, Lies, and Headlocks: The Real Story of Vince McMahon and the World Wrestling Federation*, a 2002 book by Shaun Assael and Mike Mooneyham, the researchers counted 1,658 instances of crotch grabbing, 157 obscene gestures, and 128 instances of simulated sexual activity. McMahon clearly understood what America wanted—or at least what appealed to a certain rowdy seam of the national population—and he knew how to package it, televise it, and milk it for cash. According to McMahon's wrestling organization, his operation in its prime was generating about $100 million in quarterly revenues, with a weekly viewership around the world estimated at 500 million.

As McMahon surveyed the American landscape from his peculiar rung on the ladder during the winter of 2000, he sensed a softening in the public's ardor for NFL-style football. Between 1999 and 2000, the NFL saw its television ratings slip as part of an overall sports ratings malaise, and even venerable *Monday Night Football* was losing viewers to McMahon's wrestling extravaganzas in head-to-head broadcasts. From that Mc-Mahon concluded that the red-meat crowd was ready for a new brand of football.

For decades, the NFL had been one of the most reliable magnets for the nation's young male viewers. Those viewers are prized because their buying habits are not yet established, and the shows they watch are the place the advertisers of beer, hemi pickup trucks, Doritos, and similar products want to be. McMahon knew the denizens of Guy Culture not already tuned to his wrestling shows were prowling their TV dial for offerings such as *The Man Show* on Comedy Central, which in 1999 began offering unapologetically sexist slow-mo video of girls jumping on trampolines, a regular crew of big-breasted women known as the "Juggies," and recurring skits such as "Household Hints of Adult Film Stars."

In those reliable appetites McMahon sensed an opportunity to make even more money. The NFL enjoyed the biggest slice of the American sports money pie, with annual revenues in 2002 estimated at $4.8 billion—more than twice what it had been five years before, with projected increases of $1 billion a year during the three years that followed. But the NFL was losing part of its young male audience to new players in the entertainment world, including video games, the Internet, and extreme sports competitions such as the X Games. In 1999, *Monday Night Football* was drawing about 20 million viewers per game. It's an impressive number, but the average *Monday Night Football* viewer also was forty-four years old with an income of more than $50,000—terrific for some advertisers, but not quite right for the ones trying to reach those coveted young males. "In sports, old and rich is not necessarily a good thing," noted *U.S. News & World Report* in an optimistic XFL preview article in September 2000.

McMahon imagined a football league that would appeal more directly to those beer-drinking, hemi-driving Doritos munchers. And during his February 2000 news conference announcing plans to create the XFL, McMahon went straight at what he perceived as the NFL's soft spot. All but thumping his chest like a silverback gorilla, he described the established league as a haven of "pantywaists" and "sissies," and promised to return professional football to a Neanderthal time when "the whole idea was to kill the quarterback." It was a remarkable public challenge for the most lucrative prize in American sports, and never mind that, at that point, McMahon had no teams, no coaches, no players, no equipment—just an idea, publicly announced. Perhaps the most successful thing about the XFL is that in the year that followed, McMahon actually put together something that looked remarkably like a professional football league, at least from a distance.

His wasn't the first attempt to knock the NFL off its perch, of course, but the omens weren't good. The World Football League, begun in 1973, lasted only a season and a half before its collapse. The United States Football League, created in 1983, lasted only three seasons. The Arena Football League, established in 1987, remained viable well into the new century with its potent blend of fast action, small venues, and low expectations, and even launched the NFL career of quarterback Kurt Warner, who went on to become the NFL's Most Valuable Player and lead the St. Louis Rams to victory in Super Bowl XXXIV. But unlike the XFL, it never aspired to displacing the NFL.

McMahon had no patience for small dreams. He wanted nothing less than to meld the excitement of pro football with the melodrama of pro wrestling, creating a hybrid that would electrify the lives and libidos of young American men. It's a testament to the strength of McMahon's vision that Ebersol, the head of NBC's sports operation, got caught up in the excitement. His network no longer was broadcasting professional football games, having lost its coveted NFL contract to a rival network after the 1997 season, and in mid-2000 it was also the only major network without one of the new reality television shows that were becoming so popular. NBC desperately needed programming for the Guy Culture, and McMahon's XFL seemed like just the ticket.

McMahon was talking about bone-jarring mayhem on the field and salacious player-cheerleader fraternization off it. He wanted to do away with some of the NFL's less-than-hairy-chested institutions, including the "fair catch" rule that was designed to protect punt returners from serious injury. Ebersol convinced the network to jump in with both feet, and NBC became an equal partner with McMahon in the XFL. The league's games were suddenly on NBC's schedule for prime-time Saturday night.

McMahon and the network worked hard in the months before launch to cement the league's image as both a legitimate rival to the NFL and a brand of football that promised more violence, more sex, more controversy, more everything. The XFL hired NFL legend Dick Butkus as director of football competition and former pro wrestler and then-sitting Minnesota governor Jesse Ventura as its primary color commentator for game telecasts. It culled nearly four hundred athletes from the roughly four thousand players who applied or sent videotapes of their performances to the league's offices. It announced plans for eight franchises, some in major media markets with established NFL teams, others in cities that were hungry for professional sports action. It dreamed up deliberately edgy names for those teams, including the Memphis Maniax, the Orlando Rage, and the Chicago Enforcers. It began recruiting cheerleaders with just the right joie de vivre. It hired Emmy-winning NBC veteran John Gonzalez to oversee technical aspects of the game broadcasts, including pioneering use of miniature microphones on players, refs, and coaches; on-field camera operators; and the so-called Skycam overhead camera that would give TV viewers a fresh perspective on the game. The XFL encouraged players to put their nicknames on the backs of their jerseys, leading to incomprehensible monikers such as "He Hate Me," "Chuckwagon," and "Thoro," and on the eve of the league's first game, McMahon and Ebersol even decided to inject a little mayhem into what had been an overlooked opportunity for player injury—the coin toss. In the XFL, the first possession would be determined by something called the "Scramble," a whistled two-player sprint for a stationary ball.

While the league's visionaries were clearly making things up as they went along, the NFL nonetheless watched it all with growing concern. In a preemptive move, ABC installed comedian Dennis Miller in the broadcast booth of *Monday Night Football* in the fall of 2001 to contribute smirking commentary and obscure cultural references to its telecast, and Fox added Jimmy Kimmel, the founding host of *The Man Show,* to add a bit of juvenilia to its NFL pregame show. The fight was joined, but as it turned out, it was a really short fight.

They Came, They Saw, They Surfed

From the beginning, little went right. The first-game broadcast, a one-sided snoozer featuring the Las Vegas Outlaws and the New York/New Jersey Hitmen, was a comedy of technical errors, uninspired football, and Ventura's bellowed tripe from the broadcast booth that was intended to establish the league as edgy and full of attitude. The problem with that approach, ESPN pundit Dan Patrick noted later, is that "you can't force being 'edgy.' You either are or you're not. It's not something you announce or declare about yourself."

True, the audience saw and overheard some amazing and innovative things during the broadcast: unprecedented camera perspectives, including from overhead and inside the huddle; plays radioed from the coach to the quarterback; wide shots in which camera operators "ran in and out of the picture like drunks on a dare," wrote Forrest. But they also saw and heard things that suggested the XFL was launched a wee bit prematurely. Lead commentator Jesse Ventura took every opportunity to hype the league rather than describe the action, giving the broadcast the desperate air of a doorstep sales pitch. His exchanges with co-commentator Matt Vasgersian came across, at best, as unhelpful, and at worst as chummy frat-boy innuendo. ("Lot of heavy breathing out there," Vasgersian said as the field mikes transmitted the sound of the players huffing and puffing. "Sounds like a prank call.") McMahon and Ebersol had identified Outlaws coach Rusty Tillman as potentially volatile on the sidelines, and the commentators kept hyping an explosion that never came. In uncomfortably extended shots of the cheerleaders, the women came across less as enthusiastic supporters of the battling teams and more as unemployed centerfolds auditioning for a pole-dance gig. On cue, NBC cameras panned the crowd to create the impression that the XFL was a magnet for celebrities, but the best they could do was find one of the network's own, *Saturday Night Live* and future *Just Shoot Me* star David Spade.

To the home audience, those things didn't come across as sideshows to the tepid football on the field. Rather, they actually seemed to *be* the show. Plus, 19–0 blowouts aren't exactly must-see TV, which is why NBC switched to a more competitive secondary game broadcast, anchored by blustery former pro wrestler Jerry Lawler, before the primary game was even finished.

When those February 3, 2001, games were over, though, the television ratings were encouraging—actually, more than encouraging. The broadcast drew an overall 9.5 rating, with each rating point representing roughly a million U.S. households. That was more than twice as many viewers as NBC had guaranteed its advertisers, and it bested even *Monday Night Football* and ESPN's Sunday night NFL coverage among men between the ages of eighteen and thirty-four. But a closer inspection of the numbers was revealing. When the game began, the national rating was 11.7 as the curious tuned in to see what all the noise was about. "Within an hour, the number had dropped to 10.1, the loss of a couple million viewers," wrote Forrest in *Long Bomb*. "By the end of the game, the rating had fallen to 8."

They came, they saw, they surfed away.

The next-day media reviews were a disaster. Newspapers around the country crawled over one another to offer the most scorching critique of the new league. The *New York Times* compared the XFL to "a blight that has crept from the low-rent fringes of cable to network prime time" that "suggests how the lowest television culture is gaining mainstream respectability." McMahon had previously said that the X in XFL signified nothing in particular, so sportswriter Mike Penner of the *Los Angeles Times* suggested possibilities such as "Xceptionally Xaggerated Xpectations" and "Xtravagantly Xcruciating Xecution" and "Xcessively Xcitable Xperts Xuding Xasperation." Everything about the XFL was fair game for critics, including the logo of the L.A. Xtreme, which at least one Web site compared to a stylized swastika.

The rest of the one and only XFL season is remembered mostly for its grim and relentless television ratings slide. The two games broadcast the following day received only a 4.2, already below the 4.5 rating that NBC had guaranteed its advertisers, which were paying an average of $130,000 for each thirty-second spot. By the third week, the XFL broadcasts were the 89th-ranked television show in the country. By the fourth week, Honda, one of the league's original sponsors, had withdrawn its ads and the league was providing free airtime for other advertisers to compensate for its promise of higher ratings. Even exuberantly promoted—and ultimately empty—promises that XFL cameras would take viewers on a fleshy tour of the cheerleaders' locker room at halftime of a game during Week Six brought only minor, and temporary, relief. In the seventh week, the XFL received a 1.6, earning it the dubious distinction as the lowest network prime-time rating in the history of Nielsen Media Research.

The rating for the Million Dollar Game was 2.5, well below the 3.3 rating that the league averaged during its twelve-week season. (By contrast, Super Bowl XXXIX in February 2005 got a 41.3 rating, representing 143.6 million American fans.) Adding insult to injury was the coincidence that the NFL draft was held the same weekend as the Million Dollar Game, and even that mind-numbing auction of high-priced horseflesh drew a 2.65. Or, as Forrest put it in *Long Bomb,* "If ever there was a thing called active disinterest, this was it—several million football fans opting to watch NFL executives gum doughnuts and slurp coffee . . . instead of a living, breathing football championship."

So spectacular was the XFL's failure that in 2004 *Sports Illustrated* included it among the ten "dumbest sports moments" of the past fifty years, along with boxer Mike Tyson's decision to twice bite off chunks of Evander Holyfield's ear during their 1997 bout and the Cleveland Indians' riotous 1974 Ten-Cent Beer Night promotion (see Lesson #13). Still, the careers of McMahon and Ebersol were mostly unaffected, perhaps because they were smart enough to walk away early from the steaming heap they had created.

That's not to say the league hasn't left its mark. The NFL today was shaped by failed leagues that served as laboratories for ideas and innovations, including names on the backs of jerseys and the two-point conversion (the American Football League, which was later absorbed into the NFL), the instant replay (USFL), and the fifteen-minute overtime period (WFL). Many NFL broadcasts now include players wearing tiny microphones that bring their every grunt and grumble to the home viewers, and the cable-guided overhead Skycam shot has become a staple of NFL telecasts. Both innovations flourished first in the XFL. Plus, for years after the league's demise, its cheerleaders lived on in digital form on a Web site (www.officialxfl.com) that recalled nothing so much as catalog of S&M accessories and bondage wear.

In the end, though, the XFL is not remembered just as a failed television sports enterprise, but as a symbol of something far bigger than itself: a cynical attempt to lower the bar for culture in general. As designed, the league was the electronic equivalent of flypaper, an attraction geared to the basest human impulses. Its attempt to use sex and violence to sell second-rate sports came across as pandering even to those who enjoy watching sex and violence. At least *The Man Show* had no pretense. Some even saw in the XFL's demise hope for the future of the nation. As Jay Mariotti put it in the May 21, 2001, issue of the *Sporting News:* "A note of gratitude goes out to the masses for smacking down this farcical disgrace to civilized culture. My faith in the American condition has been restored."

"OH, THE HUMANITY!"

There were unmistakable hints of doom in the weeks before the nascent XFL kicked off its first and only season. One of those hints was more difficult to ignore than the others.

The new league was working hard to establish itself as a credible rival to the NFL, which partners Vince McMahon and Dick Ebersol hoped to dethrone as the undisputed heavyweight champion of television sports. On January 6, 2001, less than a month before the XFL's opening games, the league unleashed its most provocative secret weapon—a four-thousand-pound, 143-foot-long blimp painted to look like the league's patented black-and-red football.

RECIPE FOR DISASTER
Overheated Mediocrity

Ingredients

1 blustery wrestling promoter with Big Idea
1 desperate television network
Hundreds of second-tier football players
Tons of unjustified hyperbole
Gratuitous sex
Mindless violence

Pair wrestling promoter and network executive in television fishbowl. Recruit players. Combine with hype about sex and violence and let steep for one year, or until overheated. Serve prematurely.

It soared that day over the Oakland Coliseum during an NFL play-off game between Oakland's Raiders and the Miami Dolphins, followed by a plane towing a banner that read: "XFL: The Toughest Football Ever." Despite a chilly reception from the stadium's NFL faithful, the XFL provocateurs planned a second outing for the blimp during the American Football Conference's championship game in Oakland the following Sunday.

But the blimp, like the league, was doomed to an inglorious end. According to Brett Forrest in *Long Bomb,* a gust of wind caught the blimp as its pilot tried to dock at Oakland International Airport three days after its maiden flight. The ground crew was unable to control the craft, and its crew bailed out. The blimp rose unmanned into the sky, drifted for about twenty minutes, and "slammed nose-first into a fish-and-chips shack." The resulting ridicule got the league a lot of attention, though hardly the kind McMahon and Ebersol had in mind.

the quixotic quest for the flying car

As they have for generations, aviation wonks and Popular
Mechanics *subscribers continue working toward the Holy
Grail of private transportation: the flying car. Never
mind that nobody needs one anymore.*

THE LAKEWOOD YACHT Club in Seabrook, Texas, thirty minutes
south of Houston, sponsors an annual "Keels & Wheels" benefit during
which the local swells are invited to display their vintage wooden boats
and exotic antique cars for the benefit of the Boys & Girls Clubs of Greater
Houston. Since 1995, lovingly restored classics have littered the club
grounds and the palm tree–lined inner harbor at the eastern end of Clear
Lake, just three miles from the NASA Space Center, during a weekend of
elegance, wealth, and Texas hospitality.

It says a lot about the enduring nature of an American obsession
that the biggest buzz during the 2003 event was not the collection of
wood-hulled Chris-Craft boats or stunning array of gleaming chariots
from industrial age America, but the appearance of Ed Sweeney, owner of
what he describes as the world's only working flying automobile. Those
attending the event on Saturday looked skyward and saw Sweeney's restored 1950s-era "Aerocar" pass overhead, marveling at what looked like
a cross between a pug-ugly European subcompact and a green-and-yellow
dragonfly. Hundreds of them gathered around the Aerocar as it squatted

on the club grounds, eager to gawk at a technology that was both as quaint as a poodle skirt and as current as the NASA operations just down the road. It wasn't just a nostalgia trip, either; Sweeney brought with him that day a model of the next-generation flying car that he was building using a two-seater Lotus Elise.

At the time, Sweeney was among dozens of entrepreneurs, aircraft engineers, private corporations, and even government agencies that continued to chase the fanciful dream of a practical flying car for the masses—a peculiarly American fascination that combines the relentless quest for independence with the sexy allure of dangerous new technology. The idea of personal air transportation first entered popular culture at an aircraft exposition in 1917, and by 1940 even Henry Ford was predicting the inevitability of flying cars, saying, "Mark my words, a combination of airplane and motorcar is coming. You may smile, but it will soon come." The technofantasy persisted in countless ways, from its cover treatment in *Popular Mechanics* in February 1951, to its futuristic debut on *The Jetsons* cartoon show in 1962, to the flying car in 1968's *Chitty Chitty Bang Bang* and the soaring midcentury Ford Anglia in J. K. Rowling's Harry Potter books and movies. It's hard to imagine an American infatuation that has proved more durable.

That durability, though, is what today makes the ongoing efforts to build a practical flying car so—oh, how should we put this? Poignant? Pointless? What other fantasy has been so steadily pursued and yet so noticeably unfulfilled for so long? The quest for flying cars has outlasted nearly a century of progress as automobiles evolved from rickety contraptions for the few to air bag–studded, fuel-efficient marvels for the masses. It outlasted the evolution of airplanes from cloth-winged death traps into flying buses where the most common aggravations are security checkpoints and dull in-flight movies. There's just something irresistible about the idea of having it all: a home in some pastoral Eden, and a garaged car that can carry you vast distances by air to an office in a teeming modern metropolis or commercial center, then home again in time for dinner.

Of course, in an age when a toll-free tech support call from a frustrated computer user in Indiana is answered by a reassuring English-speaking technician in India, when a buyer in California can order tamales from Texas for next-day delivery to Pennsylvania, when virtually any transaction short of actual coitus can take place with a few computer mouse clicks, one might reasonably wonder if anyone, anywhere, actually still needs a flying car.

But don't expect those modern-day realities to deter the dedicated souls who have committed themselves, sometimes for decades, to achieving the dream. As divined from the never-ending stream of news reports about their various projects and progress, the collective mantra of the flying-car devotees seems to be: *We're going to have a practical flying car one day, damn it, whether we need one or not.*

The Millennium's "Least Important Achievement"?

Summing up that quixotic quest in a special millennium section it published, oddly, in 1990, the *Chicago Tribune* included the flying car on its list of "Least Important Achievements" of the past century, along with the Maginot Line (the defensive perimeter that France built in the 1930s to keep Germany from invading), the antilightning hat, and the eight-track tape deck. "Several of the hybrid machines, part car and part airplane, were actually made," noted *Tribune* writer Frank James. "But despite growing gridlock on the nation's highways, the flying car never got off the ground."

James was writing metaphorically, of course, because certain variations of the flying car have, in fact, flown. Some have even flown high enough to do significant harm to their inventors, including the fabled flying Ford Pinto that in 1973 artlessly detached from its wing structure during takeoff and claimed the lives of its fiercest proponents, Henry Smolinski and Hal Blake of Van Nuys, California. Despite those occasional setbacks, the fantasy has persisted since at least 1917, when aircraft pioneer Glenn Curtiss designed a three-seat flying car for the Pan-

American Aeronautic Exposition in New York. It flew, but like a wounded chicken, and the design understandably failed to achieve widespread public support. But the public imagination caught fire, and in the years after World War I the U.S. government dumped a lot of money into aviation research and design. While that funding mostly went to develop better airplanes, a certain breed of entrepreneur—does the term "pocket protector" conjure any images?—set to work personalizing the dream.

Building a flying car is much like trying to build a brick that will float. "The automobile and the airplane, as we know them, are incompatible in many ways," wrote Lionel Salisbury, the editor of *Roadable Times*, an Internet magazine devoted to the colorful history of flying cars and "roadable aircraft," and a brimming well of optimism about the future of the idea. "Some of [the challenges] may seem insurmountable, but we believe creativity and persistence can be made to prevail."

The main problem is that cars usually perform better when they're heavy, and airplanes perform best when they're not. Plus, a flying-car design must accommodate the unhelpful reality that the ideal center of gravity in a car is different than it is in an airplane. Airplane controls must be designed to operate a vehicle in three axes—roll, pitch, and yaw—while its engine pushes it forward; car controls need only power the car forward or backward, and turn it left or right. What you end up with after combining the two concepts is a vehicle that manages to be both a crappy airplane and a crappy car. Those primary issues overshadow a host of other confounding problems, including convertibility, aesthetics, and marketing.

Still, other wounded chickens began emerging from private garages and hangars between the two world wars, including Waldo Waterman's Studebaker-powered Arrowbile, which in 1937 vividly demonstrated the differing aerodynamic requirements of ground and air vehicles, and an autogyro designed by Juan de la Cierva called the Pitcairn PA-36 Whirlwing, a helicopter-style contraption that in 1939 toyed with the notion of vertical takeoffs and landings. The phenomenon really took off in the heady days after World War II, during a boom in private aviation that writer Bill Yenne dubbed "the golden age of the flying automobile." During those years, according to Palmer Stiles, author of the 1994 book *Roadable Aircraft: From Wheels to Wings,* most of the seventy-plus U.S. patents for flying cars were filed. That was also when "suddenly the vista was endless, promising limitless possibilities," according to Timothy Jacobs, author of *The World's Worst Cars.* "The world was abuzz with new solutions to old problems, and among the many wonders held up was the bright prospect of 'an aircraft in every garage.' "

One of the men who embodied that age was Moulton B. Taylor, who invented the Aerocar in 1949. He recalled for the *Seattle Times* in 1990 that he rounded up fifty investors willing to put up $1,000 each to support his sketch fantasies about a vehicle that would enable them to "fly to the airport, fold up the wings and remove the tail, then leave them at the airport while you drive to wherever you have your business." He built the prototype Aerocar with that money in less than a year at his workshop in Longview, Washington, and it was both an engineering marvel and profoundly unattractive—"a real head-turner, for all the wrong reasons," wrote the Seattle paper. Taylor, a savvy promoter, rolled it out for investors following nine months of development and, to demonstrate its abilities, drove it to a local airport, attached the wings and tail, and flew it back. His success led to an oil company–sponsored promotional tour and an appearance on television's *I've Got a Secret,* during which Taylor and an assistant answered questions from the blindfolded panel for three minutes while they converted the Aerocar from a road vehicle into an airplane. Taylor also raised $750,000 by selling stock in Aerocar Inc. and began the expensive process of government certification, which finally was approved by federal aviation officials on December 13, 1956.

To goose public interest in his odd vehicle, Taylor sold one of the six Aerocars his company produced to actor Robert Cummings, who, according to the *Seattle Times,* "used the Aerocar almost as his co-star in the

'Love That Bob' television series"—an early and generally overlooked example of product placement. Demand for the Aerocar was brisk, and by 1970 no less than Ford Motor Company was talking to Taylor about building twenty-five thousand Aerocars a year.

But at that point, as has become the pattern, the flying-car dream crashed headlong into reality. Seems the only people not enthralled by the idea of a sky full of Aerocars were the nervous folks who managed the nation's air-traffic control system. "There was no way they were going to let us put an additional 25,000 of anything up in the air," said Taylor, whose dream pretty much ended there.

Another dominant figure to emerge from the golden age of flying cars was Connecticut inventor Robert Edison Fulton Jr., who not only was the first man to circumnavigate the globe on a motorcycle, but who began work on his own version of the flying car in 1945—a vehicle which became the first-ever government-certified roadable aircraft three years before Taylor's Aerocar. His two-seat "Airphibian" was based on the same detachable-wing concept as the Aerocar, and it was capable of cruising aloft at 113 miles per hour and driving at 55 miles per hour. Despite that and an endorsement from famed aviator Charles Lindbergh, though, Fulton didn't have Taylor's commercial and promotional instincts, and the Airphibian never went into production. One of the few existing Airphibians ended up in the Smithsonian National Air and Space Museum, which notes that the prototypes were driven more than two hundred thousand miles and made more than six thousand car/plane conversions. Each of those conversions was a lengthy and complicated pain in the butt, which ultimately made the Airphibian impractical.

As of early 2005, according to *Roadable Times*'s Salisbury, the Aerocar and the Airphibian were the only two "roadable aircraft" to have been certified by federal aviation authorities. Not that others haven't tried. Among the other post–World War II designs were a sixteen-foot car with a thirty-five-foot wingspan called the Boggs Airmaster; a quickly convertible critter called the Hervey Travelplane; the ill-fated Convair Model

118 ConvAirCar (which never quite recovered from publicity surrounding a mishap in which a prototype ran out of gas and crashed); and the Whitaker-Zuck Planemobile, which according to one description carried its folded wings on its back "like a hermit crab carries his shell."

Even today, entrepreneurs, engineers, and undeterred aviation wonks—including some backed by major corporations such as Boeing, Honda, and Toyota—continue to invest time, effort, and personal and corporate fortunes in the effort to build and market flying cars. And the public remains fascinated by the possibility, its visions stoked by everything from movies such as *Son of Flubber* and *Blade Runner,* to the promise of lightweight composite materials and powerful rotary engines, to Harry Potter's ride. In early 2005, the production crew of the Discovery Channel's hit custom-car show *Monster Garage* set to work trying to build a flying car out of a Panoz Esperante in just five days for an episode scheduled to air as the show's special two-hour season finale.

Perhaps no one bought into the dream more fully than California aeronautical engineer Paul Moller, who devoted more than forty years and spent tens of millions of dollars—some accounts estimate that he has raised as much as $200 million since the 1960s—trying to build an affordable flying car capable of vertical takeoffs and landings. His M400 Skycar, a sleek cherry red four-seater that looks like a James Bond wet dream, has been far more successful as a public-relations tool than anything else. Its appearance on the covers of magazines such as *Popular Science, Forbes FYI,* and the *Los Angeles Times Magazine* have made it the modern-day poster child for flying-car buffs and kept investor money flowing into Moller's research and development efforts. And to Moller's credit, it actually flies, if primarily in demonstrations during which it has risen and hovered like Harry Potter's magical Anglia, though tethered safely to a crane. There's something unspeakably sad about seeing a magnificent dream so close to reality, but leashed like a dog to a post because the world, after more than a century of dreaming, still isn't ready for it.

Like Cockroaches, Styrofoam, and Disposable Diapers

When the world's inventors were trying to develop practical airplanes in the late 19th and early 20th centuries, they had an obvious advantage over today's flying-car visionaries. If those early aviation pioneers wanted to put something in the air, they simply had to find a place to do it and make a daring leap into the empty sky. Today, though, American airspace is far from empty. Time and again, the nation's air-traffic control system has been strained by the task of managing the existing amount of commercial, military, and civilian aircraft. The thought of launching tens of thousands more aircraft into those overcrowded skies—vehicles owned and operated by the same people who drive their cars while jabbering on cell phones, applying eyeliner, and ingesting Egg McMuffins—gives even the most dedicated flying-car believers pause.

In short, the cart is solidly before the horse on this one. What good are flying cars if no system exists to manage them–especially in a post-9/11 world where the threat of terror from above is a proven reality. The eternally optimistic Moller managed to spin 9/11 as a possible boon to the development of flying cars (since traveling on commercial airlines from regional hub airports has become such a time-consuming hassle), but even he concedes that the infrastructure must be in place before his dream machines become practical. The multibillion-dollar national investment required to build such a system seems about as likely as President George W. Bush's ambitious—but vaguely outlined and achingly underfunded—plan to colonize the moon and undertake a manned mission to Mars, which became a national priority for the entirety of his eighteen-minute speech to NASA on January 15, 2004. And that's where the fantasy and reality collide.

That unavoidable collision finally spelled the end of the flying-car fantasy, right? Well, not quite. The ongoing efforts to push the idea forward may be the greatest demonstration that the dream probably will outlive us all, like cockroaches, Styrofoam cups, and disposable diapers. Beginning in 1999, and with an estimated $69 million in funding, a five-year research project got under way using the combined resources of NASA, the Federal Aviation Administration, and the private National Consortium for Aviation Mobility. The purpose of the Small Aircraft Transportation Systems, or SATS, project: to demonstrate that, by using the approximately 3,400 small airports around the country, "there could be a future safe and affordable travel alternative to driving by auto or flying on commercial airlines." Most Americans live within twenty miles of one of those airports, the SATS researchers claim, and they envision a decentralized air-transportation system that relies more on computer-guided "air taxis" than on scheduled high-volume commercial carriers flying into regional hubs. One concept under discussion, according to a NASA researcher, is navigational technology that would make air taxis and flying cars behave more like a horse—a creature that instinctively avoids other objects and may even know how to find its way home.

In June 2005, the SATS researchers culminated their research by inviting aviation entrepreneurs and enthusiasts, business executives, congressional leaders, state and local economic development officials, and members of key science and aviation agencies to Danville, Virginia, for a weekend celebration of possibilities called "SATS 2005: A Transformation in Air Travel." There, today's most avid proponents of the dream conjured tantalizing evidence that a flying-car future is finally within reach. They were not dissuaded by Mark Moore, head of the Personal Air Vehicle Division of the Vehicle Systems Program at NASA's Langley Research Center in Hampton, Virginia, who cautioned that anything "remotely Jetsons-like" is at least twenty-five years away.

Even that seems hopelessly optimistic. Fixated on the technological challenges, the culture hasn't even begun to grapple with the many other issues that would arise if cars began to fly—pollution, noise, energy efficiency. In a litigious society where neighbors sue one another about barking dogs, imagine the problems that gale-force wind wash from a hovering Skycar might cause along Main Street USA. In an age when full Internet access is as close as your cell phone, when computers seamlessly link homes and offices, when staggering gas prices make even the cost of terra firma commuting prohibitive, who needs the aggravation?

Maybe the continuing quest for flying cars is the culture's subconscious yen for something we can understand and embrace as more complicated technological wonders rush toward us. The *actual* future, in many ways, came without warning. The things that radically changed the world as we know it—instant messaging, picture phones, Napster, scoop-shaped tortilla chips—don't turn up in the sci-fi visions into which we all bought while reading Jules Verne or George Orwell.

But a flying car? Now that's cool.

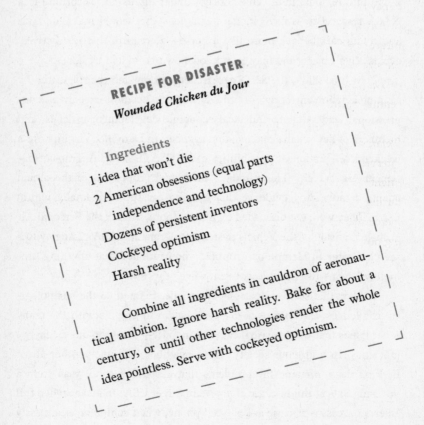

RECIPE FOR DISASTER
Wounded Chicken du Jour

Ingredients
1 idea that won't die
2 American obsessions (equal parts independence and technology)
Dozens of persistent inventors
Cockeyed optimism
Harsh reality

Combine all ingredients in cauldron of aeronautical ambition. Ignore harsh reality. Bake for about a century, or until other technologies render the whole idea pointless. Serve with cockeyed optimism.

AND STILL, THE DREAM PERSISTS

If you're looking for a logical expiration date on the American flying-car fantasy, you might try 1996. That was the year when America Online launched a series of television commercials that, in a subtly subversive way, heralded the real technology that made the notion of flying cars seem *so* last century.

The fast-paced spots depicted a modern family embracing the future by using computers, the Internet, cell phones, and other communications technologies to conduct their lives and careers. To score the ads, the agency that created them, TBWA Chiat/Day New York, convinced AOL to pay Hanna-Barbera $1 million for the rights to a song that, at one point in American history, represented a very different view of the future, a future where every home had a spaceport and flying cars folded neatly to the size of a briefcase. The commercial's sound track was the theme song to *The Jetsons,* and it might well have served as ironic punctuation for a century of dreaming.

But dreams die hard. Three years later, in 1999, writer Kristina Stefanova of the *Washington Times* conducted random man-on-the-street interviews and asked passersby what marvels they thought the future might hold. After more than a century of flying-car experimentation, during which even the few that actually got off the ground proved commercially impractical, two of the six respondents focused on the intriguing possibility of . . . flying cars.

fiascoes that failed to qualify for oops

FOR EVERY FIASCO that met the high qualification standards necessary for inclusion in *Oops*—spectacular failure, undeniable cultural impact, a certain inspired goofiness—recent history contains scores of mistakes that are not quite as momentous or influential (though they often are mind-bogglingly outlandish). Since our readers tend to be at least as obsessed with weird trivia as we are, here is a sampling of *Oops* also-rans that we considered, but which didn't quite make the final cut.

We've left out some of the more familiar ones, such as New Coke, Michael Dukakis's 1988 presidential campaign, and Michael Jordan's baseball career. But we're confident that the following still have the potential to stimulate pleasurable frontal-lobe activity while you're caught in a traffic jam, sitting in your dentist's waiting room, or feigning enthusiasm for your nephew's rendition of "Stairway to Heaven" on the ocarina.

The "Crash at Crush"

This was perhaps the dumbest publicity stunt in history. In 1896, the Missouri, Kansas & Texas Railroad hired William G. Crush, a protégé of P. T. Barnum, as its promoter. His idea to draw attention to the struggling railroad was to stage a spectacular collision between two speeding locomotives. Most of the fifty thousand people who gathered for the 1896 spectacle survived, though many with painful injuries from the rain of hot metal upon the makeshift frontier town of Crush after the locomotives' boilers exploded. Willie Crush was fired the same day, but the disaster ultimately *did* boost the railroad's name recognition, launching the loathsome "any publicity is good publicity" public-relations ethic that still persists today.

CIA Assassination Plots Against Castro

Incensed by the failure of the Central Intelligence Agency–organized invasion of Cuba in 1961, the Kennedy White House let the agency know that it wanted something done about the island's defiant, hirsute dictator. CIA men developed about six hundred different proposals for eliminating Fidel Castro, many of them involving gadgetry better suited for Rube Goldberg than James Bond—an exploding seashell, a poison-lined wet suit, a ballpoint pen–hypodermic needle filled with poison, botulism-laced Cuban cuisine. One particularly inane plot would have contaminated his shoes with thallium salts, a depilatory, to make his beard fall out—the theory being that without his trademark facial hair, Castro would seem less powerful. Not surprisingly, El Presidente continued to thumb his nose safely at the U.S. for decades.

G.I. Nurse Action Girl

After the twelve-inch "action figure" G.I. Joe became a hit for Hasbro in the mid-1960s, the toymaker sought to expand the franchise, with mixed results. One particularly short-lived spin-off was G.I. Nurse Action Girl, a bendable blonde clad in a white uniform and nylon stockings. G.I. Nurse had a few design flaws—from the chest down, as one collector has noted, she was actually identical to a male G.I. Joe, only smaller. "It was an extraordinarily ugly doll," toy-collecting expert Sharon Korbeck said in a 2004 interview with *Nurse Week*. "It basically looks like a soldier in a wig." Presumably, elementary-school male G.I. Joe enthusiasts considered G.I. Nurse as yucky as actual females their age, and she quickly disappeared from the market.

The Amphicar

Produced in Germany between 1961 and 1968, the Amphicar was the only mass-produced amphibious passenger automobile (and the only car ever to include a bilge pump as standard equipment). In the water, the Amphicar relied upon twin propellers, with its front wheels functioning as rudders. With a sticker price of about $3,000, the Amphicar was a pretty good deal, and the convenience of being able to go boating and see a drive-in movie on the same outing could not be denied. But when new environmental and safety regulations blocked importation into the United States, the manufacturer, which sold 90 percent of its cars to American customers, soon went under.

The AMC Pacer

Sold between 1975 and 1980, American Motors' egg-shaped Pacer was perhaps the worst-designed, worst-performing American car ever built—a clunker that made the Edsel look like a Porsche 911. AMC scrapped its original plan to give the car a rotary engine, and instead went with a cheaper, underpowered six-cylinder engine. As a result, the Pacer got just fifteen miles per gallon on the highway—bad for any car, horrible for a compact. The car also had a steering system that would occasionally freeze, and an easy-to-pick rear-hatch lock that made the car vulnerable to car thieves, except that there probably weren't many dumb enough to steal one.

The Village People Movie

Hollywood seldom resists the urge to push the latest pop music sensation in front of the camera and churn out a movie. But it's crucial to move quickly. Producer Allan Carr didn't. *Can't Stop the Music,* featuring the none too sexually ambiguous superstars of the late 1970s disco scene, no doubt seemed like a brilliant idea when it was conceived. By the time it hit the theaters in 1980, however, the dance-music craze was dead, and the movie's awfulness only served to shovel more dirt on disco's coffin.

Can't Stop the Music remains a video-store cult curiosity. It's notable not only for its lack of a coherent plot and its gratuitous splashing-in-the-pool beefcake scenes, but for the acting debut of former Olympic gold-medal winner Bruce Jenner—of whom one Web movie reviewer notes, "He has no discernible acting ability, but seems like Kenneth Branagh compared to the rest."

The Smokeless Cigarette

In the early 1980s, with smokers' lawsuits presenting a threat to the tobacco industry's survival, cigarette manufacturer RJ Reynolds spent $800 million on a top secret product-development effort. The result was Premier. It looked like a regular cigarette, but contained only a tiny amount of tobacco, which was heated, rather than burned, by a special device in the tip and then filtered through "flavor beads" when a smoker inhaled. Premier created almost no smoke and few of the carcinogens that had gotten the industry into so much trouble. The problem was that smokers hated the taste, which a Japanese focus group described by repeating an expression in their language that company officials translated into English as "tastes like shit." Premier flopped so quickly that Reynolds pulled it from the market after only a year.

The Worst Oscars Telecast Ever

The 61st Academy Awards in 1989, also produced by disco auteur Allan Carr (see "The Village People Movie," above), featured a twelve-minute opening musical extravaganza that included dancing cocktail tables, a high-kicking chorus line, Merv Griffin serenading Doris Day and Vincent Price with a rendition of "I've Got a Lovely Bunch of Coconuts," and then-rising young movie star Rob Lowe's Vegas lounge–style version of "Proud Mary," which he sang as a duet with an actress costumed as the Disney version of Snow White—sans permission from the studio, a faux pas that later led to litigation. Other highlights of the broadcast included an even longer production number featuring a Michael Jackson impersonation and a swordfight between actors Christian Slater and Errol Flynn Jr. Gregory Peck, Paul Newman, and other Hollywood greats wrote an open letter to show-business trade papers, calling the show "an embarrassment." Peck even threatened to give back his two statuettes if subsequent shows were as bad.

Miller Lite's "Dick" Campaign

There's such a thing as being too clever. The beer brand's trademark commercials featuring former athletes and bikini-clad models seemed a bit too tame to lure Generation-X consumers, who favored *South Park*–style sarcasm and irony-drenched references to kitschy pop culture. Miller's answer in the late 1990s was a series of commercials that it presented as the work of "Dick," a fictional slacker who was compensated with free beer. The spots featured Dadaesque images and situations, such as an actor in a beaver costume who devoured a log cabin, and another who inexplicably lost control of his arm every time he picked up a bottle of Lite. Instead of reinvigorating the brand, sales dropped. Executive heads rolled, and pretty soon clones of the old commercials were back.

Corporate Theme Songs

For reasons that remain unclear, some technology start-ups in the 1990s Internet boom saw the need to have company anthems, almost as if they were developing nations dreaming of their first Olympic medal ceremonies. Many of the companies, alas, have vanished, but their musical legacies endure, if only as ironic MP3 artifacts traded among Internet wags. One of their faves is the theme of a now-defunct Silicon Valley business software outfit, "Asera Everywhere," which, for want of a better analogy, sounds a bit like early 1980s old-school hip-hop, as interpreted by Pat Boone. But evocative lyrics such as "We're lean and mean, we're takin' control of the e-biz scene" and "you gotta think big, or getcha butt off the pot" are worth savoring.

The Chin Putter

A patent was issued in 2003 for this ingenious, albeit unorthodox, remedy for golfers afflicted with nervous twitches while putting. In the patent sketch, the putter resembles an upside-down Y. The top slides under a golfer's chin, and one of the prongs serves as a stabilizer while the other strikes the ball. Clever, yes, but it's hard to imagine the Royal and Ancient Golf Club of St. Andrews ever approving this one.

Equine Sushi Ice Cream

Unlike wasabi spice and teriyaki-style cooking, Bashasi vanilla ice cream has yet to be imported to America—and it's unlikely that it ever will. The flavor, which reportedly was offered in 2004 at Toyko's Ice-Cream City trade fair, has a special ingredient: chunks of raw horsemeat.

THINK WE BLEW IT?

IF WE OVERLOOKED a terrific fiasco or other pivotal moment that helped shape contemporary culture, please let us know about it. Just visit our Web site, www.oopsbook.com, and drop us an e-mail explaining the idea and how you feel it influenced the world in which we now live.

chapter notes
OR, HOW WE LEARNED THESE TWENTY LESSONS

CREDIBILITY IS EVERYTHING when you're writing a cultural history that includes flaming elephants, government-funded psychics, and a cutting-edge cinematic technology known as Smell-O-Vision. The fact is, we couldn't have made this stuff up, even if we wanted to.

But we also don't expect you to take us at our word, so we've compiled the following chapter notes that identify all of the material we used to research and write this book, or at least all of it we can remember. The notes cite the sources of information we culled from books, newspaper and magazine articles, and Web sites, as well as information we developed by doing our own reporting and interviews.

Rather than bog down the chapters with footnotes, endnotes, or cumbersome attribution, we stuffed all that into this easily avoidable section and hid it way in the back of the book. The information is here if you need it, but really, it's pretty dull stuff, except maybe the citation of the Web site (www.camerashoptacoma.com/narrows.asp) where you can watch video of the Tacoma Narrows Bridge dance the Watusi just before it fell down. That one's kind of fun.

1. *The Eroto-Utopians of Upstate New York*
"About Oneida." www.oneida.com (Dec. 6, 2004).
"About Oneida: Heritage." http://www.oneida.com/static/Heritage.
    ASP?UniqueURL=656811977-2004-12-6-11-41-3/ (Dec. 6,
    2004).

Carden, Maren Lockwood. *Oneida: Utopian Community to Modern Corporation.* Baltimore: Johns Hopkins University Press, 1969.

Dziamka, Kaz. "Rational Sex? The Oneida Community Revisited." http://www.infidels.org/org/ar/articles/dziamka2.html (Dec. 6, 2004).

Fogarty, Robert S. *Desire and Duty at Oneida: Tirzah Miller's Intimate Memoir.* Bloomington and Indianapolis: Indiana University Press, 2000.

Foster, Lawrence, ed. *Free Love in Utopia: John Humphrey Noyes and the Origin of the Oneida Community.* Urbana and Chicago: University of Illinois Press, 2001.

Kern, Louis J. *An Ordered Love: Sex Roles and Sexuality in Victorian Utopias—the Shakers, the Mormons, and the Oneida Community.* Chapel Hill: University of North Carolina Press, 1981.

Noyes, John Humphrey. Letter to David Harrison. Published in the *Battle-Axe and Weapons of War,* newspaper, Aug. 1837.

2. How Thomas Edison Invented Trash Talk

Beals, Gerald. "Major Inventions and Events in the Life of Thomas Alva Edison." http://thomasedison.com/Inventions.htm (Aug. 30, 2004).

Davis, L. J. *Fleet Fire: Thomas Edison and the Pioneers of the Electric Revolution.* New York: Arcade Publishing, 2003.

"Elephant Burial Ground." http://www.roadsideamerica.com/pet/eleph.html (Sept. 9, 2004).

Essig, Mark. *Edison and the Electric Chair: A Story of Light and Death.* New York: Walker & Company, 2003.

Jonnes, Jill. *Empires of Light: Edison, Tesla, Westinghouse, and the Race to Electrify the World.* New York: Random House, 2003.

Moran, Richard. *Executioner's Current: Thomas Edison, George Westinghouse, and the Invention of the Electric Chair.* New York: Alfred A. Knopf, 2002.

Patton, Philip. "Negativity and Product Advertising." *Marketing & Media Decisions*, June 1990.

"PW Forecasts." *Publishers Weekly*, Mar. 24, 2003.

Vanderbilt, Tom. "They Didn't Forget." *New York Times*, July 13, 2003.

Wicks, Frank. "Full Circuit." *Mechanical Engineering—CIME*, Sept. 2000.

3. The Global Underarm Deodorant Disaster

"Antarctic Ozone Hole 20% Smaller This Year." *Los Angeles Times*, Oct. 3, 2004.

Bryson, Bill. *A Short History of Nearly Everything.* New York: Doubleday, 2003.

Cagin, Seth, and Philip Dray. *Between Earth and Sky: How CFCs Changed Our World and Endangered the Ozone Layer*. New York: Pantheon Books, 1993.

"Call for Nominations for Thomas Midgley Award." http://pubs.acs.org/cen/awards/8122/html/8122awardsW.html (Oct. 4, 2004).

Humes, Edward. "The Man Who Saved the World." *Orange Coast Magazine*, Feb. 1996.

Kitman, Jamie Lincoln. "The Secret History of Lead." *Nation*, Mar. 20, 2000.

McNeill, John. *Something New Under the Sun: An Environmental History of the 20th Century*. New York: W. W. Norton, 2000.

Midgley IV, Thomas. *From the Periodic Table to Production: The Life of Thomas Midgley, Jr*. Corona, Calif.: Stargazer Publishing, 2001.

"National Inventors Hall of Fame Announces Seventeen Inductees in 2003." News release from the National Inventors Hall of Fame, Feb. 11, 2003.

Roan, Sharon L. *Ozone Crisis: The 15-Year Evolution of a Sudden Global Emergency*. New York: John Wiley & Sons, 1989.

Thomas, Steve. "How UCI Chemist F. Sherwood Rowland Saved the World." *OC Metro*, May 18, 2000.

4. *Kudzu: A Most Tangled Tale*

Academy Awards Database. http://awardsdatabase.oscars.org/ampas_awards/DisplayCatChron.jsp?curTime=1104449611911 (Dec. 30, 2004).

Alderman, Derek H., and Donna G'Segner Alderman. "Kudzu: A Tale of Two Vines." *Southern Cultures,* Fall 2001.

Aoyugi, Akiko, and William Shurtleff. "The Kudzu Connection." *Mother Earth News,* Mar.–Apr. 1979.

Auchmutey, Jim. "Super-Aggressive Imported Vine Gives a Whole Region the Creeps." *Atlanta Journal-Constitution,* Dec. 12, 1993.

"Bermuda: 'War' Declared on Kudzu, the Quick-Growing, Invasive Japanese Vine." British Broadcasting Corporation, May 15, 2004.

"Cash on the Vine." *Business Week,* Feb. 19, 1944.

"Geography of Massachusetts." http://www.netstates.com/states/geography/ma_geography.htm (Jan. 1, 2005).

Gough, Buddy. "Alien Invaders: Non-Native Eyeing Ozark Ecosystems." *Arkansas Democrat-Gazette,* June 3, 2004.

Gower, Stephen M. *The Art of Killing Kudzu: Management by Encouragement.* Tacoa, Ga.: Lectern Publishing, 1991.

Hipps, Carol Bishop. "Kudzu: A Vegetable Menace That Started Out as a Good Idea." *Horticulture, the Magazine of American Gardening,* June–July 1994.

Kinbacher, Kurt E. "The Tangled Story of Kudzu." *Vulcan Historical Review* 4, Spring 2000.

"Kudzu: *Pueraria lobata.*" Virginia Tech Weed Identification Guide, http://www.ppws.vt.edu/scott/weed_id/puelo.htm (July 12, 2004).

"Kudzu Timeline." http://www.prince.org/msg/100/63795?jump=14 (Dec. 29, 2004).

Lembke, Janet. *Despicable Species: On Cowbirds, Kudzu, Hornworms, and Other Scourges.* New York: Lyons Press, 1999.

"The 100 Worst Ideas of the Century." *Time,* June 14, 1999.

"The Pulitzer Prize Winners 1988." http://www.Pulitzer.org/cgi-bin/
     year.pl?type=w&year=1988&FormsButton2=Retrieve (Dec. 30,
     2004).

"September Events." http://birminghamtrackclub.com/races_Sept.2004.
     html (Dec. 30, 2004).

Stewart, Doug. "Kudzu: Love it—or Run." *Smithsonian,* Oct. 2000.

5. *The Preposterous Collapse of "Galloping Gertie"*

Carson, Rob. "Tacoma's Titanic: Galloping Gertie's World of Wonders."
     Tacoma (Wash.) News Tribune, Aug. 10, 2003.

Duncan, Don. "The Day Gertie Tumbled Down." *Seattle Times,* Nov. 4,
     1990.

George, Kathy. "It Has Been 50 Years Since Gertie Galloped into His-
     tory." *Seattle Post-Intelligencer,* Nov. 2, 1990.

Hobbs, Richard. E-mail interview with Martin J. Smith, Nov. 9, 2004.

Hobbs, Richard. "Lessons from the Failure of a Great Machine." http://
     www.wsdot.wa.gov/TNBhistory/Machine/machine3.htm (Nov. 8,
     2004).

Hobbs, Richard. " 'Most Beautiful in the World'—Art and the 1940s
     Narrows Bridge." http://www.wsdot.wa.gov/TNBhistory/Art/
     art1.htm (Nov. 8, 2004).

Hobbs, Richard. "People of the 1940s Narrows Bridge." http://www.
     wsdot.wa.gov/TNBhistory/People/people1.htm (Nov. 8, 2004).

Hobbs, Richard. "Proposed Bridges for the Tacoma Narrows: A Chro-
     nology." http://www.wsdot.wa.gov/TNBhistory/Connections/
     prop_bridges.htm (Nov. 8, 2004).

Hobbs, Richard. "Tacoma Narrows Bridge Aftermath—a New Begin-
     ning, 1940–1950." http://www.wsdot.wa.gov/TNBHistory/
     Connections/connections4.htm (Nov. 6, 2004).

Hobbs, Richard. "Tacoma Narrows Bridge Aftermath—a New Begin-
     ning, 1940–1950." http://www.wsdot.wa.gov/TNBHistory/
     Connections/connections2.htm (Nov. 10, 2004).

Hobbs, Richard. "Tacoma Narrows Bridge: Weird Facts." http://www.
wsdot.wa.gov/TNBhistory/weirdfacts.htm (Nov. 6, 2004).

Honeycutt, Kirk. "Film Registry Announces 25 New Additions to Select
List." *Hollywood Reporter/Seattle Post-Intelligencer,* Nov. 27, 1998.

Janberg, Nicholas. "Bronx-Whitestone Bridge." *Structuræ: International Database and Gallery of Structures.* http://www.structurae.
net/structures/data/index.cfm?ID=s0000010 (Nov. 11, 2004).

Janberg, Nicholas. "Deer Isle Bridge." *Structuræ: International Database
and Gallery of Structures.* http://www.structurae.net/structures/
data/index.cfm?ID=s0000558 (Nov. 11, 2004).

Janberg, Nicholas. "Leon Solomon Moisseiff (1872–1943)." *Structuræ:
International Database and Gallery of Structures.* http://www.
structurae.net/persons/data/index.cfm?ID=d000067 (Nov. 8,
2004).

Janberg, Nicholas. "Menai Straits Bridge." *Structuræ: International
Database and Gallery of Structures.* http://www.structurae.net/en/
structures/data/s0000091/index.cfm (Nov. 11, 2004).

Janberg, Nicholas. "Niagara Clifton Bridge." *Structuræ: International
Database and Gallery of Structures.* http://www.structurae.net/en/
structures/data/s0000528/index.cfm (Nov. 10, 2004).

Larson, Erik. "A New Science Can Diagnose Sick Buildings—Before
They Collapse." *Smithsonian,* May 1988.

Martin, Rachel. "Coatsworth's Account of the Collapse." http://www.
eng.uab.edu/cee/reu_nsf99/rach_coatsworth.htm (Nov. 10, 2004).

"People & Events: Leon Moisseiff (1872–1943)." *The American Experience.* http://www.pbs.org/wgbh/amex/goldengate/peopleevents/
p_moisseiff.html (Nov. 6, 2004).

Peterson, Ivars. "Rock and Roll Bridge: A New Analysis Challenges the
Common Explanation for a Famous Collapse." *Science News,* June
2, 1990.

Petroski, Henry. *Design Paradigms: Case Histories of Error and Judgment
in Engineering.* New York: Cambridge University Press, 1994.

Petroski, Henry. "Success and Failure in Engineering." *National Forum,* Winter 2001.

Petroski, Henry. *To Engineer Is Human: The Role of Failure in Successful Design.* New York: St. Martin's Press, 1985.

Sullivan, Louis H. "The Tall Office Building Artistically Considered." *Lippincott's Magazine,* Mar. 1896.

"Tacoma Narrows Bridge Failure." http://www.camerashoptacoma.com/narrows.asp (Nov. 11, 2004).

Zasky, Jason. "Suspended Animation: The Tacoma Narrows Bridge." *Failure Magazine.* http://www.failuremag.com/arch_science_tacomanarrows.html (Nov. 6, 2004).

6. The Screeching Diva

Brindle, Marc. "Florence Foster Jenkins, *Even More Glory (???) of the Human Voice.*" http://www.musicweb.uk.net/classrev/2002/May02/FFJ.htm (Feb. 15, 2005).

Browne, David. "Hung Out to Dry: There's Nothing Funny About the Debut CD from American Idol's Most Laughed-at Star." *Entertainment Weekly,* June 23, 2004.

Bryk, William. "A Diva's Carnegie Hall Debut." *New York Sun,* Oct. 6, 2004.

"Caruso, Enrico." *Encyclopaedia Britannica.* http://www.britannica.com/eb/article?tocId=9020571&query=caruso&ct=eb.

Chusid, Irwin. *Songs in the Key of Z: The Curious Universe of Outsider Music,* Chicago: Chicago Review Press, 2000.

Copeland, Libby. "Songs in His Head; Wesley Willis Is Haunted by Voices. His Music Helps Drown Them Out." *Washington Post,* November 24, 2000.

"Cosme McMoon's Recital." *New York Times,* Mar. 23, 1936.

Dixon, Daniel. "Florence Foster Jenkins: The Diva of Din." *Coronet,* Dec. 1957.

"Dreamer." *Time,* Nov. 19, 1934.

"From 'American Idol' Washout to Web Celebrity, William Hung Proves That Nice Guys Finish First." *PR Newswire,* Mar. 4, 2004.

Gardner, Lee. "Irwin Chusid Reveals What's So Good About Playing Badly." *Baltimore City Paper,* Feb. 7, 2001.

Harper, Marques G. "W-B Woman's Off-Key Voice Claim to Fame." *Wilkes-Barre Times Leader,* Nov. 21, 2004.

"Historic Opera." http://www.historicopera.com/jsingerd_D1_page. htm (Feb. 19, 2005).

Hubler, Shawn. "Off-Key, on the Map." *Los Angeles Times,* Feb. 6, 2004.

"Joaquín 'Quinito' Valverde Sanjuán." http://www.zarzuela.net/com/ valverde2.htm (Feb. 16, 2005).

"Julia Friedman Gallery Presents Pablo Helguera Parallel Lives." http:// www.juliafriedman.com/press22.html (Feb. 16, 2005).

"Lady Florence's Triumph." *Newsweek,* Nov. 6, 1944.

MacIntyre, Fergus Gwynplaine. "Happy in Her Work." *New York Daily News,* June 23, 2004.

McMullen, Randy. "Idols' William Hung Inspires an Angry Rant." *Contra Costa Times,* June 4, 2004.

Meimer, Mel. "My New York." *Vidette Messenger* (Valparaiso, Ind.), Apr. 10, 1954.

"Mrs. C. D. Foster Dies; Member of 42 Clubs." *New York Times,* Nov. 8, 1930.

"Mrs. Florence F. Jenkins." *New York Times,* Nov. 27, 1944.

"Mrs. Jenkins Dies; Founder of Verdi Club." *New York Herald Tribune,* Nov. 27, 1944.

Nevin, Ethelbert. "Florence Foster Jenkins & Friends on Naxos." http://www.lafolia.com/archive/nevin/nevin200309jenkins.html (Feb. 16, 2005).

"Outsider Music Mailing List." http://wlt4.home.mindspring.com/ outsider.htm (Feb. 19, 2005).

Orlean, Susan. "Meet the Shaggs." *New Yorker,* Sept. 27, 1999.

Oxman, Steven. "Souvenir." *Variety,* Dec. 13, 2004.

Peter, Laurence J. *Peter's Quotations.* New York: HarperCollins, 1993.

Peters, Brooks. "Florence Nightingale." *Opera News,* June 2001.

Pitou, Spire. *The Paris Opera: An Encyclopedia of Operas, Ballets, Composers, and Performers.* Vol. 3, part 1. Westport, Conn.: Greenwood Press, 1983.

"Recital Mill." *Time,* Nov. 2, 1942.

Robinson, Francis. "Liner Notes from the CD *The Glory (????) of the Human Voice.*" http://www.maxbass.com/Florence-Foster-Jenkins.htm (Feb. 16, 2005).

Social Security Death Index. http://www.ancestry.com/search/db.aspx?dbid=3693 (Feb. 20, 2005).

"St. Clair Bayfield, Actor, Is Dead at 91." *New York Times,* May 21, 1967.

Transcript of Interview with Cosme McMoon, KALW-FM, May 26, 1991, posted at http://listproc.ucdavis.edu/archives/mlist/log0402/0004.html (Feb. 21, 2005).

Tuttle, Raymond. "Léo Delibes: Lakmé." http://www.classical.net/music/recs/reviews/e/emi56569a.html (Feb. 16, 2005).

"Who Is Mrs. Miller?" http://www.mrsmillersworld.com/whois_bin/WhoIs.html (Feb. 20, 2005).

"The Will of Charles D. Foster." http://www.rootsweb.com/~paluzern/patk/cfoster.htm (Feb. 15, 2005)

"William Hung Sells 100,000 of Album." United Press, June 14, 2004.

7. The Kaiser-Hughes Flying Boat

Adams, Stephen B. *Mr. Kaiser Goes to Washington: The Rise of a Government Entrepreneur.* Chapel Hill: University of North Carolina Press, 1997.

Barlett, Donald L., and James B. Steele. *Empire: The Life, Legend, and Madness of Howard Hughes.* New York: W. W. Norton, 1979.

Barton, Charles. *Howard Hughes and His Flying Boat.* Fallbrook, Calif.: Aero Publishers, 1982.

Bellis, Mary. "Howard Hughes and the Spruce Goose." http://inventors. about.com/library/inventors/blduramold.htm (Sept. 15, 2004).

Fowler, Raymond D. "Howard Hughes: A Psychological Autopsy." *Psychology Today*, May 1986.

Hack, Richard. *Hughes: The Private Diaries, Memos and Letters.* Beverly Hills: New Millennium Press, 2001.

"David Grant (obituary)." *Los Angeles Times*, Sept. 26, 2001.

"Howard Hughes' Flying Boat." American Society of Mechanical Engineers, http://www.asme.org/history/brochures/h219.pdf (Dec. 3, 2004).

"Howard Hughes' Giant Flying Boat—Popularly Called the Spruce Goose." http://www.air-and-space.com/sprucea.htm (Sept. 15, 2004).

Peltz, James F. "End of an Era: Closure of Building 15 Shuts Book on Hughes Aircraft Complex." *Los Angeles Times*, May 26, 1994.

Rosenfeld, Ira. "Off Target: From the Spruce Goose to Disposable Gliders, the Air Cargo Industry's Success Has Come Among Some Misguided Failures." *Journal of Commerce*, Sept. 29, 1997.

"Spruce Goose Reborn." *Forest Products Journal*, Apr. 2000.

Sterngold, James. "Dreamworks Plans to Build Vast New Lot to Make Films." *New York Times*, Dec. 14, 1995.

"Then and Now: Western Building Empire Spawned Kaiser HMO." *Los Angeles Times*, Oct. 5, 2003.

8. The 1955 Dodge La Femme

Birnbaum, Jane. "Big Three Hope People Will Go Plum Crazy for Purple." *St. Louis Post-Dispatch*, Mar. 26, 1995.

Bonsor, Ken. "How the Volvo 'Your Concept Car' Works." http://auto.howstuffworks.com/volvo-concept2.htm (Dec. 16, 2004).

Bowden, Robert. "Car for Females Left Detroit Pink-Faced." *Tampa Tribune*, Oct. 23, 1995.

"Color by numbers—Research Data Concerning Color, Demographic Trends." *American Demographics,* Feb. 1, 2002.

Cooke, Patrick. "It's a Scarab! It's a Strato Streak! It's a Nucleon! FYI Lovingly Salutes the Biggest Design Misfires in Automotive History." *Forbes FYI,* Mar. 5, 2001.

De Paula, Matthew. "Autofocus." *Bust,* Fall 2004.

"Dodge La Femme Brochure." http://www.duricy.com/~firetone/lafemme/images/55broc3.jpg (Dec. 14, 2004).

"Edith Wharton Chronology from the Edith Wharton Society." http://guweb2.gonzaga.edu/faculty/campbell/wharton/wchron.htm (Dec. 14, 2004).

Harmon, Amy. "U.S. Auto Firms Wonder: What Do Women Want?" *Los Angeles Times,* June 19, 1992.

Heasley, Jerry. "Weird Mustang Facts." *Mustang Monthly,* http://www.mustangmonthly.com/thehistoryof/5866/ (Dec. 14, 2004).

Hindes, Martha. "Supersizing Influence: Women's Needs Shaping GM's New Trucks." http://www.roadandtravel.com/roadtests/buyersguides/companybg/gmtrucks/2003 gmtrucks.htm (Dec. 14, 2004).

Kennedy, Mark. "Autos Once Made Fashion Statements." Associated Press, July 10, 1997.

Lamm, Michael, and David Hollis. *A Century of Automotive Style.* Stockton, Calif.: Lamm-Morada Publishing, 1996.

Lopez, Michael. "Haute Car-ture: An Exhibit in New York City Shows How Automakers in the '50s Tried to Make Interiors Appealing to Women." *Times Union* (Albany, N.Y.), Sept. 20, 1997.

MacKenzie, Angus. "Good Rear End Holds Equal Appeal for Sexes." *Times* (London, U.K.), Dec. 8, 2001.

"Milady Gets a Car of Her Own." *Valley News* (Van Nuys, Calif.), Jan. 10, 1956.

Miller, Chuck. "Highway Hi-Fi: Chrysler's 1950s Car Phonograph

Add-On." *Goldmine,* http://ookworld.com/hiwayhifimiller.html (Dec. 15, 2004).

Motovalli, Jim. "Driving: Pink Power." *New York Times,* Apr. 26, 2002.

"New Airbag Regulation Requires New Family of Dummies." Press release, May 5, 2000. http://www.ftss.com/press_releases. cfm?article=4 (Dec. 14, 2004).

"1954 Imperial Specifications, Equipment, and Historical Notes." Online Imperial Club, http://www.imperialclub.com/Yr/1954/specs. htm (Dec. 14, 2004).

"Peterson Dream Car Display." http://www.river-road.net/oldcars/ petersen/50dreams/08.html (Dec. 14, 2004).

"Putting What Women Really Want in a Car." *Ergonomics Today,* Mar. 19, 2004.

Scharff, Virginia. *Taking the Wheel: Women and the Coming of the Motor Age.* Albuquerque: University of New Mexico Press, 1999.

Sherman, Debra. "Automakers Design with Women in Mind." *Philadelphia Inquirer,* Feb. 11, 1995.

Siuru, Bill. "1955–56 Dodge La Femme." *Auto Week,* Mar. 28, 1994.

Sparke, Penny. *A Century of Car Design.* London: Mark Reazby, 2002.

"Technologies, Challenges, and Research and Development Expenditures for Advanced Air Bags." General Accounting Office, June 12, 2001.

Trentacosta, Rick. "Where Have You Gone, Mrs. Cleaver?" *Forward: The American Heritage of Daimler-Chrysler,* Fall 2000.

Vance, Bill. "Chrysler's Failed Pitch to Women Included Pink Interior, Handbag." *Toronto Star,* Feb. 25, 1989.

9. *The Lingering Reek of "Smell-O-Vision"*

Arnold, Gary. "100% Polyester." *Washington Post,* July 6, 1981.

"Around the World in Eighty Days." http://www.tvguide.com/movies/ database/showmovie.asp?MI=19386 (Jan. 8, 2005).

Banes, Sally. "Olfactory Performances; Aroma in Theatrical Representations." *TDR,* Mar. 22, 2001.

Barrie-Anthony, Steven. "On Scent, We've Barely Scratched the Surface." *Los Angeles Times,* Nov. 4, 2004.

Bone, Paula Fitzgerald. "Does It Matter If It Smells?" *Journal of Advertising,* Winter 1998.

Brown, Geoff. "Broadly Speaking, a Failure." *Times* (London, U.K.), Jan. 26, 1993.

Brown, Janelle. "Scent with Your Site? A New Company Bets on Odor Technology." *Salon,* Oct. 14, 1999.

Camp, Todd. "More Than a Movie: The Best Bits of Ballyhoo." *Fort Worth Star-Telegram,* July 24, 2003.

Chung, Winnie. "Director 'Nose' How to Tell a Love Story." *South China Morning Post,* Dec. 21, 2000.

Chung, Winnie. "Producers Take Whiff of 'Smelly' Movies." *BPI Entertainment News Wire,* July 7, 2000.

"Cinerama Adventure—Michael Todd." http://www.cineramaadventure.com/todd.htm (Jan. 8, 2005).

Conner, Floyd. *The Top 10 Book of Lucky Breaks, Prima Donnas, Box Office Bombs, and Other Oddities.* London: Brassey's, 2002.

Crowther, Bosley. "How Does It Smell?" *New York Times,* Feb. 28, 1960.

Crowther, Bosley. "On Making Scents." *New York Times,* Dec. 13, 1959.

Ewoldt, John. "Fragrance Causes a Stink at Work; for Many, Those Scented Products Can Be Sickening." *San Diego Union-Tribune,* Nov. 26, 2001.

"Exploit-O-Scope: Promotions and Commotions in the Theater." http://www.bampfa.berkeley.edu/pfa_programs/exploit/content.html (Jan. 8, 2005).

"Five Films Will Open Here During Week." *New York Times,* Feb. 15, 1960.

Frumkes, Roy. "An Interview with Michael Todd Jr." http://www.in70mm.com/news/2004/todd_jr/interview.htm (Jan. 8, 2005).

Gerald, Harold. "Audiences Like Perfumed Pictures." *Edwardsville (Ill.) Intelligencer,* Mar. 11, 1943.

Gilles, Midge. "No Sniffing Allowed During the Movie, Please." *Los Angeles Times,* June 17, 1997.

Jones, Stacy. "Odors Added to Films and Video, Even Those of Oranges and Ham." *New York Times,* Nov. 23, 1957.

Jones, Stacy V. "Times Square Conveyor System to Replace Shuttle Is Patented." *New York Times,* Sept. 26, 1959.

Krier, Beth Ann. "The Scenting of America." *Los Angeles Times,* Sept. 8, 1988.

Lewis, Paul. "Michael Todd Jr., 72, a Creator of Smell-O-Vision for Movies." *New York Times,* May 8, 2002.

Lightman, Herb A. "This Movie Has Scents!" *American Cinematographer,* Feb. 1960.

Lovell, Glenn. " 'Odorama' Flap Seems to Favor Nickelodeon over John Waters." *San Jose Mercury News,* June 17, 2003.

"Michael Todd." Wikipedia, http://en.wikipedia.org/wiki/Michael_Todd (Jan. 8. 2005).

"Michael Todd Jr." *Daily Telegraph* (London, U.K.), May 15, 2002.

"Michael Todd Jr." *Register* (London), May 11, 2002.

Moh, Lim Chang. "No Cure for This Stinker." *Malay Mail* (Wilayah Persekutuan), Feb. 7, 2004.

"The Mystery of Smell: The Vivid World of Odors." Howard Hughes Medical Institute, http://www.hhmi.org/senses/d110.html (Jan. 5, 2005).

Nason. Richard. "Smellovision to Get Film Test." *New York Times,* Aug. 19, 1959.

Nason, Richard. "Todd 'Smell' Film May Be Scooped." *New York Times,* Oct. 17, 1959.

"Notes on Science." *New York Times,* July 14, 1946.

"Odor Fatigue." http://www.macalester.edu/~psych/whathap/UBNRP/Smell/odor.html (Jan. 6, 2005).

"Peter Lorre Desperately Ill." *New York Times,* May 11, 1959.

Platt, Charles. "You've Got Smell." *Wired,* Nov. 1999.

"Plot Summary for Lilac Time." http://www.imdb.com/title/tt0019098/ plotsummary (Jan. 6, 2005).

Quigg, Doc. "Movie Producers in Race to Put Out First 'Smelly' Film." United Press, Nov. 5, 1959.

"Reported from the Field of Science." *New York Times,* Feb. 23, 1941.

Rothaus, Steve. "Divine's Mother Looks Back on His Life." *Miami Herald,* Dec. 13, 2001.

" 'Scent of Mystery' Is the First Movie in . . . Smell-O-Vision." *Lima (Ohio) News,* Apr. 4, 1959.

"Sensurround." http://web.uflib.ufl.edu/spec/belknap/exhibit2002/ sense.htm (Jan. 8, 2005).

Slaton, Joyce. "Inane Attractions." *SF Weekly,* July 14, 2004.

"Swiss Inventor Announces New Gadget 'Smellivision.' " United Press, Apr. 22, 1946.

Szabo, Julia. "A Nose with an Eye." *New York Times Magazine,* Apr. 1, 2001.

"Terra Lycos's Wired News Unveils the Year's Most Overhyped New Technologies That Never Were with the 2001 Vaporware Awards." *Business Wire,* Jan. 7, 2002.

Thomas, Bob. "Hollywood Highlights." *Manitowoc (Wis.) Herald Times,* Jan. 28, 1960.

"THX." http://en.wikipedia.org/wiki/THX (Jan. 12, 2005).

"The Thrill Killers." http://www.imdb.com/title/tt0058653/ (Jan. 8, 2005).

"Trivia for The Broadway Melody (1929)." http://www.imdb.com/title/ tt0019729/trivia (Jan 6, 2005).

Uter, W., et.al. "Association Between Occupation and Contact Allergy to the Fragrance Mix: A Multifactorial Analysis of National Surveillance Data." *Occupational and Environmental Medicine,* June 2001.

Vallance, Tom. "Obituary: Michael Todd Jr., Pioneer of 'Smell-O-Vision.' " *Independent* (London, U.K.), May 10, 2002.

Weiler, A. H. "By Way of Report." *New York Times,* Feb. 18, 1962.

Weiler, A. H. "Passing Picture Scene." *New York Times,* July 12, 1959.

Wilson, Earl. Syndicated column, Feb. 3, 1958.

10. *The Paper Dress*

Barkett, Cy. "Paper Dress Business Needs Much More Testing." *Elvira (Ohio) Chronicle-Telegram,* May 11, 1967.

Bitz, Karen. "Safety First; Comfort Second." *Nonwovens Industry,* Feb. 1, 2004.

Bowman, Sylvia E. *The Year 2000: A Critical Biography of Edward Bellamy.* New York: Bookman Associates, 1958.

Budge, Rose Mary. "Fast Forward to the Future." *San Antonio Express-News,* Sept. 5, 1999.

Carleton, Helen. "The Wastebasket Dress Has Arrived." *Life,* Nov. 25, 1966.

Cassini, Oleg. "Oleg Cassini Says. . . . Paper Dress Fad Appeals Most to Attention Seekers." *Mansfield News Journal,* Jan. 15, 1967.

"Disposable." http://www.2wice.org/issues/uniform/disp.html (Sept. 20, 2004).

Huckbody, Jamie. "Starship Trooper." *Independent* (London, U.K.), Mar. 8, 2003.

"KAYCEL Scrim Reinforced Material Provides Absorbency and Strength for Disposable Towels." http://www.kcnonwovens.com/kaycel.html (Jan. 1, 2005).

"Kimberly-Clark Initiates Changes in Paper Machines." *Appleton (Wis.) Post-Crescent,* Dec. 13, 1965.

LaRue, Arlene. "Want to Paper a New Dress?" *Syracuse Herald Journal,* July 27, 1956.

Niepold, Mary Martin. "Designing Women: Fashion at the End of the Century." Copley News Service, Feb. 28, 1999.

"Nonwovens Time Line." *Nonwovens Industry,* Dec. 1, 1994.

Palmer, Alexandra. "Paper Clothes: Not Just a Fad." In *Dress and Popular Culture,* ed. Patricia A. Cunningham and Susan Voso Lab. Bowling Green, Ohio: Bowling Green University Popular Press, 1991.

"The Paper Caper Dress." http://www.kimberly-clark.com/aboutus/paper_dresses.asp (Sept. 20, 2004).

"Paper Dress Here to Stay." *Bucks County (PA) Courier Times,* Aug. 11, 1967.

"Paper Dress Passes Fire Safety Dress." Associated Press, Dec. 23, 1966.

"PFFC 75th Anniversary Timeline." http://pffc-online.com/news/paper_Sept._timeline_3/ (Jan. 1, 2005).

"Potpourri." *Great Bend (Kans.) Daily Tribune,* July 10, 1966.

Schaer, Sydney C. "Recycling a Fad into Fashion." *Newsday,* Feb. 12, 1999.

"Scott Paper Starts New Fashion Look." *Advertising Age,* Mar. 29, 1999.

Stezzi, Mary Ellen. "The New, New, Paper Dress—Color It Fashion." *Bucks County (Pa.) Courier Times,* April 22, 1966.

Strasser, Susan. "A Look At . . . What We Throw Away." *Washington Post,* Oct. 17, 1999.

"Style.com Fashion Shows: Collections: S2005RTW Review." http://www.style.com/fashionshows/collections/S2005RTW/review/UNDERCOV (Jan. 2, 2005).

Taylor, Angela. "Whatever Happened to the Paper Dress?" *Syracuse Journal-American,* July 1, 1969.

"They Wear Paper Sacks to the Ball." *Walla Walla Union Bulletin,* Oct. 24, 1966.

"Wardrobe Fire Danger Possible." United Press, July 27, 1967.

11. *The U.S. Psychic Friends Program*

ABC News Nightline, Transcript, Nov. 28, 1995.

"American Taxpayer Losing War on Waste." Congressional Press Releases, July 28, 1997.

"Analysis of a Remote-Viewing Experiment of URDF-3 (Author's Name Redacted)." Central Intelligence Agency, Dec. 4, 1975. http://www.gwu.edu/nsarchiv/NSAEBB/NSAEBB54/st36.pdf (Mar. 10, 2005).

Broad, William J. "Pentagon Is Said to Focus on ESP for Wartime Use." *New York Times,* Jan. 10, 1984.

Druckman, Daniel, and John A. Swets. *Enhancing Human Performance: Issues, Theories, and Techniques.* Committee on Techniques for the Enhancement of Human Performance, Commission on Behavioral and Social Sciences and Education National Research Council, 1988.

Geller, Uri. "Psychic and Paranormal." *Jerusalem Post,* Oct. 29, 1999.

Kale, Wendy. "Clairvoyant Discusses Details of 'Remote Viewing.' " *Colorado Daily* (Boulder), Jan. 9, 2002.

"Kazakhstan: Semipalatinsk Test Site." http://www.nti.org/db/nisprofs/kazakst/weafacil/semipala.htm (Mar. 10, 2005).

LaMothe, John D. *Controlled Offensive Behavior—USSR.* Defense Intelligence Agency, July 1972. http://www.dia.mil/Public/Foia/cont_ussr.pdf (Mar. 11, 2005).

Leblanc, Pamela. "Remote Viewing Keeps Attracting Believers." Cox News Service, July 12, 2002.

Lumpkin, John J. "CIA Satellites Worked, Spy Cats Didn't, Recently Declassified Documents Show." Associated Press, Sept. 10, 2001.

McMoneagle, Joseph. *The Stargate Chronicles.* Charlottesville, Va.: Hampton Roads Publishing, 2002.

Monk, John. "CIA Lifted Astral Lid for Rose." *Charlotte Observer,* Dec. 10, 1995.

Mumford, Michael D., Andrew M. Rose, and David S. Goslin. "An Evaluation of Remote Viewing Research and Applications." National Institutes of Research, Sept. 29, 1995.

Neimark, Jill. "Do the Spirits Move You?" *Psychology Today,* Sept.–Oct. 1996.

Osgood, Charles. "Mind Games; Taking a Look at America's Passion for the Paranormal." CBS News, Apr. 28, 2002.

Puthoff, H. E. "CIA-Initiated Remote Viewing at Stanford Research Institute." http://www.irva.org/papers/CIA_RV_SRI.html (Mar. 11, 2005).

Sandaine, Kerri. "Psychic Search 'on Right Track.' " *Lewiston (Idaho) Morning Tribune,* July 13, 2004.

Sanger, David A. "Intelligence: Why a Fix Is So Elusive." *New York Times,* Aug. 15, 2004.

Smith, Paul H. "RV History: A Brief Time Line of Remote Viewing History." International Remote Viewing Association, http://www.irva.org/papers/RVTimeline.html (Mar. 10, 2005).

Smith, Paul H. "What Is Remote Viewing?" International Remote Viewing Association, http://www.irva.org/papers/WhatisRV.html (Mar. 10, 2005).

Smith, R. Jeffrey. "Senators Kept Psychic Intelligence Program Alive, Staff Aides Say." *Washington Post,* Dec. 1, 1995.

Squires, Sally. "The Pentagon's Twilight Zone." *Washington Post,* Apr. 17, 1988.

Vistica, Gregory. "Psychics and Spooks." *Newsweek,* Dec. 11, 1995.

Waller, Douglas. "The Vision Thing." *Time,* Dec. 11, 1995.

12. *The 1967 Jimi Hendrix–Monkees Concert Tour*

Avasthi, Surabhi. "Q and A: The Monkees' Mickey Dolenz." *New York Daily News,* July 21, 1996.

Bahls, Roy A. "Monkees 30th Anniversary Tour Brings Out Fans." *Norfolk Virginian-Pilot,* Aug. 7, 1996.

Baker, Glen A. (assisted by Tom Czarnota and Peter Hogan). *Monkeemania: The True Story of the Monkees.* London: Plexus, 1986.

Black, Johnny. *Hendrix: The Ultimate Experience.* New York: Thunder's Mouth Press, 1999.

"BruceBase 1974." http://www.brucebase.shetland.co.uk/gig1974.htm (Mar. 8, 2005).

"Buddy Miles Bio and Photo Page." http://www.buddymiles.com/bio.html (Mar. 8, 2005).

Dolenz, Micky, and Mark Bego. *I'm a Believer: My Life of Monkees, Music, and Madness.* New York: Cooper Square Press, 1993.

"Douglas DC-6." http://www.flyinghigher.net/douglas/NC90739.php (Nov. 6, 2004).

Duff, S. I. "Jimi and the Monkees." *Guitar World,* Mar. 1988.

"Electric (Late 1960s, Early 1970s)." Shasta College Music Department, http://www3.shastacollege.edu/music/hrj/chap22.html (Nov. 18, 2004).

"A FANtastic weekend! City Vibrated with Music from Hip-hop to Gospel." *Chicago Defender,* Apr. 10, 2002.

Friedlander, Paul. *Rock and Roll: A Social History.* Boulder, Colo.: Westview Press, 1996.

Handelman, Jay. "Hey Hey, They're the Monkees." *Sarasota Herald Tribune,* Jan. 20, 1997.

Henderson, David. *'Scuse Me, While I Kiss the Sky: The Life of Jimi Hendrix.* New York: Doubleday, 1978.

Ivry, Bob, and Barbara Jaeger. "Glory Days." *Record* (Bergen County, N.J.), Mar. 14, 1999.

Kulick, Bob, and Art Thompson. "Hendrix at the Crossroads; Spirit of '66: When Jimi Was Jimmy James." *Guitar Player,* Sept. 1995.

Lefcowitz, Eric. *The Monkees Tale.* San Francisco: Last Gasp of San Francisco, 1989.

McDermott, John, and Eddie Kramer. *Hendrix: Setting the Record Straight.* New York: Warner Books, 1992.

Mitchell, Mitch. *Hendrix: Inside the Experience*. New York: Harmony Books, 1990.

"The Monkees." http://en.wikipedia.org/wiki/The_Monkees (Nov. 19, 2004).

"The Monkees." http://www.nostalgiacentral.com/music/monkees.htm (Nov. 15, 2004).

"Monkees Truth: Interesting Facts." http://www.loveisonlysleeping. com/Monkees/MonkeesTruth/ (Mar. 8, 2005).

" 'N Sync Get Intimate on Tour." http://www.rollingstone.com/news/ story/_/id/5931661 (Nov. 21, 2004).

Pesant, Steven C. "There Was an Attraction to Hendrix: He Was Hot! One on One with Dick Clark." *Experience Hendrix*. http://www. jimihendrix.com/magazine/601/601,interview,dickclark.html (Nov. 21, 2004).

Redding, Noel, and Carol Appleby. *Are You Experienced: The Inside Story of the Jimi Hendrix Experience*. London: Fourth Estate, 1990.

Shapiro, Harry, and Caesar Glebbeek. *Jimi Hendrix: Electric Gypsy*. New York: St. Martin's Press, 1990.

"Sgt. Pepper's Lonely Hearts Club Band." http://en.wikipedia.org/wiki/ Sgt._Pepper's_Lonely_Hearts_Club_Band (Nov. 14, 2004).

"Tour Diary." http://www.smashmouth.com/diary_mar_02.html (Mar. 8, 2005).

"Touring." http://www.psycho-jello.com/monkees/tours.html (Mar. 8, 2005).

"The Walker Brothers." http://www.vh1.com/artists/az/ walker_brothers/bio.jhtml (Mar. 8, 2005).

Wooten, Frank. "Hey, Hey: Monkees Are Back to Set Their Records Straight." *Charleston (S.C.) Post and Courier*, Jan. 16, 1997.

13. *The Cleveland Indians' Ten-Cent Beer Night*

Barnes, Bart. "Mickey Mantle, Legend of Baseball, Dies at 63." *Washington Post*, Aug. 14, 1995.

Dyer, Bob. *Cleveland Sports Legends: The 20 Most Glorious & Gut-Wrenching Moments of All Time*. Cleveland: Gray & Company, 2003.

Felton, Bruce, and Mark Fowler. *The Best, Worst, and Most Unusual: Noteworthy Achievements, Events, Feats, and Blunders of Every Conceivable Kind*. Edison, N.J.: Barnes & Noble Books, 1976.

Fimrite, Ron. "Take Me Out to the Brawl Game." *Sports Illustrated*, June 17, 1974.

Fisher, Eric. "Drunken Fans Pose Ongoing Problem for Baseball Teams." *Washington Times*, May 28, 2000.

Gershman, Michael. *Diamonds: The Evolution of the Ballpark*. Boston: Houghton Mifflin, 1993.

Hans, Dennis. "The Budweiser National Pastime." http://www.alternet.org/module/printversion/9422 (Oct. 22, 2004).

Hruby, Patrick. "Love Story: Beer and Sports, So Happy Together." *Washington Times*, June 17, 2003.

Kitman, Jamie. "Baseball's New Family Image." *Nation*, Apr. 26, 1986.

Lamb, David. "Dennis J. Kucinich: The Onetime Boy Mayor of Cleveland Is Still a Maverick After All These Years and Proudly Wears the Liberal Label." *Los Angeles Times*, July 13, 2003.

Latimer, Clay. "Abusive Fans Turn Ballparks into Battle Zones." *Rocky Mountain News* (Denver), May 31, 2000.

Lewis, Jerry M. "Fan Violence: An American Social Problem." In *Research in Social Problems and Public Policy*, ed. Michael Lewis and Joann L. Mille. Greenwich, Conn., and London: JAI Press, 1982.

Lewis, Jerry M. Telephone interview with Martin J. Smith, Oct. 15, 2004.

"MADD Milestones." http://www.madd.org/aboutus/1,1056,1179,00.html (Oct. 7, 2004).

Nemec, David. *The Beer and Whiskey League*. New York: Lyons & Burford, 1994.

O'Connor, Ian. "Alcohol Puts Damper on Fun and Games." *USA Today,* Apr. 17, 2003.

Rushin, Steve. "Dumbest Sports Moments." *Sports Illustrated 50th Anniversary Issue,* Sept. 27, 2004.

Scanlan, Wayne. "When Promotions Go Bad, They Really Go Bad." *Leader-Post* (Regina, Saskatchewan, Canada), May 14, 2004.

Smith, Martin J. "Retake on the Lake." *Pittsburgh Press Sunday Magazine,* Mar. 24, 1985.

Torry, Jack. *Endless Summers: The Fall and Rise of the Cleveland Indians.* South Bend, Ind.: Diamond Communications, 1995.

Verducci, Tom. "Blood and Guts: In Their Quest to KO the Cardinals—and the Curse—Curt Schilling and the Red Sox Got Off on the Right Foot." *Sports Illustrated,* Nov. 1, 2004.

14. *The Sixty-Story John Hancock Guillotine*

"Broken Glass, Soaring Costs; Travails of a Skyscraper—Last of Its Kind?" *U.S. News & World Report,* July 12, 1976.

Campbell, Robert. "Builder Faced Bigger Crisis Than Falling Windows." *Boston Globe,* Mar. 3, 1995.

Cox, Christopher. "Hub Walking Tour Offers Dark Passage to Calamities." *Boston Herald,* Sept. 3, 2004.

"Famous Properties: Boston's Signature Skyscraper." *Journal of Property Management,* July 1, 2004.

Feeney, Mark. "Initially Plagued by Controversy, the John Hancock Tower Has Become a Prized Part of the City's Skyline." *Boston Globe,* Apr. 29, 2003.

Fuller, Tony, and Lynn Langway. "The Glass Menagerie." *Newsweek,* Apr. 26, 1976.

Hales, Linda. "Architect at the Apex; I. M. Pei's Pyramids and Sharp Angles Have Taken Him in One Direction: To the Top." *Washington Post,* Oct. 5, 2003.

"Hancock Tower Sold for $910 million." Associated Press, Mar. 14, 2003.

Janberg, Nicolas. "John Hancock Tower." *Structuræ: International Database and Gallery of Structures.* http://www.structurae. net/structures/data/index.cfm?ID=s0000035 (Jan. 5, 2005).

Petroski, Henry. *To Engineer Is Human: The Role of Failure in Successful Design.* New York: St. Martin's Press, 1982.

"The New John Hancock Building: An Example of Public and Private Decision-Making." Boston Architectural Center Conference, Boston, Mass., May 4, 1968.

"The Top Technological Blunders of the (Just Past) 20th Century." *Business Week,* Jan. 17, 2000.

Washburn, Gary, and Terry Wilson. "Skyscraper Glass Falls, Kills Mother; Young Girl at Her Side in Loop Nightmare." *Chicago Tribune,* Oct. 9, 1999.

Wiseman, Carter. *I. M. Pei: A Profile in American Architecture.* Rev. ed. New York: Harry N. Abrams, 2001.

15. *Male Fashion's Fabulous Faux Pas*

Adato, Allison, and David Burnett. "Life Goes to . . . a Leisure Suit Convention." *Life,* Feb. 1996.

Ad from *Lincoln (Neb.) Star,* June 1, 1975.

Ad from *Sheboygan (Wis.) Press,* Mar. 26, 1973.

Ad from *Syracuse Herald Journal,* Mar. 23, 1975.

Bachhuber, Billie. "Who Killed Leisure Suits? Men, Media and Manu- facturers." *Chicago Daily Herald,* Jan. 31, 1978.

Bakke, Bruce. "Improving the Image of Polyester." United Press, May 5, 1983.

Becker, Bart. "Leisure Look in Bold Prints Will Catch His Eye." *Lincoln (Neb.) Evening Journal,* Dec. 15, 1974.

Barmash, Isadore. "Retailers Are Pushing Early Summer Clearance Sales." *New York Times,* June 21, 1976.

Beicher, Elisa, Paul N. Keaton, and William A Pollman. "Casual Dress at Work." *ASAM Advanced Management Journal*, 1999.

Beyette, Beverly, and Gaile Robinson. "Esther Williams Suiting Up Again." *Los Angeles Times*, June 10, 1991.

Botto, Louis. "The Great Safari Suit Flap." *New York Times*, Sept. 15, 1974.

"Brave New Items." *New York Times*, Sept. 21, 1952.

Brennan, Tom. "Skip the Necktie: Leisure Suit Popular." *Mansfield (Ohio) News Journal*, Nov. 16, 1974.

Cartner-Morley, Jess. "Style: The Dear Leader's Look (and How to Get It)." *Guardian* (London, U.K.), May 4, 2001.

Dougherty, Philip H. "From the Jungle to Main Street, Emergence of the Safari Suit." *New York Times*, June 26, 1975.

Dougherty, Philip H. "The University Shop Falls Victim to the Undressed-Up Look." *New York Times*, Feb. 24, 1975.

Dowling, Denise. "The Seventh Annual International Leisure Suit Convention." http://desires.com/1.4/Style/Docs/leisure.html (Oct. 6, 2004).

Ettorre, Barbara. "Businessmen and Buttonholes." *New York Times*, Oct. 28, 1979.

"Fresh Fields for Corduroy." *New York Times*, Sept. 13, 1964.

Fritsch, Jane. "Cabbies Told to Clean Up Their Act." *Los Angeles Times*, Mar. 30, 1990.

"Goodbye to Wingtips: Public Opinion on Menswear Swinging Toward the Splashy." *Time*, Nov. 19, 1973.

Johnson, Craig, and Brian Mullen. *The Psychology of Consumer Behavior*. Hillsdale, N.J.: Lawrence Erlbaum Associates, 1990.

Haggie, Helen. " 'Esquire' Fashion Chief: Gray Suit Long Gone." *Lincoln (Neb.) Evening Journal*, Oct. 31, 1975.

"Hart Schaffner Says 2nd Period Net About Equal to Year Ago." Dow Jones News Service, June 20, 1980.

Hix, Charles. "Leisure Suits Are Now Coming of Age." *Fond du Lac (Wis.) Reporter,* Apr. 7, 1976.

Hollander, Ann. "Clothes Make the Man—Uneasy." *New Republic,* Sept. 7, 1974.

"How to Wear Suit Important to Men." *Newark (Ohio) Advocate,* Dec. 4, 1975.

Klaffke, Pamela. "Ladies of Leisure (Suits) Back in Style." *Calgary Herald,* Oct. 3, 2002.

Klages, Karen E. "Let's Get Comfy! Corporate America Begins to Say a More 'Casual Look' Suits Them Just Fine." *Chicago Tribune,* June 17, 1992.

Kron, Joan. "A Few Daring Dressers Risk Sneers to Push Menswear into the Future." *Wall Street Journal,* Mar. 11, 1986.

Lause, Kevin, and Jack Nachbar, eds. *Popular Culture: An Introductory Text.* Bowling Green, Ohio: Bowling Green State University Popular Press, 1992.

"Leisure Seizure." *People Weekly,* Apr. 20, 1992.

"Leisure Suit Lovers Boogie Down." Jan. 8, 1996. http://www.cnn.com/STYLE/9601/leisure/ (Oct. 6, 2004).

Levy, Lawrence. "Office Dress: Not Quite Anything Goes." *New York Times,* Dec. 28, 1975.

"Louis XIV." http://mars.acnet.wnec.edu/~grempel/courses/wc2/lectures/louisxiv.html (Jan. 8, 2005).

Machlowitz, Marilyn. "Dressing Up for the Executive Suite." *New York Times,* Dec. 5, 1976.

Macomber, S. Gray. "The Manmade Fiber Industry Comes on Stream." Parsippany (N.J.) *Daily Record,* May 22, 1992.

"New Look Suited for Leisure." *Mansfield (Ohio) News Journal,* June 15, 1975.

"The Now Look Ken." http://www.manbehindthedoll.com/nowlook.htm (Jan. 23, 2005).

Podmolik, Mary Ellen. "Men Bridge Fashion Gap as Tailored Sales Rise." *Chicago Sun-Times,* Oct. 27, 1997.

Raine, George. "Suiting the Public." *San Francisco Chronicle,* July 21, 2001.

Rivenburg, Roy. "The New Wrinkle in Polyester." *Los Angeles Times,* Nov. 25, 1992.

Rubenstein, Ruth P. *Dress Codes: Meanings and Messages in American Culture.* Boulder, Colo.: Westview Press, 1995.

Schor, Juliet B. *The Overworked American: The Unexpected Decline of Leisure.* New York: Basic Books, 1993.

Sloane, Leonard. "Suiting Up for Leisure." *New York Times,* Oct. 27, 1974.

Stern, Gabriella. "Police Will Suit the Man." *Omaha World-Herald,* Jan. 30, 1984.

"Suit." *Encyclopaedia Britannica,* http://www.britannica.com/eb/article?tocId=9070204 (Jan. 22, 2005).

Suplee, Kurt. "Hung Up on Brooks Brothers." *Washington Post,* Nov. 20, 1977.

Walker, Sam. "Fashion's Latest Victims: Men." *Wall Street Journal,* Dec. 1, 2000.

Weiner, Steve. "Tacky but a la Mode." *Wall Street Journal,* Feb. 8, 1985.

"Welcome to Black Light Vintage Clothing!" http://www.vintage70sclothing.com/Mens/Pants/leisure.htm (Jan. 26, 2005).

"When It Comes to Fashion, North's New Leader Marches to Own Drum." Associated Press, July 17, 1994.

Willig, John M. "Report on Men's Wear." *New York Times,* Sept. 14, 1969.

"Winston Churchill." http://www.museumofworldwarii.com/TourText/Area04a_Churchill.htm (Jan. 20, 2005).

Worthington, Christina. "An American Original." *New York Times,* Sept. 18, 1988.

16. The Abbreviated Reign of "Neon" Leon Spinks

Baker, Chris. "So Fast, So Far to Go: After 3 Years of Homelessness, McTear Is Rebuilding His Life." *Los Angeles Times,* Nov. 26, 1988.

Benjamin, Amalie. "Grinning and Bearing." *New Orleans Times-Picayune,* Sept. 14, 2004.

Coffey, Wayne. "Leon Spinks, Trying to Get Back on His Feet, Says Regrets Are Overwhelming." Knight Ridder/News Tribune Service, Jan. 1, 1997.

Dahlberg, Tim. "Memories Strong 40 Years After Ali Won Title." Associated Press, Feb. 24, 2004.

Davies, Sean. " 'Neon Leon' Hits Wales." BBC Sport, April 4, 2004.

Gerbasi, Thomas. "Cory Spinks: Not Jinxing the Future." http://www.maxboxing.com/Gerbasi/gerbasi083004.asp (Dec. 3, 2004).

Green, Michelle. "The Road May Not Be Ready, but Denny McClain and Leon Spinks Are Getting Their Acts Together." *People Weekly,* Feb. 13, 1989.

Greenberg, Alan. "A Day with Leon Spinks, the Well-Known Aviator." *Los Angeles Times,* Apr. 18, 1979.

Hawn, Jack. "Ali Finally Taps Out in Las Vegas." *Los Angeles Times,* Feb. 16, 1978.

"Leon Spinks Has a 'Lost Weekend.' " *Los Angeles Times,* Mar. 20, 1978.

Maher, John. "Next Generation Spinks Family Takes Shot in the Ring." *Austin American-Statesman,* Feb. 23, 2001.

"Michael Ray Richardson's Tough Journey Leads Him Back to the NBA." *Jet,* Oct. 20, 2003.

Miller, Stuart. "The Time of Their Lives." *Inside Sports,* Aug. 1995.

Murray, Jim. "The Other Spinks Lives in Slow Lane." *Los Angeles Times,* Sept. 27, 1987.

Murray, Jim. "Spinks' Meteoric Fall." *Los Angeles Times,* Sept. 17, 1978.

Murray, Jim. "There Is No Fight Anymore." *Los Angeles Times,* June 30, 1988.

"Newsmakers: Where Are They Now?" *People Weekly,* Nov. 28, 1994.

"Spinks Banned from Fighting in Florida," *St. Petersburg Times* (Fla.), Jan. 19, 1987.

"Spinks Dethrones Ali." *Los Angeles Times,* Feb. 16, 1978.

Springer, Steve. "Mayorga Falls to Spinks." *Los Angeles Times,* Dec. 3, 2004.

"Walking Tall: Johnny Knoxville Q&A." http://www.cinemas-online. co.uk/films/walkingtall/quanda/knoxville.html (Nov. 12, 2004).

Wharton, David. "Scrambling for His Life." *Los Angeles Times,* Apr. 13, 2001.

17. *Clippy—Microsoft's Relentless Software Irritant*

Baker, M. Sharon. "Bob Brings Microsoft's Suite Approach to Home PC." *Puget Sound Business Journal,* Jan. 6, 1995.

Bekker, Scott. "Clippy Has a Dark Side, Microsoft Says." http://www. entmag.com/news/article.asp?EditorialsID=861 (Feb. 4, 2005).

Bickmore, Timothy W., and Rosalind W. Picard. "Establishing and Maintaining Long-Term Human Computer Relationships." http://affect.media.mit.edu/pdfs/04.bickmore-picard-tochi.pdf (Feb. 14, 2005).

Blythe, Rory. "Clipped: An Interview with the Fallen Celebrity of Office Suite." http://neopoleon.com/blog/posts/5130.aspx (Feb. 4, 2005).

Catrambone, Richard, John Stasko, and Jun Xiao. "Embodied Conversational Agents as a UI Paradigm: A Framework for Evaluation." http://www.vhml.org/workshops/AAMAS/papers/xiao.pdf (Feb. 13, 2005).

"Clippy the WD 97 Office Assistant Deserves to Die and Be Tortured!!!!!" *microsoft.public.word.general,* Feb. 22, 1999.

"Clippy v.1.00." http://www.rjlsoftware.com/software/entertainment/ clippy/ (Feb. 4, 2005).

"Clippy's Come-uppance." *Financial Times,* Apr. 7, 1999.

"Create a Fake Clippy." http://j-walkblog.com/blog/index/P16638/ (Feb. 4, 2005).

Deegan, Peter. "Kill Clippy! (The Microsoft Office Assistant)." *ZDNet Reviews and Solutions,* Dec. 19, 2000.

DePompa, Barbara, Caryn Gillooly, David Needle, Joseph C. Panettieri, and Clinton Wilder. "Say Goodbye, Bob." *Information Week,* Feb. 26, 1996.

"Die Clippy!" http://entries.the5k.org/1126/ (Feb. 4, 2005).

Dyck, Timothy. "Microsoft Gives Clippy the Ax." *eWeek,* May 1, 2001.

Enrico, Dottie, and Paul Wiseman. "Techno Terror Slows Info Highway Traffic." *USA Today,* Nov. 14, 1994.

"Explaining Bayes' Theorem." http://mathforum.org/library/drmath/view/56622.html (Feb. 12, 2005).

"Farewell Clippy: What's Happening to the Infamous Office Assistant in Office XP." http://www.microsoft.com/presspass/features/2001/apr01/04-11clippy.asp (Jan. 8, 2005).

Goodley, Simon. "Intimations of Immortality." *Daily Telegraph* (London, U.K.), Aug. 16, 2001.

"GREAT Switcher Shirt Idea." http://www.mac-forums.com/forums/showthread.php?t=13436&page=1 (Feb. 12, 2005).

"Here We Go Again." http://diveintomark.org/archives/2003/02/12/here_we_go_again (Mar. 5, 2005).

Ishizuka, Mitsuru, and Helmut Prendinger. "Introducing the Cast for Social Computing: Life-Like Characters." http://www.springeronline.com/sgw/cda/pageitems/document/cda_downloaddocument/0,10900,0-0-45-99908-0,00.pdf (Feb. 4, 2005).

Lewis, Peter. "Xploring the new Office XP." *Fortune,* July 9, 2001.

Linn, Allison. "Microsoft Anti-Marketing Campaign Aims to Sell Office XP." Associated Press, May 2, 2001.

Locke, David. "RE: F1 for Help." Mar. 22, 2000. http://www.techwr-l.com/techwhirl/archives/0003/techwhirl-0003-01262.html (Feb. 13, 2005).

Loftus, Peter, and Maxwell Murphy. "Microsoft Unveils New Software, Buries a 'Friend.'" Dow Jones News Service, May 31, 2001.

Luening, Erich. "Microsoft Tool 'Clippy' Gets Pink Slip." *CNET News,* http://news.com.com/Microsoft+tool+Clippy+gets+pink+slip/ 2100-1001_3-255671.html (Jan. 28, 2005).

Manne, Alan S. *Economic Analysis for Business Decisions.* New York: McGraw-Hill, 1961.

Marble, Ann M. "The Screwtape Letters (Was Re: A Lot of Stuff)." *rec. arts.sf.composition,* Jan. 4, 2000 (Feb. 12, 2005).

Markoff, John, with Stewart Elliot. "Humor Is at Center of Microsoft's New Campaign." *New York Times,* Apr. 11, 2001.

"Microsoft Office XP Launch: Remarks by Bill Gates, May 31, 2001." http://www.microsoft.com/billgates/speeches/2001/ 05-31officexplaunch.asp (Feb. 14, 2005).

Mossberg, Walter S. "Some Computer Users May Find a Refuge in the House of Bob." *Wall Street Journal Europe,* Mar. 31, 1995.

Nass, Clifford, and Youngme Moon. "Machines and Mindlessness: Social Responses to Computers." *Journal of Social Issues,* Spring 2000.

National Science Foundation. http://www.nsf.gov/sbe/srs/issuebrf/ sib00314.htm (Feb. 13, 2005).

"OFF97: One Office Assistant Installed with Complete Setup." http:// support.microsoft.com/default.aspx?scid=kb;en-us;155143 (Feb. 14, 2005).

Papadakis, Maria C. "Complex Picture of Computer Use in the Home Emerges." National Science Foundation, http://www.nsf.gov/sbe/ srs/issuebrf/sib00314.htm (Feb. 13, 2005).

Pratley, Chris. "Clippy and User Experiences." http://weblogs.asp.net/ chris_pratley/archive/2004/05/05/126888.aspx (Feb. 13, 2005).

Raap, Jamie. "Cute: A Container, Insensitive to Content and Context?" Thesis for European master's of media arts, Merz Akademie, Stuttgart, Germany, Feb. 2004. http://www.zeitguised.com/wear/ work/cute/cute.html (Feb. 13. 2005).

Reichenbach, Bruce R. *Evil and a Good God.* New York: Fordham University Press, 1982.

Rose, Dan. "Windows® 1.x/2.x/3.x Abandonware: Microsoft 'Bob.' "
http://home.pmt.org/~drose/aw-win3x-16.html (Sept. 28, 2004).

Sidener, Jonathan. "Where's Clippy? Know-It-All Icon Missing from
New Office." *Arizona Republic* (Phoenix), May 22, 2001.

"So Much for the Friendly Assistant." http://news.zdnet.com/
2100-9595_22-520809.html (Feb. 5, 2005).

Stenger, Richard. "Microsoft's 'Clippy' Headed for the Trash." CNN,
Apr. 12, 2001. http://archives.cnn.com/2001/TECH/ptech/04/12/
office.clippy/ (Feb. 4, 2005).

Sullivan, Tom. "Gates: Companies Should Spend on Research During
Downturn." *InfoWorld*, Jan. 9, 2005. http://www.infoworld.com/
articles/hn/xml/01/09/05/010905hngates.html (Feb. 12, 2005).

"Thomas Bayes." Wikipedia, http://en.wikipedia.org/wiki/
Thomas_Bayes (Feb. 4, 2005).

Thomson, Susan B. "SIUE Student Researches Why So Many People
Hate Clippy." *St. Louis Post-Dispatch*, Sept. 22, 2003.

Warner, Jack. "Microsoft Bob Holds Hands with PC Novices, Like It or
Not." *Austin American-Statesman*, Apr. 29, 1995.

Wilcox, Joe. "Reports of Clippy's Demise Exaggerated." *CNET News*,
http://news.com.com/Reports+of+Clippys+demise+exaggerated/
2100-1001_3-267631.html (Feb. 5, 2005).

18. *The Y2K Scare*

Anson, Robert Sam. "The Y2K Nightmare." *Vanity Fair*, Jan. 1999.

Barr, Stephen. "On a Snowy Day, Looking Back at Y2K." *Washington
Post*, Jan. 28, 2000.

Bemer, Bob. "The Powerful ESCAPE Character—Key and Sequences."
http://www.bobbemer.com/ESCAPE.HTM (Mar. 5, 2005).

"Benefits Emerge from Y2K Hype." *On Wall Street*, Feb. 2000.

Boys, Don. *Y2K*. Lafayette, La.: Huntington House, 1999.

Burmeister, Dale R. "Ignorance Is No Defense—When They Should

Have Known About the Y2K Computer Glitch." http://www. harveykruse.com/ignorance.htm (Mar. 5, 2005).

Catastrophic Cooking." http://www.amazon.com/gp/product/ product-description/0966980042/ref=dp_proddesc_0/ 104-0668126-9411101?%5Fencoding=UTF8&n=507846 (Mar. 5, 2005).

Chang, Yi-Hsin. "Once in a Millennium: The Year 2000 Problem." *Motley Fool,* Sept. 15, 1998. http://www.fool.com/features/1998/ sp980914y2k002.htm (Mar. 5, 2005).

Christensen, John. " 'Nobody Wins If the Public Freaks Out.' " CNN Interactive, Mar. 23, 1999. http://www.cnn.com/TECH/specials/ y2k/stories/y2k.goldrush/ (Mar. 5, 2005).

Falwell, Jerry. "Ten Things I See in 1999." Sermon at Thomas Road Baptist Church, Jan. 3, 1999. http://sermons.trbc.org/990103. html (Mar. 6, 2005).

"Falwell Says God May Be Responsible for Y2K Bug." Associated Press, Nov. 24, 1998.

Farrar, Steve. *Spiritual Survival During the Y2K Crisis.* Nashville: Thomas Nelson, 1999.

Farrell, Chris. "The Costs of Y2K." American Radio Works, http:// americanradioworks.publicradio.org/features/y2k/b2.html (Mar. 6, 2005).

Feder, Barnaby J. "For Computers, the Year 2000 May Prove a Bit Traumatic." *New York Times,* May 7, 1988.

Feder, Barnaby J. "You've Tried the Rest, Now Try the Y2K-Ready." *New York Times,* Feb. 28, 1999.

Feder, Barnaby J., and Andrew Pollack. "Trillion Dollar Digits." *New York Times,* Dec. 27, 1998.

"Gary North's Y2K Links and Forums—Category: Introduction." http://web.archive.org/web/19980521104649/garynorth.com/y2k/ results_.cfm/Introduction (Mar. 6, 2005).

Gomez, Lee. "Y2K Countdown: Will the Bug Bite?" *Wall Street Journal,* Dec. 23, 1999.

Grady, Sandy. "The Y2K Furor Flop and Other Reflections." *Philadelphia Daily News,* Dec. 28, 2000.

Greenemeier, Larry. "Businesses Still Feeling Sting from Y2K Bug—an Increasing Number of Glitches Are Surfacing, Though Most Are Termed Insignificant." *InformationWeek,* Jan. 10, 2000.

Harrar, George. "Computers in Crisis, by Jerome T. Murray and Marilyn J. Murray." Book review. *Computerworld,* June 11, 1984.

Heard, Alex, and Peter Klebnikov. "Apocalypse Now. No, Really. Now!" *New York Times Magazine,* Dec. 27, 1998.

Hoffman, Thomas. "Tarnished Image." *Computerworld,* May 12, 2003.

"Introduction to COBOL." http://www.csis.ul.ie/cobol/Course/COBOLIntro.htm (Mar. 5, 2005).

"Investigating the Year 2000 Problem: Telecommunications." Special Committee on the Year 2000 Technology Problem, U.S. Senate, Feb. 24, 1999. http://www.senate.gov/~y2k/documents/report/Telcom.pdf (Mar. 5, 2005).

Kratofil, Bruce. "The Impact of the Y2K Bug—Year 2000 Computer Problem." *Business Economics,* Jan. 1999.

Kliesen, Kevin L. "Was Y2K Behind the Business Investment Boom and Bust?" *Federal Reserve Bank of St. Louis Review,* Jan.–Feb. 2003.

Lacayo, Richard. "The End of the World As We Know It." *Time,* Jan. 18, 1999.

Levy, Steven, and Katie Hafner. "The Day the World Shuts Down." *Newsweek,* June 2, 1997.

Machalaba, Daniel, and Carrick Mollenkamp. "Companies Struggle to Cope with Chaos, Breakdowns and Trauma—Y2K Plans Pay Off at Last as Businesses Use Bunkers, Backups, 'Hardened' Rooms." *Wall Street Journal,* Sept. 13, 2001.

Mandel, Michael J. "Zap! How the Year 2000 Bug Will Hurt the Economy." *Business Week,* Mar. 2, 1998.

McClintock, Mike. "Y2K Scams on the Internet." *Washington Post,* Sept. 30, 1999.

McMillan, Dan. "Y2K Hype Became the Biggest Story of 1999." *Business Journal–Portland,* Jan. 7, 2000.

"Millennium Bug: Most Companies Preparing for Year 2000 Systems Issue." *EDGE: Work-Group Computing Report,* June 3, 1996.

"National Poll Determines Phrases of 2000 That Make Americans Want to Crunch Something." *PR Newswire,* Dec. 18, 2000.

Murray, Jerome T., and Marilyn J. Murray. *Computers in Crisis: How to Avert the Coming Worldwide Computer Systems Collapse.* New York: PBI, 1984.

Ordonez, Jennifer. "The World Doesn't End." *Wall Street Journal,* Jan. 3, 2000.

Pease, Meredith, et al. "Memory Distortions for Pre-Y2K Expectancies: A Demonstration of the Hindsight Bias." *Journal of Psychology,* July 2003.

Prendergast, Alan. "Profits of Doom: How a Costly Computer Glitch Turned into a Once-in-a-Millennium Bonanza for High-Tech Companies." *Denver Westword,* Feb. 12, 1998.

Reimold, Frieder. "Computer Pioneer Bob Bemer, Who Published Y2K Warnings in '70s, Dies of Cancer." *AP Online,* June 24, 2004.

"Reverend Jerry Falwell Discusses the New Millennium." ABC News, Jan. 1, 2000.

"Satellites Blinded by Y2K Bug." *NewsBytes,* Jan. 13, 2000.

Schwartz, Mat. "A Millennium Disaster: NBC's Y2K: The Movie." *Computerworld,* Nov. 22, 1999.

"Securities Broker-Dealer Sanctioned in 'Failure to Supervise' Case; Agent Was Simi Valley Investment Adviser Who Lost $6 Million in Y2K Bet." *Business Wire,* Feb. 1, 2001.

"Senate Report Says Y2K Would Not Pose Major Disruptions." *Allpolitics,* http://www.cnn.com/ALLPOLITICS/stories/1999/03/02/senate.y2k/ (Mar. 5, 2005).

Surkan, Michael. "What's All the Y2K Panic About?" *PC Week,* Dec. 1, 1997.

Von Sternberg, Bob. "Millennium Bug Fear Sends Many to Woods." *Minneapolis Star Tribune,* July 5, 1998.

Webster, Mark. "Y2K Plans Had New Use in Dealing with Disaster." *Business First of Buffalo,* Nov. 5, 2001.

"White House—'We Squashed Y2K Bug.'" *Newsbytes,* Feb. 24, 2000.

"Who Is Michael S. Hyatt?" http://web.archive.org/web/ 20001025182937/www.y2kprep.com/editorials/hyatt/bio.htm (Mar. 5, 2005).

Wilson, Tim. "In Final Assessment, Y2K Did Leave a Mark." *Internet-Week,* Jan. 8, 2001.

Winter, Catherine. "The Surprising Legacy of Y2K: Separating Hype from Reality." http://americanradioworks.publicradio.org/ features/y2k/transa.html (Mar. 6, 2005).

"Y2K." http://www.imdb.com/title/tt0196221/ (Mar. 6, 2005).

Y2K Family Survival Guide. http://www.amazon.com/exec/obidos/tg/ detail/-/6305300224/104-0668126-9411101?v=glance.

"Y2K Plans Finally Serve Their Purpose." *Financial Times,* Oct. 5, 2001.

"Y2K (II) (TV)." http://www.imdb.com/title/tt0215370/ (Mar. 6, 2005).

"Y2K Watch Products." http://web.archive.org/web/19990911181932/ y2kwatch.com/articles.html?mcat=5 (Mar. 6, 2005).

"Y2K Watch Three-Step Preparedness Plan." http://web.archive. org/web/19990911152252/y2kwatch.com/articles.html?mcat=12 (Mar. 6, 2005).

19. *The XFL's Quick Takedown*

Assael, Shaun, and Mike Mooneyham. *Sex, Lies, and Headlocks: The Real Story of Vince McMahon and the World Wrestling Federation.* New York: Crown, 2002.

"Chronology." http://www.stlouisrams.com/History/ (Jan. 27, 2005).

"Coliseum and Sports Arena History." http://www.lacoliseum.com/
content/1/col_info/history.htm (Jan. 23, 2005).

"Divas." http://www.officialxfl.com/Women/Divas/divas1.asp (Feb. 5,
2005).

"Final Gun Sounds Early for the XFL." *Mediaweek,* May 14, 2001.

Forrest, Brett. *Long Bomb: How the XFL Became TV's Biggest Fiasco.*
New York: Crown, 2002.

Grainger, David. "Football Gets an Xtreme Makeover." *Time,* Feb. 5,
2001.

"Gridiron Gladiators." *American Demographics,* Apr. 1, 2001.

Internet Movie Database, http://www.imdb.com/title/tt0202741/ (Feb.
4, 2005).

Mancini, Chad, and Keith A. Willoughby. "The Inaugural Season of
the Xtreme Football League: A Case Study in Sports Entertainment." *International Journal of Sports Marketing & Sponsorship,*
Sept.–Oct. 2003.

Mariotti, Jay. "Trashing the Garbage of the XFL." *Sporting News,*
May 21, 2001.

Martzke, Rudy. "Super Bowl Ratings Edge Up." *USA Today,* Feb. 7,
2005.

McGraw, Dan. "I Don't Mean to Rant, but What Is This XFL?" *U.S.
News & World Report,* Sept. 11, 2000.

Penner, Mike. "Now, XFL Should Start Grappling for a Quick Fix." *Los
Angeles Times,* Feb. 4, 2001.

Rushin, Steve. "Dumbest Sports Moments: It's True That Someone
Has to Win and Someone Has to Lose, but Nobody Has to Make
These Kinds of Colossal Blunders." *Sports Illustrated,* Sept. 27,
2004.

"Separated at Birth?" http://www.indignantonline.com/images/
xfl-swastika.gif (Feb. 5, 2005).

20. *The Quixotic Quest for the Flying Car*

"Aircraft Specification No. 4A16." Federal Aviation Administration certification provided by FAA media relations specialist Alison Duquette, Mar. 1, 2005.

Anton, Mike. "Can We Ever Commute as Jetsons Did?" *Los Angeles Times,* Dec. 30, 2003.

Brownlee, Nick. "Back to the Future." *People,* Feb. 6, 2000.

"Bush Calls for Manned Base on the Moon: No Price Tag Offered for Ambitious Program." http://www.npr.org/templates/story/story.php?storyId=1597182 (Feb. 20, 2005).

"Chitty Chitty Bang Bang." http://www.imdb.com/title/tt0062803/plotsummary (Feb. 17, 2005).

"Defining the Challenge." *Roadable Times,* http://www.roadabletimes.com/overview.html (Feb. 22, 2005).

"Fulton FA-3-101 Airphibian." http://www.nasm.si.edu/research/aero/aircraft/fulton.htm (Feb. 19, 2005).

Higgins, Bill. "A Pinto for Icarus: Smolinski and Blake." http://world.std.com/~jlr/doom/blake.htm (Feb. 22, 2005).

Jacobs, Timothy. *Lemons: The World's Worst Cars.* Greenwich, Conn.: Brompton Books, 1987.

James, Frank. "1,000 Years of Progress." *Chicago Tribune,* Dec. 2, 1990.

"Jesse James' Monster Garage Features Panoz Esperante." http://www.theracesite.com/04print.cfm?form_article=8694 (Feb. 25, 2005).

"Keels & Wheels." http: www.woodenkeels-classicwheels.com/index.cfm (Feb. 13, 2005).

Kharif, Olga. "A Flying Leap for Cars." *America's Intelligence Wire,* Aug. 25, 2004.

Linn, Allison. "As Gridlock Grows, Scientists Look at Adding Lanes in the Sky." *America's Intelligence Wire,* Aug. 30, 2004.

Linn, Allison. "Flying Cars Reportedly Still Decades Away." Associated Press, Aug. 27, 2004.

Nashawaty, Chris. "The Jetson Age." *Entertainment Weekly*, Nov. 1, 1996.

"The National Consortium for Aviation Mobility." http://ncam-sats.org (Feb. 12, 2005).

Oliver, Myrna. "Robert E. Fulton Jr., 95, Adventurer, Inventor." *Los Angeles Times*, May 12, 2004.

Powell, Dennis E. "Winging It: Down the Road, Through the Clouds, the Aerocar Idea Is Still Aloft." *Seattle Times*, July 15, 1990.

Raphael, Jordan. "The Audacious Mr. Moller." *Los Angeles Times*, June 25, 2000.

Salisbury, Lionel. E-mail interview with the editor of www.roadable-times.com by Martin J. Smith (Feb. 22, 2005).

Siegel, Lee. "Harry Potter and the Spirit of the Age: Fear of Not Flying." *New Republic*, Nov. 22, 1999.

Stefanova, Kristina. "Humans, Machines May Swap Roles in the Future: Robotic Dogs, Telepathic Gear, Skycars Imagined." *Washington Times*, Dec. 30, 1999.

Stiles, Palmer. *Roadable Aircraft: From Wheels to Wings*. Melbourne, Fla.: Custom Creativity, 1994.

"Tethered Skycar Hovers as It Awaits Approval." *Engineer*, Nov. 16, 2001.

Wall, Lucas. "Colorado-Based Innovator Is Working to Make Flying Car Practical." *Houston Chronicle*, May 5, 2003.

Wilson, J. R. "Future Flying Car Lends Itself to a Host of Mature Electronic Technologies." *Military & Aerospace Electronics*, Apr. 2001.

Yenne, Bill. *The World's Worst Aircraft*. As excerpted at http://www.fiddlersgreen.net/aircraft/private/aerocar/info/info.htm (Feb. 12, 2005).

The Bonus Chapter

"Amphicar FAQ." http://www.amphicar.com/AmphicarFAQ.htm (Feb. 4, 2005).

"Amphicar History." http://www.amphicar.com/history.htm (Feb. 4, 2005)

Arnold, Gary. "Disco Delirium." *Washington Post,* June 25, 1980.

Biffle, Kent. "Crush's Crash: A Stunt That Went Awry." *Chicago Tribune,* Sept. 22. 1985.

Burrough, Bryan, and John Helyar. *Barbarians at the Gate: The Fall of RJR Nabisco.* New York: Harper & Row, 1990.

"Can't Stop the Music (1980) from Johnny Web." http://www.fakes.net/cantstopthemusic.htm (Mar. 10, 2005).

Earman, J. S. "Memorandum for the Record—Subject: Report on Plots to Assassinate Fidel Castro." Office of the Inspector General, Central Intelligence Agency, May 23, 1967 (Declassified 1993). http://www.parascope.com/mx/articles/castroreport.htm (Mar. 10, 2005).

Hall, Karen J. "A Soldier's Body: GI Joe, Hasbro's Great American Hero, and the Symptoms of Empire." *Journal of Popular Culture,* Aug. 2004.

"In Search of a Safe Cigarette." *Nova,* Thursday, May 9, 2002. http://www.abc.net.au/catalyst/stories/s551901.htm (Mar. 10, 2005).

Jacobs, Timothy. *Lemons: The World's Worst Cars.* Greenwich, Conn.: Brompton Books, 1987.

Judge, Peter. "Asera Rules the World." *ZDNet,* March 7, 2003. http://insight.zdnet.co.uk/business/0,39020481,2131580,00.htm (Feb. 4, 2005).

Lewis, Leo. "The Heat's On and the Japanese Can Cool Off with Horse-Flesh Ice Cream." *Times* (London, U.K.), July 22, 2004.

"Linear Putter Device." U.S. Patent No. 6659880, issued Dec. 9, 2003. http://www.freepatentsonline.com/image-6659880-1.html (Feb. 4, 2005).

Maslin, Janet. "Can't Stop the Music." *New York Times,* June 20, 1980.

Pond, Steve. *The Big Show: High Times and Dirty Dealings Backstage at the Academy Awards.* New York: Faber & Faber, 2005.

"The Royal and Ancient Golf Club of St. Andrews." http://www.
    theroyalandancientgolfclub.org/ (Feb. 4, 2005).

Stratton, Lee. "G.I. Wish I'd Kept My Joes." *Columbus Dispatch,*
    July 15, 1994.

Thomas, Bob. "Star Watch: Bruce Jenner in 'Can't Stop the Music.' "
    Associated Press, May 30, 1980.

Vaughn, Don. "A Toy Story: Rare G.I. Nurse Action Figure a Valu-
    able Find for Collectors." *Nurse Week,* May 6, 2004. http://www.
    nurseweek.com/news/features/04-05/toystory.asp (Mar. 10,
    2005).

Ward, George B. "The Crash at Crush: Texas' Great Pre-arranged Train
    Wreck." The University of Texas at Austin (master's report),
    May 1975.

index